P3

Where is Joey?

Where is Joey?

LOST AMONG THE HARE KRISHNAS

MORRIS YANOFF

Swallow Press
Ohio University Press

Chicago • Athens, Ohio • London

Library of Congress Cataloging in Publication Data

Yanoff, Morris.
  Where is Joey?

  1. Krishna (Hindu deity)—Cult—United States.
2. International Society for Krishna Consciousness.
I. Title.
BL1220.Y36   294.5'512   81-11280
ISBN 0-8040-0414-5   AACR2

Swallow Press Books
are published by
Ohio University Press
Athens, Ohio 45701

Designed by Ann Smeltzer

To protect our friends, and in charity to those who did things for which they may now be sorry, all names (except public ones) have been changed.

While I kept a diary of the events, I wrote from memory; hence, the dialogue is not verbatim. For literary purposes, I have run some events together and combined some personalities. With these qualifications, everything in this narrative is true.

—*Morris Yanoff*

*To our dear friends
without whose help this book
would have had a different ending.*

Prologue

Two American Airlines jets were unloading at Chicago's O'Hare Airport, the world's busiest. Just my luck to be alone this morning, I thought, as I watched eight Krishnas gather eagerly to meet a crowd of passengers.

As the first stream of travelers came through, I observed tall Gadapati hold out his hand toward a sailor, and wondered how far he would get.

"Hi Buddy, welcome to Chicago." From Gadapati's manner, one might have thought he'd been sent by the mayor himself. A lonely kid in a strange city, the young sailor seemed pleased to be greeted. When he dropped his duffel bag between his feet, in order to accept the yellow-jacketed copy of the *Gita* from Gadapati, I started in their direction.

Just then, little Deva dasi, blond and smiling sweetly, deftly pinned a wine-red carnation to the lapel of an old gentleman. In a hurry to reach the sailor, I called to the old man, "Sir, it's a pitch!" He looked up, grinned his understanding, and waved Deva away.

I now stood in front of the sailor to catch his eye. Gadapati, another *Gita* in his hand, was showing him the picture pages. "You believe in God?" he asked.

"Oh, yes."

"This is all about God."

"Excuse me, son," I said to the sailor. "Do you know who these people are?"

He turned his large brown eyes on me. "No, who?"

Gadapati swung his book-laden grocery cart against my shins. I did a quick side-step but held the sailor's eyes. "These are the Hare Krishnas."

"Hairy, who?"

"Hare Krishnas, a Hindu cult."

"But he said this book is about God."

"This is their God." I held up a full-color page of their magazine, *Back to Godhead.* Emblazoned on it was a blue-skinned Krishna in red and yellow dhoti, a flower chain falling from his neck to pearl-draped ankles.

"Him, God?" He gave Gadapati a puzzled look.

Gadapati shook a finger at me. "He's a Jew. He doesn't believe in God."

I brought out a clipping from the *Chicago Tribune.* "I'm this boy's grandfather," I said, pointing to Joey's picture and the headline. The sailor's eyes scanned the bold type. "At 12, he 'disappears' into Krishna." When he looked up at me again, I told him, "We're asking people not to contribute to the Krishnas until this boy is returned to his father."

Gadapati snatched the book from the startled sailor and took off for another prospect. I followed, trying to keep him in sight. A friendly porter pointed in the direction he took.

Airport employees called us the "Where is Joey?" people because pinned to our lapels were little cards bearing that question. It was the question we had been asking since our search began more than a year before. Letters, phone calls, pleas to their Swami, picketlines, and publicity had brought us no closer to an answer. The cult continued to deny knowledge of Joey's where-abouts.

Day after day the young devotees diligently plied passengers with books or carnations, reaping thousands of dollars in dona-tions for their cult. Like the Hare Krishnas, we also kept a daily vigil at O'Hare.

Many travellers now refused to donate when they heard our story and our question, "Where is Joey?" Would cutting into the Krishna collections force an answer? It was our last hope.

Contents

1

Joey Gets His Mantra

IN A WAY, IT HAD ALL BEGUN AT O'HARE TOO. ON A warm summer afternoon, the last day of July 1975, I had driven Joey to the airport where a plane would take him to spend the month of August in Los Angeles with Miriam, his mother, my former daughter-in-law. Our family had given barely a thought to the fact that she had recently joined the Hare Krishna Society and that Joey would be staying in the temple complex, for we knew next to nothing about the group.

During the three years since Larry, our son, had assumed custody of the boy, Joey had made several trips to visit his mother. This year Larry had arranged for his own vacation in France to coincide with Joey's absence from Chicago. My wife Toby and I had promised to keep in touch with our grandson while he was away.

"Now, don't forget to phone us collect as soon as you reach Los Angeles," I reminded Joey, as we stood waiting for boarding time. "Do you know how to do that?"

He gave me a look out of blue eyes which seemed to ask, "How many more times are you going to tell me, Grandpa?"

Small for his age, Joey looked even smaller beside the tall steward who took charge of him. On entering the ramp, he turned to wave goodbye, and I felt a rush of tenderness. God, I thought, this child has been subjected to so many shocks in his short life.

When Joey did not phone that evening or the next day, Toby and I began to worry. Finally, on the third day, we called the Los Angeles temple directly; after some delay, Joey was put on the line. We learned he was not staying with his mother, as we had assumed. She lived in the women's dormitory, and he had been

1

put into the men's, the only child among them. He was awakened at 3:30 A.M. every day, given a cold shower, and before breakfast took part in temple ceremonies. For recreation he accompanied the devotees when they went chanting and dancing on the streets.

We were concerned at what he told us, since we had not expected Miriam to involve him in the cult's activities. But it's only for a month, we told ourselves. What could possibly happen? He would at least return with some interesting stories to tell.

Though Joey promised to phone a week later at the same hour, the time came and went without a call from the boy. Our concern rising, Toby and I phoned the temple next evening. We were asked to wait rather a long time, only to be told "Joey is in class. Please call back at 7:30 P.M. Los Angeles time." When we did so, the same voice first told us to wait, and then, "Joey is in bed and cannot be disturbed." We were exasperated, dismayed, and frightened too. What did all this mean?

Now anxious, we called the next evening at five and again there were delays, though our persistence finally brought Joey to the phone.

"Why didn't you call us the other night as you promised?" I demanded. He did not answer. "We were waiting all evening for your call." My voice had risen.

Toby cut in, "How are you enjoying your stay, Joey?"

"O.K., I guess," he replied.

"What do you do during the day?"

"I work in the kitchen cutting vegetables and I sweep the floor."

"Do you have time to play?"

"There's nobody here I can play with," he complained. "They're all too old."

"Aren't there other children?" Toby asked.

"Yes, but they're babies."

"No one your age?"

"No."

"Do you get to go anywhere?" I interjected.

"I take walks sometimes."

"Where do you walk?"

"Around the temple block."

"How is the food?" Toby asked.

"It's O.K."

"You told me when you ate it at the Evanston temple, you didn't like it."

"I got used to it."

2

At that point, Miriam, who unknown to us was standing by, took the phone. After the usual exchange Toby asked how Lainie was. Joey was to visit his half-sister in Dallas where she was enrolled in the sect's school. From there he would take the plane back to Chicago.

"Lainie's fine," Miriam replied. "She loves it in Dallas." We said nothing, but I wondered how a five-year-old bore separation from her mother. Then, on a note of delight, Miriam added, "Do you know what? Joey has his own mantra."

Toby and I remained silent. We did not feel we could discuss our concern with Miriam; she might become antagonized and perhaps cut us off from phone contact with Joey.

"Morris," she went on, "you're a scholar. You should read the *Bhagavad Gita*. It will tell you what we believe in." She spelled out the words for me as I wrote down the title.

Though somewhat disturbed by the conversation, we were not yet alarmed. In a perverse way, Miriam's frankness reassured me. Following her suggestion, I searched out a translation of the *Gita* in my local library. A long, religious poem of ancient India, its main purport is the promise of eternal bliss to those who devote themselves entirely to Krishna.

The alarm bells were finally set off by an article from the *Chicago Tribune*, sent to us by Toby's closest friend, Rose. It was dated August 11, 1975, a week to the day before Joey went to Los Angeles. (If only we had seen it sooner!) It began:

> Randy Sacks and Scott Berner believe some religious cults use a form of mind control to lure members. It took several years for Randy and Scott to come out from under one such influence. Randy described the Hare Krishna conversion as a three-step process: (1) on-the-spot hypnosis; (2) brainwashing; and (3) self-hypnosis. "The on-the-spot hypnosis isn't that effective, but it's very fast," he said. Hare Krishna members "stare you in the eyes, touch your hand. The objective is to get you to agree. 'Isn't school a drag?' they ask. 'Why don't you come down to our temple and eat our food? Isn't this food good? See how happy we all are?' It's like giving a kid a piece of candy.
>
> "Once you're past the first stage, they start the brainwashing, totally immersing you in their philosophy. Everything in the world is 'maya' or illusion. That includes parents, school, society, friends, money, sex,

3

your body, gambling, drinking. The Hare Krishnas
are good; they are the reality. They are right and
everyone else is wrong."

Now worried, I phoned my sister Rachel, who lived in Los
Angeles, to ask that she visit Joey at the temple during their
weekly open house. After her visit that Sunday, Rachel called
with the dramatic announcement, "Joey is being brainwashed!"

Before being allowed to see Joey, Rachel and her husband
Walter had been kept waiting several hours. The boy was participating in a ceremony, the couple were told, but they had the
feeling this long delay was a ploy to exhaust their patience so they
would leave. During their wait, Miriam, who had returned from
selling the cult's books on the streets, invited Rachel to the
women's dormitory, a three-bedroom apartment near the temple.
There were no beds; the women slept on the floor, several to each
room.

As Miriam undressed, she threw her clothes into a laundry
basket, saying, "When we come back from the outside, from the
filth, we have to cleanse ourselves; we take a shower and change
clothes."

Rachel, noted in our family for blunt speech, asked, "You take
their money. Is their money filthy?"

"The purpose the money goes for," she replied, "makes it
acceptable."

Rachel noticed that all Miriam's possessions were contained in
part of a small closet. "That's all we need," Miriam boasted.
"That's the trouble with people—buy, buy, buy." When Miriam
had changed, the two women returned to the temple lawn where
food was being served. Here Rachel and Walter finally came face
to face with Joey, with a male Krishna hovering nearby. Joey
talked of violence and drugs in the public schools, showed fear of
leaving the temple area, and expressed a desire to remain with
the cult.

"Don't you want to see your father?" Rachel asked.

"All the people here are my fathers and mothers," he replied.
"My father beats me."

"Your father beats you?" Rachel knew it wasn't true. "Did your
father ever beat you?"

Joey hesitated, "No, but he will."

Walter suggested they visit Disneyland. Joey agreed happily,
asking them to wait while he changed out of temple costume. A

4

nearby devotee, however, told Rachel she would have to get Miriam's permission. They found her and after a whispered exchange between her and the devotee, Miriam told Rachel that Joey had chores and would not be able to go to Disneyland. "Perhaps some other time," she said.

Toby and I listened to Rachel's report over the phone and fought to control our rising fears. "You'd better get him home right away," Rachel urged.

Afterward, we debated whether to call Larry in France, but decided instead to phone Joey, hoping to win reassurance from him. Once more we were told he was in class and that we should call again in an hour. There were the usual delays the second time, but finally we heard our grandson on the other end of the line. Toby told him we planned a special feast for the coming Jewish holidays when he would be home. Instead of welcoming the news, as he would normally have done, Joey was evasive.

"I learned how to make a Hindu dish," he told us.

"You'll have to show me how," Toby said.

"I'll send you a cook book," was all he would say. There was no mention of coming home. Instead he rang off with the surprising announcement: "We're having a big celebration at the temple. It's our Spiritual Master's appearance day."

Both Rachel's report and this conversation with Joey convinced us that the sooner he was brought home, the better. We cabled Larry to phone us, and when he heard what was happening to Joey, he exclaimed, "What are they doing to his head!" Larry decided to take the first flight home.

Our younger son, Ronald, and I met Larry at the airport. He was bleary-eyed and under strain, but just being together made us all feel better. As a family we had seen rough times before, the worst in 1959 when Toby's illness had been diagnosed as multiple sclerosis and within a few months she was in a wheelchair. A few years later, Ronald was in an auto accident; neck broken, his head held in place by pincers, he was turned like a chicken on a spit to prevent bed sores. Now we were facing a crisis the nature of which we could only guess.

We sat down together in the airport while I went over the events of the last four weeks. "This letter came yesterday," I told Larry. "Joey wants to stay at the temple." The letter read in part:

> Dear Daddy: I like it very much and I want to stay for
> about a year. I will go to a public school that is near

here. When you get home, send me my pajama tops, my
two pants, some long sleeve shirts, and my notebook.
Please remember I love you and that I made this
decision for myself.

Larry moaned, "God, what the hell did they do to him? This
letter is not Joey."

"Rachel thinks he was brainwashed," I said.

"Brainwashed? Just what does it mean?"

"I'm not sure what it means in this situation. That expression
was used to describe what happened to the American prisoners of
war in North Korea. They used a combination of punishment and
rewards to change people's thinking."

"Poor Joey," Larry sighed. "After all he's been through, now
this."

"We have to get him home," Ronald said. "The longer he stays,
the more they'll work on him." Larry nodded.

"Listen," I said. "Tomorrow is Sunday, when they have their
open house in the afternoon. Don't phone in advance. Just show up
there with Rachel and Walter and get Joey to come home with
you."

"He'll come with me, all right," Larry said. "What we have
between us is stronger than whatever stuff they've fed him."

Using my credit card, Larry booked the next flight to Los
Angeles. Waiting for his flight, we sat around a coffee table and
talked. Having made a decision, we were able to relax a little
until it was time for Larry to catch the L.A. flight. As he went up
the ramp, my son turned with a grin and a wave as if to say, "Don't
worry; we've been through worse."

The next night when I answered a ring, the operator asked,
"Will you accept a collect call from Los Angeles?"

"Toby," I shouted, "It's Larry!" She quickly rolled over, in her
wheelchair, to the extension. "O.K., operator, put him on."

"Hi, Dad," he said tonelessly.

"How did it go?" I asked anxiously.

"It was awful. I don't have Joey."

"Did you see him?"

"Yes, but before I could talk to him, they grabbed him."

"Grabbed him? The Krishnas?" I was shocked.

"They wrestled him away from me."

"Did they hurt you?" Toby asked.

6

"I'm all right, Ma."

"What happened? Tell us," I urged.

"Walter and Rachel drove me down in the afternoon about five. While they were parking a few blocks away for safety, I went ahead to the temple. As I came up to it, I saw Miriam."

"Miriam?" I echoed.

"She said, 'I thought you'd come.' I asked her where Joey was. 'Inside,' she said. I had to take my shoes off at the door. I went in; they were having a ceremony. I saw Joey up front and went over to him. I put my hands on his shoulders; he turned; we hugged. 'I want to talk to you,' I said, and picked him up and took him to the door. I stopped to put on my shoes. Two Krishnas came over. 'I want to talk to my son, alone,' I told them, then picked up Joey and took him out on the lawn. There I was surrounded by Krishnas. One of them yelled, 'Let's take him.' They grabbed me. I tried to hold on to Joey. He was screaming. They pinned my arms and pulled Joey away. I was knocked to the ground."

"Oh, boy," I murmured.

"Where were Rachel and Walter?" Toby asked.

"They tried to come to my help, but were held back."

"Didn't Miriam stop them?" Toby asked angrily.

"No; actually I didn't see her. We left to call the police. When they came and heard what had happened, they said, 'You can't take your son without a California court order,' and warned me not to try again."

We listened in despair, unable to muster comforting words.

"What will you do now?" I asked.

"Come home. What else can I do? They'll be watching for me now. Anyhow, they'll hide him."

I knew what he was going through and wanted at that moment to put my arms around him, to share his grief. "Yeah," I said slowly, "I guess you'd better come home. We'll figure out something."

Back in Chicago, Larry found a young attorney specializing in custody cases. The first step, he said, was to go to the Illinois courts for a temporary custody order. In the circumstances, he thought the court would quickly grant it. With this, Larry could get a California order for Joey's return. With Joey back in Illinois, the court would hold another hearing with all parties present to decide the issue of permanent custody. The attorney's opinion cheered us.

On September 9 Toby and I made another attempt to reach Joey by a person-to-person call to the temple. There was a long wait after the operator asked for him, and then came a small boy's voice, "This is Joey." The voice trembled with eagerness, "Is this my mother?" Toby choked up, so I took over. The boy turned out to be another child named "Joey." When had he last spoken to his mother that he could not recognize her voice?

And *our* Joey, where was he?

2

Family Chronicle

LARRY HAD MET MIRIAM LASHER WHILE VISITING A friend in Boston some thirteen years before. He was then twenty-three and had just been drafted into the Army. She was twenty, tall and with a serious face somewhat marred by acne scars. Dressed up and in a happy mood, she was attractive.

Miriam and Larry saw each other a few times and corresponded. When he finished basic training and was assigned to Hawaii, they decided to marry and leave together. Her parents were against the marriage, and we had our own misgivings. "You hardly know each other," Toby said to Larry, who insisted they were in love. And so we arranged for a home wedding to which we invited a few close friends, enough for a "minyan," the ten males prescribed by Jewish law.

After a long, emotional long-distance call, Miriam's parents reluctantly agreed to come. Did they simply object to this sudden wedding to a strange soldier? Or did they have insights into their daughter's unpredictable character?

In November of 1963, Joey was born in Hawaii. Five months later, Larry's service over, they returned to Chicago and moved into an apartment a mile from ours. We helped with a loan to enable Larry to complete college and become a teacher. He augmented their income with part-time jobs in the neighborhood.

Within a month after their arrival, the disturbing episodes began. At a backyard picnic arranged to introduce the young couple to our friends, Miriam would not come out of the house to join the party until most of the guests had gone; there was no

9

explanation. Another time I saw her smash one of Joey's toys in a fit of anger because the child had been slow to put it away. Once she phoned Toby, troubled because she had lost her head and beaten Joey. Finally, there was the quarrel which broke out between Miriam and her neighbor on the floor below. Later, we heard the details partly from Miriam and partly from Larry. When the neighbor woman complained of some noise Joey was making, Miriam became so abusive that the woman took fright, locked her door, and phoned her husband to come home. When Miriam repeated the language she had used "to put her in her place," my wife and I, no puritans, were shocked by its brutality and the relish with which our daughter-in-law relived the incident. Alarmed by the affair, the building's owner ordered Larry to move.

Yet, when Miriam was in control of her moods, she could be charming. Her voice would take on a soft, melodious quality; she sang sweetly. Often she made a very pleasing first impression. But the dark side of her showed itself more and more until, eventually, she required counseling. It was only then that Larry learned she had a history of such care.

When Joey was four, Miriam left her husband and son for a man she had met that summer at a lake resort. Within three weeks, however, she was back again, and Larry was persuaded to try and patch up their marriage. To escape gossip, they moved to another apartment. However, their efforts at reconciliation were in vain; after seven years of marriage, the two finally had to call it quits. On the advice of his attorney, Larry took the blame to expedite the divorce. As is usual in such cases, Miriam received legal custody of Joey, then five. The year was 1969.

Joey and his mother moved to an old two-story house in a West Side slum area, sharing it with friends of Miriam. Soon after, she married Robert Jefferson, a widower. Miriam's friends moved out; Jefferson moved in with his two small children. They were of different worlds; he a poorly educated, unemployed black; she from a middle-class Jewish background, a high school graduate with considerable self-education. We met Bob on our visits. He was about thirty, thin, of medium height. We never really got to know him; he was quiet when we were around.

Larry took Joey for weekends, picking him up on Friday after school and returning him Sunday evening. He also visited him on Wednesdays. When Toby and I visited Joey, we were heartsick at the squalor in which the Jeffersons lived. Their main sources of

10

income were from Miriam's part-time work and Larry's child care allowance. I recommended Bob for a shipping job with my company, but the traveling distance was too great and he quit. Thus, except for odd jobs, he remained unemployed.

To relieve Larry of the long drive to and from the West Side, I sometimes took Joey home after a weekend with his father. I remember one late Sunday afternoon in the fall, when Joey was eight years old. Glancing at him sitting quietly beside me on the front seat, I smiled with pleasure. He noticed my smile out of the corner of his eye and turned his head slightly in acknowledgment. Just to look at my grandson gave me joy. At the same time my love for him—and my pity—made me want to weep. He sat at the far edge of the seat next to the window so he could look out. He was too small to see out the windshield without standing up, and I told him not to, in case of sudden braking.

After half an hour we turned up the street on which the Jeffersons lived, a mean block of old houses stacked against one another like moldy boxes. There was a car-wreck along the curb, and garbage littered street and sidewalks. The garden patches in front of the houses were rank, and where there were many children and the patch unfenced, the grass had been trampled into dirt. Many of the houses had broken or rudely repaired windows; almost all were in need of repair and paint. This, I thought to myself, is where my grandson lives, the kind of street I once lived on when I was his age, in Brooklyn, New York. We've made progress I reflected bitterly, from slum to slum in two generations.

I pulled up to the curb near his house. "So long, Joey, I'll see you next Friday."

He looked up at me. "Don't I live on a nice street, Grandpa?"

I was taken by surprise, but I smiled and said, "I guess you do, Joey." He wrestled the door open, got out, and ran up the steps of his house to open the door, which lacked a handle.

Whenever Toby and I visited, we would take Joey and his half-sister and brother for a ride and treats. Larry sometimes brought the Jefferson children to our home on Friday evenings to join in our family get-togethers. At first shy, they eventually warmed up, imitating Joey in calling Toby "Bubbie." Pronounced in Southern drawl, it gave us a chuckle.

Meanwhile there were signs that Miriam's marriage to Bob Jefferson was running into difficulties. At one point the Jefferson children were sent to live with "Granny." Another time, alone with me, in our kitchen during one of his weekend visits, Joey suddenly asked, "Do you and Bubbie fight?"

He surprised me, since the question seemed to come out of the blue. "Sometimes," I said, "but not often. Why do you ask?"

"I never see you fight," he said.

What scenes had he witnessed to prompt the question? Already a child of divorce, where could he find stability? Could we, his grandparents, fill that need when we saw him but a few hours a week?

At the dinner table that night, we noticed Joey had developed a rapid, nervous eye-blinking. At our suggestion, Larry promised to take him to a doctor.

Once, sitting on my lap, he interrupted my reading to ask, "Grandpa, are whites as good as blacks?"

"Of course. Did anyone tell you different?"

"Gloria wouldn't play with me because she says I'm a 'whitey'."

"Who's Gloria?"

"She's in my class."

When a business appointment took me near the West Side at about three in the afternoon one day, I stopped outside Joey's school building, hoping to meet him. The children, black and Latino, came tumbling out, laughing and yelling. Among the last, Joey emerged quietly, and alone.

"Joey!" I called joyfully from across the street. He looked up, recognized me, and slowly came over. I took his hand to walk him home. "Everything O.K.?" I asked. He nodded noncommittally.

After two years Miriam left Bob Jefferson. Taking Lainie, the child of their union, and Joey, she rented a small apartment on the North Side of Chicago. When Miriam got a full-time job, Lainie was sent to an all-day nursery and Joey became a latch-key child, on his own from nine to six-thirty. Very much troubled, Toby, after a great effort, found a family with a boy Joey's age who lived across the street from his school. The mother agreed to give Joey an after school snack and supervise his play until it was time for him to go home.

When the Jeffersons managed a reconciliation and moved into an apartment on Chicago's South Side, it was much too distant for Toby and I to visit, and so we kept in touch by phone. During one week we called several times a day when Joey, home with the mumps, was left alone.

12

One Friday in October 1972 Larry came as usual to pick up Joey for the weekend and found Jefferson alone. Miriam had disappeared, he knew not where, and she had taken Joey and Lainie with her. Miriam being unpredictable, we worried. After two anxious weeks on our part, Miriam phoned Larry from Boston, her home town. Miriam made Larry promise not to let Jefferson know where she was. Larry pointed out that the removal of Joey from the jurisdiction of the Illinois court was in violation of the divorce decree. He persuaded her to let him come to Boston to talk things over.

In Boston, Larry could not convince her to return. She was terrified of Jefferson. She fled, she said, because he tried to harm her; he had fired a gun at her. She was afraid that no matter where she lived in Chicago, he would find her. She agreed, however, to transfer custody of Joey over to Larry, provided he be sent to her for three yearly visits: at Christmas, spring vacation, and for the month of August.

Thus began a new, stable life for Joey. Larry took a larger apartment so Joey could have a room of his own. Being a teacher at a nearby high school, Larry arrived home every afternoon soon after Joey. Father and son chatted and had a snack together before Joey went out to play with his friends. His school work was good; his sixth grade teacher enrolled him for an enrichment program; and he was appointed patrol boy to guard a street crossing. For the first time in his life, Joey settled down for an extended period in one home and one school. In contrast, during the previous three and a half years, he had lived at four addresses and attended as many schools.

In spite of all the shifts and shocks, Joey retained a healthy capacity to enjoy life. We attributed it to the child's resiliency, Larry's constancy ("I'm your only dad; I'll always be around," he had assured a worried Joey when Miriam married Jefferson), and the anchor our family and home gave Joey. With few exceptions, we were all together Friday evenings and holidays. From the moment he walked into our apartment on the North Side of Chicago, the boy knew himself on safe and familiar ground. His coat and shoes off, he ran into the kitchen to sniff at the cooking, asking to be lifted to peer into the pots. At the table, he had the peculiar habit of smelling his food before putting it into his mouth; he sniffed at books too, as if to judge their contents by some indefinable odor. He could always find his toys in their

13

accustomed place, and his books on the lowest shelf of the breakfront in our living room.

I loved to read to him, beginning when he was about three years old. When he grew tall enough to reach the bookshelves, he would make his own selection and back up to me to be lifted into my lap. It was a delight to read to Joey because he was so responsive, especially to word play. After many readings, he had memorized his favorites and I would purposely commit reading errors so he could gleefully catch me. On those times when he spent the night with us, he would demand a story from me upon being tucked into bed and then he would summon Toby for lullabies.

Friday evenings our sons would often bring their instruments to our regular family get-together: Larry, guitar; Ronald, banjo and recorder. Toby and I loved to sing—we first met at a summer songfest—and our sons shared the love. Larry and Ron resembled each other physically, but were very different in temperament. Larry was outgoing, quick to make friends; Ron was more shy. Larry loved adventure, had hitchhiked twice across the country and to Alaska. He had been to France, England, Latin America, and talked of settling in Canada one day. He liked teaching and was well esteemed by his colleagues. Ronald, who worked in a bank as a systems analyst, spent his spare time developing a graphic language. A work of his—a mathematical equation in graphic form—was exhibited at a biennial show at the Chicago Art Institute. Although Larry had not remarried, he often dated. Ronald did so seldom. Toby loved to joke about her male harem, though she always dreamed of a daughter-in-law with whom she could also be close.

I had first met Toby at a cooperative summer camp outside New York City. Alone and shy, I was attracted by her radiant, ingenuous smile. With easy grace she drew me into her small circle of friends. Toby took delight in the world around her and wanted to share her pleasure. On the first evening of our meeting, her group sang union songs in which I joined, and then went on to Jewish tunes unfamiliar to me. She sang sweetly and with feeling for the songs of the East European *shtetl*. She cannot walk now, but in my memory I see her striding toward me, her loose, burnished hair catching the light of day, her smile radiating simplicity and goodwill.

As her face, so was her character. It knew no sham. She went to the heart of what really mattered—decent human relations. She

14

was good for me, her common sense cutting through pretense and wishful thinking. When I wanted an honest opinion, I got it from Toby. Not having my wider experience, she was sometimes wrong, but I respected her judgment.

When, during the war, the white-collar union I worked for asked me to take charge of the Midwest Region, she willingly left her devoted family to join me in Chicago. With her came our first child, Larry, then three years old. I was on the road a lot, visiting local unions from Denver to Wichita. The burden of managing our household and two small children, Ronald being born a year after we moved to Chicago, fell on her.

When Toby became ill, I had taken over the shopping and dinner preparation. My first criterion was speed of execution, which she laughingly alleged was my only one. She had wide interests and scores of friends. Before her illness and when our boys were still in school, Toby had been an officer of her Parent-Teachers Association and got it to initiate a cultural exchange program with a black high school chapter. That was considered so far-out in the mid-fifties that the story made the front page of the *Chicago Daily News.*

For the last fifteen years Toby had been in a wheelchair, although she could stand for short intervals with the aid of a walker or with some other support. She liked to go through the daily press and bring items of political and social interest to my attention. We were both active with an independent voters group and considered ourselves left-of-center. We had maintained an active concern for world peace, and for many years I was a public speaker for the United Nations Association.

We were a close-knit family and our love surrounded Joey. Toby mothered him, while he made a boy's show of protest. From what we could see, he was a happy child yet we ached for him, knowing that a mother's love was irreplaceable.

Visits to Miriam at the appointed times went well. She would phone in advance to set the date and give her current address—always a new one—and Larry would make the plane arrangements. Joey enjoyed the visits to his mother, complaining only that he had to babysit for Lainie.

Christmas of 1974 came and went without Miriam's usual call, however, and Joey's disappointment was apparent. We heard no word from her until June of 1975 when she phoned Larry to request that the boy visit her during August in Los Angeles. She

15

said she had joined the Hare Krishnas and was living in their Los Angeles temple. We had never heard of the sect.

To prepare him for the visit, Larry took Joey on a Sunday afternoon to the Krishna temple in Evanston, a suburb which adjoins Chicago to the north. They listened to a lecture, watched a ceremony, and shared the food. Larry reported that Joey wept that his mother was involved with such a strange group. Still, the boy wanted to visit her.

3

I Chant with the Krishnas

NOW WE WERE TORMENTED BY THE QUESTION,
"What is happening to Joey?" Efforts to phone him at the Los
Angeles temple were unavailing. "We don't know anyone by that
name," the answering voice said—yet his name had been known
well enough before the episode on the temple lawn. To learn
something—anything—of what the boy might be experiencing, I
too decided to visit the Krishna temple in Evanston.

Having learned that the temple had open house at five every
Sunday, I drove to the converted YMCA building on Emerson
Avenue one September afternoon. Painted yellow and with the
Hare Krishna mantra in red letters across the front, the temple
stood in sharp contrast to the small store fronts which flanked it
and to the large new senior citizens' housing complex facing it
from across the street.

A clutter of shoes inside the entrance door induced me to
remove mine. Unshod, I went painfully on callused feet into the
large, rather bare reception room. Other than two easy chairs,
there was a large table covered with the sect's literature—the
books and magazines vividly illustrated with scenes from Hindu
mythology.

A young male devotee in saffron dhoti (baggy, diaper-like
pants), head shaven except for a little pigtail at the back, called
out, "Hare Krishna," to which I stiffly replied, "How d'ye do?"
When I introduced myself, he gave me his Sanskrit name and
wished me a happy new year. Was he Jewish, I wondered?

By now, there were several other visitors. We were led down a
flight of stairs into a brightly lit, high-ceilinged hall which must

17

have been the former basketball court of the YMCA. Its walls were painted cream, the floor covered with black and white tile. At the north end was a dais on which stood a large framed picture of the aged founder and head of ISKCON (International Society for Krishna Consciousness), Swami Prabhupada (pronounced Prá-bu-pod). It was hung with floral wreaths and propped upon colorful cushions. The south end of the hall was screened by drapes. As there were no chairs, everyone sat on the floor. About twenty visitors, mostly young, a few with children, arranged themselves along the east wall facing the center. Along the west wall were a few women devotees in flowing, gaudy saris. All the devotees moved silently and swiftly on bare feet.

A devotee came to the middle of the floor and sat down cross-legged before a microphone facing the visitors. His dark eyes were sunken; his high cheek bones, large nose, and shaven head gave a skull-like appearance. Introducing himself as Purana, he launched into an explanation of the Krishna Consciousness movement. Meanwhile, more and more visitors kept arriving until there were about fifty, half of whom were East Indians who came in family groups. With the exception of one black, all the devotees were white.

The speaker interlarded his talk with Sanskrit phrases. "We are not our bodies," he began. "We are atmans, spirit souls. Suppose I amputate my arm," he proposed, making a motion of cutting at his left elbow. "There is my arm." He looked at the ground to his left. "It is lying there rotting. Is that me? No. I am not my arm. Neither am I my body. That too will die and rot eventually. I must be something else, something indestructible which continues after I shed my body. That something is atman, a tiny particle of the universal Atman, Krishna. When the body dies, the atman leaves to enter another body and begin a new cycle." He paused to let the thought sink in.

"The real you is your spirit soul, your atman. It yearns to reunite itself with Krishna from whence it came. But the atman is burdened by karma, by its previous lives, by materialism, which is attractive to the body; by the senses, seeking self-gratification. Thus, we find it difficult to get off samsara; we are doomed to continue on the wheel of birth, misery, old age, and death.

"This world," he continued, "is maya, illusion. The real world, the one the soul yearns for, is Krishna, with whom there is eternal

18

bliss. How can we get off samsara and unite with Krishna? Through Krishna consciousness, the way taught by our Spiritual Master, who comes to us from Krishna himself through a five-thousand-year succession of spiritual masters. That way is not difficult. We have only to chant the holy name of God, Krishna, stop eating the flesh of living things, refrain from illicit sex, smoking, gambling and frivolous sports. In whatever we do, we need to have Krishna in our thoughts; do everything for Krishna."

He asked for questions. A young woman with two children asked, "May we not be both body and soul?"

"The body," he replied, "is of no importance. It is like a suit of clothes. When it's worn out, you take it off and throw it away."

I raised my hand. "Perhaps this life is all there is to enjoy and once dead there is nothing else?"

"If you believe that," he said, "I can tell you nothing."

A young woman, who said she was Catholic, asked why all the devotees were young.

"What do you mean, 'young'?"

"Under thirty."

"We have some devotees over thirty; our Spiritual Master is seventy-nine."

"Another question," she continued, "how do you define illicit sex?"

"All sex is illicit, except between husband and wife, and only for procreation. All our troubles are due to this material body which seeks only to gratify itself through sex, animal flesh, empty amusements, drink, and dope. If we give in, we are bound to samsara, to eternal misery, birth after birth without end."

He stopped, turned slowly to look at the Swami's portrait and then back again to the audience. "Our Spiritual Master teaches us to become devotees of Krishna, the Supreme Personality of Godhead. This is far more beneficial than any of the material things we are conditioned to like. If a person overcomes this disease of his soul, he attains the Supreme Lord's abode and never has to come back to this miserable, material world. He will have achieved eternal bliss."

He dealt with their dietary rules which prohibit the meat of cows, sheep, fowl, even the eating of eggs. At some length he described the usefulness of the cow. He rhapsodized over a long list of dairy products from cheese to yogurt. "How do we show our gratitude to this wonderful animal?" he asked. "We murder it."

He concluded with a reference to the ceremony we were to participate in, after which we would have "prasadam, the remnants of the food offered to Krishna."

A devotee with a two-ended hand drum stepped up to the microphone and rehearsed us in the Hare Krishna mantra, the mahamantra. We chanted after him, phrase by phrase: "Hare Krishna, Hare Krishna, Krishna, Krishna, Hare, Hare; Hare Rama, Hare Rama, Rama, Rama, Hare, Hare." He interjected, "Our Spiritual Master teaches that all we need to do to be blissful is chant Hare Krishna and take prasadam." He beat the drum slowly with his hand and we chanted after him. He took steps from side to side in rhythm; we followed. He speeded up chant and step. I had no stomach for it and after a few rounds stopped and merely looked on. No one seemed to notice, or to care. Most of the visitors, however, got into the swing; some who seemed to have had previous experience raised their voices and stepped with verve.

More devotees appeared, mostly men. As they entered on bare feet, they came to their knees before Prabhupada's picture, bringing foreheads to the floor, posteriors high. The men were in the center of the floor, the women grouped along the west wall chanting dignifiedly, demurely stepping from side to side. They began to jig as the chant speeded up and the sound volume rose.

After fifteen minutes, at a signal from the drummer, the devotees turned to the south wall. The draperies pulled back revealed a spotlighted scene of portrait paintings, flowers, and fruits. The center picture, standing on brightly colored pillows, was of a youthful couple whom I guessed to be Krishna and his consort (their word), Radharani. On either side were pictures of Prabhupada's predecessors. They were painted in the naive style and gaudy colors of the book covers on the reception room table.

When the curtains parted, there was a heightening of excitement; the chanting increased in tempo and volume. The drummer at the microphone, from whom the chanters took their cue, varied the chant. The jigging had turned into dancing, becoming wild as the drummer increased speed. Some of the men at the very center leaped straight up, arms thrust high. A devotee, clanging small cymbals in time to the chant, ran madly around the room, head thrown back, shouting, his throat straining. The women members, graceful in their saris, kept up the side-step on the outskirts of the men's group, adding their voices to the volume

20

of sound. Several of the male visitors, all young, joined in the leaping, but none of the East Indians. They remained in place, chanting and jigging.

When the leaping and shouting reached an unbearable peak, the drummer sounded a new variation in reduced tempo. It was a relief. But, as the new tune continued, the pace increased and again came strenuous, ecstatic leaps. Sari billowing, a woman devotee stepped up to the altar, her hands making motions before the portraits. The pungent odor of incense saturated the hall. It was the signal for the sound system to be turned up. The din of chant, drum, cymbals, and at the climax, the wild cry of a conch shell, rose to such a level I had to cover my ears. The dancers' faces shone with sweat, their eyes were frenzied. But when the chanting abated, they gradually assumed a normal mien. A half-hour had passed since the drapes had been drawn back. A voice invited us upstairs for prasadam.

A neighbor who worked in a health food store had given me the name of a customer who had recently joined the cult. Catching sight of the devotee who had greeted me earlier, I asked if Tom was here today.

"I was telling Joan at the health food store that I would like to know more about Krishna consciousness," I said to Tom, when he was brought over to me. "She suggested I talk to you." Barefoot and dressed in yellow dhoti, he was cordial and invited me to come upstairs for the food.

The room above the temple was of the same size but with a low ceiling. Paper plates with food were spread over the floor and alongside each place was a cup of fruit liquid. My dish consisted of a scoop of saffron rice, an eggplant mixture, cooked fruit, and a fried dough cake. The eggplant was spiced with curry, the rest bland but too sweet for my taste. We ate with our fingers, the devotees licking theirs clean after each mouthful. Many went to the large pots at the front of the room for second and third helpings.

Tom and I were joined by a big devotee, over six feet, and unlike others, paunchy. His plate was filled to overflowing; he caught the drippings and carried them to his mouth. Tom introduced him by his "spiritual" name and, at my blank look, said, "Call him Don."

21

Don did most of the talking. He was filled with proselytizing zeal and had difficulty talking and eating at the same time. Directly behind us was a black woman devotee passionately explaining her beliefs to a husky, young black man. He looked dubious; she sounded impatient. All over the large room there were similar clusters of visitors and devotees. Sunday open house seemed to be the cult's occasion for winning converts.

Don returned with a second plateful. "We are eating prasadam," he said, "food blessed by the Lord Krishna. If we eat prasadam and chant Hare Krishna, that's the remedy for all the evils in this material world." Tom listened with the eager look of the novitiate.

"I'm Jewish," I said, "and religious Jews also thank the Lord for their food." I tried to be pleasant.

"But they eat meat," Don said accusingly. "They don't follow their own commandments: thou shalt not murder."

"Perhaps that commandment was not meant to apply to animals," I responded.

"It's murder though, any way you look at it, the taking of life."

I turned to Tom. "How come there are no Hindus among the devotees?" He smiled wryly; it must have been a sore point. Don answered. "They say they know all about Lord Krishna, so they don't have to join. They come only for the ceremony on Sundays."

"And for the food," Tom added sarcastically.

I asked if the center picture on the altar was a representation of Krishna and his wife. Tom started to answer when Don interrupted. An exchange followed which I couldn't understand.

"That's not a representation," Don said, "that's Krishna himself." I looked puzzled. "We don't worship a symbol, only the real thing. Those are the deities you saw, the Supreme Lord Krishna Himself and his Consort. I couldn't love a symbol. Could you?"

He stared at me for an answer. I was at a loss for a reply which would not offend. A thought popped into my head. "I read somewhere about a Greek philosopher who said that if horses had a god, he would look like a horse."

"A soul may go into a horse," Don said solemnly.

"A man's soul?"

"That's right. At death it can go into anything, any other form of life, even into an insect. You heard Purana earlier. The atman, that's the soul, leaves the body at death and enters another form."

"Unless you're in Krishna consciousness," Tom explained, "then the soul flies directly to Krishna's abode."

22

"Are children subject to the same laws?" I asked.

"Of course," Don answered. "Children are responsible for their own souls. The main thing is to teach them about Krishna, otherwise they don't serve God, and instead waste their lives doing nonsense. They become victims of self-gratification—movies, sports, TV."

"What about learning math? Or the sciences?"

"When one has Krishna, he needs nothing else," Don replied. "He may think he has everything, but without Krishna he has nothing. Prabhupada said it is our duty to teach how to love God and worship him in our daily lives. All other aims in life are useless, temporary." Don's face glowed with conviction.

"Don," I said, "you speak of God and of Krishna, using the names interchangeably. Other people worship God but not Krishna."

"Such people are to be commended. But the *Gita* says, 'Abandon all varieties of religion and just surrender unto Me.' Other ways of worshipping God are wasteful. One who is serious should come to us."

"Tell me about Prabhupada."

"He's our Spiritual Master," Don said.

"Like a guru?"

"More than that; much more."

"Is he your Christ?"

"Something like that," Don said. "He gets his knowledge directly from Krishna. Something like Moses, who spoke to God on Sinai. Some of us think he is an avatar of Krishna."

"An avatar?"

"A manifestation of Krishna."

"The man who led the chanting said that all one needs to do to reach Krishna consciousness is chant and eat prasadam."

"That's right. If you do enough chanting, you won't be troubled by the material world, by sex and other distractions. Chanting purifies."

"How much is enough?" I asked.

"Well, they say that Prabhupada chants all the time, even in sleep. But every devotee is required to chant the mahamantra sixteen rounds a day; a round has 108 beads, so your total is 1,728."

I was amazed. "1,728 times a day?"

"At a minimum," Don said.

"How long does it take?"

"To one who is proficient, two, two and a half hours."

I tried to imagine Joey chanting for two and a half hours, but couldn't. "Children, too?" I asked.

"We start them young. By the time they're nine or ten they do the whole bit."

"What does that do to you?" I asked impulsively, thinking of the deadening effect of the endless repetition.

Don did not catch the implicaton of my question. "You are repeating the names of God—Rama and Krishna. 'Hare' addresses the energy of God. You are fixing your mind on Him. If, for example, you are chanting His name at the time of death, you will go to a spiritual life and never be reincarnated again. If you are thinking of your dog at the time of death, you will become a dog in the next life. If you are thinking of your wife, you will become a woman."

"What's so bad about that?" I laughed.

He did not share my humor. "Prabhupada says that women have half the brains of men."

When I could not restrain a smile, he added, "You may smile, but it's a fact." I wasn't going to argue with him. "You cannot understand what chanting does," he continued, "because there's no way to explain it in words. Words are only symbols for the real thing. The mahamantra, however, does not consist of ordinary words. For instance, if you are thirsty and say 'water,' will your thirst be satisfied? Of course not. But when you say 'Krishna,' He is actually present. We experience Him. We experience His qualities of eternity, knowledge, bliss in the sound vibrations of His name." He took in my incomprehension. "You cannot grasp this intellectually; you have to experience its transcendental meaning for yourself."

"How would I know if it's working for me?"

"It will be self-evident," he said with certainty. "If you eat a meal, you know when you're satisfied. Right? When you chant Hare Krishna, you will know beyond a doubt that it's working for you."

Corroboration came from Tom who had been listening avidly. "That's right."

"Are you suggesting I try it?"

"Why not," Tom urged. "No one's too old for Krishna."

"Let me ask you this, Don. Purana spoke only of birth, old age, misery, and death as man's cycle on earth. What about joy?

Surely, everyone has some happy moments, even some great ones."

Don replied, "The pig lies in the filth of his pen swilling garbage. He thinks to himself, 'This garbage is great; I'm happy.' Do you think he's happy? People confuse happiness with self-gratification."

"You suggest the pig as a comparison with our lives?"

"I've lived both ways," Don said, "I should know."

By this time, very few were left on the floor. Still wanting to talk to Tom alone, I thanked Don for his explanation of doctrine and for his patience.

"We have a class at the temple in *Bhagavad Gita*," he said. "Visitors are welcome."

"I've read the *Gita*," I said.

"Have you?" He was delighted. "You'll like the class."

"I'll think about it," I said. Tom walked me to the door. Outside, the night was warm and I suggested that we sit on the temple steps for a moment. Several devotees were standing around on the upper step; we seated ourselves on the lowest.

"Joan says you no longer visit her food store," I said.

"No need to now. I get my food here at the temple."

"Tom, how did you get to meet the Krishnas?"

"I was on State Street downtown one Saturday afternoon, and I ran into them dancing and chanting. They looked so happy." His face lit up at the recollection. "I hung around and talked to them. They invited me to the temple. I came the next day, a Sunday, to their open house. I came again the next Sunday. I began to look forward to Sundays; that used to be the worst day for me. Then I took a class. It got so I wanted to stay all the time." He talked readily like one who is glad to testify for his new-found religion.

"Were you employed?"

"I worked in Skokie for the Regulator Company."

"I know their plant," I said. "I was in real estate before I retired. I represented an investor group which bought sixty acres and developed them into an industrial park. Your company was just west of our park. It's a big outfit."

"Sure is; over a thousand people. You feel lost; a tiny part in a big machine."

"Didn't you have friends?"

"I wouldn't call them friends, just people to say 'Hi' to."

"What does your family think of your joining the temple?"

"Not much. My older brother visited me last week. 'It's your life,' he said."

"What about your parents?"

"My father died a couple of years ago. He was the one I really cared for."

"Was your family church-affiliated?"

"I was born Catholic, but it didn't mean much to me. I didn't know what religion really meant until I joined the Krishnas."

"Can you explain your feeling?"

"Like Don said, it's hard to put into words. Once during arotik—that's the temple ceremony—we were sitting before the altar, a few of us, chanting under our breaths. I felt a strange sensation as if Krishna were present. It gave me goose-pimples." He fell silent. Sensing his mood, I too kept still.

A red Thunderbird powered down the street and came to a screeching halt before a red light. Inside was a young man with a girl by his side. The car radio was booming disco music.

"At one time," Tom resumed, "I would have given my right arm to be in his place. Now I have nothing and desire nothing. When I joined, I turned everything over to the temple. It wasn't much. Now I own nothing, not even these clothes. Everything belongs to the temple. I eat what's provided; sleep on the floor."

"It must have been quite a change."

"It wasn't easy. It was rough getting up before dawn, cold showers, the change of diet. And the dancing! My feet are still swollen." He looked down at his bare feet, wiggling his toes. "But they're toughening."

"Do you have a temple job?"

"For now, I'm setting up their library. It's a mess. People borrowing; no records. I'm cataloguing the books, setting up a loan system."

I turned our conversation to what was on my mind. "I saw a few children tonight, the boys with shaved heads."

"We have some marrieds. They live in separate quarters."

"Do their kids go to school?"

"They're too young. When they are five, they are sent to our Dallas school."

"They're sent off by themselves, without the parents?" I showed surprise.

Tom nodded. "Kind of rough, I guess, at that age." I thought of the little boy who, over the phone, asked Toby, "Is this my mother?"

"What of the older children, ten, twelve?"

"I think when they're that age they are sent to our farms. We have one in Mississippi and another in West Virginia."

The devotees who had been lounging above us had gone in. Tom was becoming restive. I liked him for his honesty, his willingness, on the basis of a tenuous relation to a mutual friend, to discuss his intimate thoughts. I wanted to know him better, to deepen our relationship. I desired profoundly to understand, if I could, the nature of his experience.

"I would like very much for my wife to meet you," I said. "She's in a wheelchair. Is there any chance of you visiting us? We live fifteen minutes away by car."

He hesitated. "I would have to get permission." Seeing my disappointment, he added, "I'll tell them I'll be spreading the word. That should do it." I gave him our phone number; we shook hands cordially and parted.

4

Letter from Joey

NOT LONG AFTER MY GLIMPSE INTO KRISHNA LIFE
at the Evanston temple, Larry obtained a court order granting
him temporary custody of Joey and empowering him to bring his
son back into the jurisdiction of the Illinois Court. Once he was
back, the court would hold another hearing at which Miriam and
Joey would be present. At that time the issue of permanent
custody would be decided.

The next day a troubled Larry came to discuss an unforeseen
development. "I asked Earl Massin, my attorney, how I was
supposed to get Joey. 'Just serve the order on Miriam and take the
boy,' he said. But, I don't know where in the temple she lives. If I
go to the temple office and ask, you know what'll happen, Dad.
They'll tip her off and she'll be gone before I can get to her."

"I don't understand this," I said. "Where are the teeth in the
court order? Aren't the police supposed to enforce it?"

"I asked Massin the same thing: why can't I have the police
come with me? That's when Massin checked with California law.
It seems that California will not issue a warrant for Joey based on
an order for temporary custody, only if it's permanent."

"Oh boy," I moaned. "Now we find out. How can we get a
permanent order for custody before we've acted on the temporary?"

"Massin thinks he can get it because of the special circumstances in this case."

More delay, more costs, I thought. "There must be a better
way," I said. "Maybe we ought to take the chance and try with the
temporary order. After all, it is a court order and Miriam and the
Krishnas may respect it."

"Dad, we may never get another chance."

"What do you mean?" His desperation disturbed me.

"If I miss, they may ship Joey off where we can never find him."

I was chilled by the thought. "We'd better move carefully."

While we were deliberating, my sister Rachel called from Los Angeles. She had talked to a detective agency in Van Nuys which specialized in cases like ours. By surveillance, it would establish Joey's movements, call Larry when they were ready, supply three men to protect him when he picked up Joey, and escort him to the airport. The fee was reasonable.

Toby and I listened but did not know what to say to Rachel. We were on strange ground—detectives, surveillance, child-snatching. We winced at the implications. Rachel, on the other hand, urged us to act quickly, to get Joey before they hid him away.

Larry consulted his attorney, who advised that Rachel's proposal was perfectly legal. Larry was authorized by his temporary order to find Joey and return him, by whatever means, to Illinois.

Larry called the detective agency to learn more of their methods. How would they proceed? he asked. They would chart Joey's pattern of activity. Then, anticipating where he would be at a particular time—for example, going from his dormitory to the temple—they would help Larry take him from the street into a waiting car. Suppose Joey resisted? They would force him into the car. Suppose devotees surrounded them before they could get him to the car? Three men would be available to take care of that contingency; they knew their business. Could that mean a fight on the street? It could, but that was their concern. Suppose someone got hurt? That was their worry, not his.

Yet Larry did worry, and not only about that, but about the traumatic effect on Joey of forcibly being grabbed off the street. He decided against using the agency and instead authorized his lawyer to petition the court for a permanent order.

While we were waiting for action on Larry's petition for permanent custody, three events occurred to deepen our gloom. On October 28, we received a second letter from Joey. It was to be his last:

I like it here in Krsna consciousness better than the life
I led with you. I have found a higher state. Two years
ago I told you I was tired of the same old drab routine.
Well now I have broken away from all that. Each day is
a new adventure in Krsna....

You want to take me back but I don't want to go....If
you take me back to Chicago, I will run away from you.

Evidently it had been written to discourage Larry from
proceeding with his custody suit. (Miriam had been notified by
the court to appear.) This letter was in Joey's handwriting, but
were they his words?

On November 1, we received a phone call from our niece Carrie,
who lived in San Diego. While on a visit to Los Angeles, she and
her husband, Sam, had caught sight of Joey and Miriam with a
group of thirty Krishnas on Hollywood Boulevard. Joey was up
front with the men, chanting and dancing; Miriam was at the
rear among the women. Joey's head was shaved except for a pony
tail at the back. He was dressed in the same garb as the others:
loose, pale-pink pants and a sweatshirt. Not knowing what to do,
Carrie and Sam did not approach him.

The news hit us hard. Joey had become one of them; he had
permitted his head to be shaved.

The third event confirmed our fears. On Sunday, November 10,
we received another call from San Diego, this time it was Doris,
Toby's younger sister, Carrie's mother. The day before she had
seen and talked to Joey!

Hearing on the radio that there would be a Krishna festival in
Balboa Park, and on the chance that a delegation including Joey
might come from Los Angeles, she had gone to the park. Sure
enough, Doris ran into Joey.

"He startled when he saw me," Doris said, "and looked
uncomfortable. To reassure him, I asked if his mother was there.
He led me over to Miriam, who had Lainie with her too. After
awhile, Joey became relaxed and quite talkative. His hair was
closely cropped, with a small pony tail at the back. He wore a
striped polo shirt and orange temple pants.

"When Miriam saw me, she was hostile at first. She said, 'We'll
have to send Joey away again so he can't be found.' I assumed she
meant that after the incident on the temple lawn, Joey had been
sent somewhere for a time. She blamed me for Larry's attempt

30

because I had spoken to her on the phone a few days before. And then she said something which shocked me. 'You can tell Larry he'll never find us. You know, they can send us to any one of thirty cities, or even to India.'"

Toby and I heard these dreadful words in silence. Could Miriam be so cruel? It was beyond understanding. Yet, she was treating Bob Jefferson the same way; he hadn't seen or heard from Lainie in three years.

"As we talked," Doris went on, "Miriam loosened up. I asked Joey if he was going to school. He said, 'No, all they teach is junk. They don't teach about Krishna.' Miriam said I shouldn't worry about Joey's education, he'd be sent to one of their schools. Lainie, who had been listening, told her mother she didn't want to go back to Dallas, the 'gurukula,' she called it. 'I want to stay with you,' she said to Miriam. She kept repeating she didn't want to go back, and cried. It hurt me to hear her pleading with her mother. How could she send a child of five to a school a thousand miles away? She said to Lainie, 'You're going to go to a nice new school in Illinois.' I asked Joey what he had heard from his father and grandparents. He said, 'They don't write or phone me.'"

We had suspected that Joey was cut off from all communication with us. Not only had we and Larry written, but two of Joey's friends had also done so.

"I told Joey I couldn't believe you wouldn't try to keep in touch with him. Miriam said, 'Maybe their letters got lost in the shuffle.' I said to Joey, 'You'll be twelve on November 17. We'd like to come to Los Angeles and celebrate your birthday with you.' Miriam quickly put in, 'I don't know where he'll be then.'"

"How did Joey look?" Toby asked.

"He's grown an inch or so and he looks thinner. But is he articulate! He told me if I joined the Krishnas I would quit the smoking habit. I asked him where he lives and what he does. He said he lives in the men's quarters of the temple and works in the kitchen cutting vegetables. He complained that he's bored and wants to go to school.

"I asked Miriam what she does, and learned she works for their publications, doing research and writing. She told me she's found what she's been looking for.

"I invited them to come home with me, but Miriam said they had to go back to Los Angeles with their group. Carrie and Sam joined us for awhile during the conversation and Carrie snapped a picture. I'll send you a copy as soon as it's developed."

31

The Balboa Park picture showed Miriam, Lainie, Joey, Doris, and Sam. In the three years since we had seen Miriam, she had grown much heavier and older looking. Tilaka (white clay) was smeared on her nose bridge and from her neck hung a bead bag containing the string of 108 beads on which she daily chanted the cult's mahamantra. Lainie looked tall for her five years; her Afro haircut came up to Joey's ear. She wore large eyeglasses and also had tilaka painted on nose and forehead.

Joey's face appeared pinched, troubled; his eyes half closed. A bead bag hung from his neck too. Was it possible that after only three months they had him chanting the Hare Krishna mantra 1,728 times daily? Could that lively, inquisitive mind be harnessed to hours-long repetition of "Hare Krishna, Hare Krishna, Hare, Hare"?

In the long months which followed, I would ponder Joey's image in the Balboa Park photo scores of times, seeking to read the thoughts behind the small, troubled face. Eventually that picture would look back at me from newspapers and TV screens. It became a picture to indict the Krishnas, proof that Joey had been inducted into the cult, without the consent of his father, at the age of twelve.

The hearing on Larry's petition for permanent custody had taken place October 23, about a week prior to the Balboa Park incident. Our whole family came to court that morning, each of us eager to see Joey and at the same time fearful of what he might do or say. How would he greet us? Had his mind been poisoned against us? Had he been told that we didn't care for him anymore? Would he ask to remain with the cult? It was a tense moment for us when the clerk called our case, and then a deep disappointment when we saw that Miriam and Joey had simply not shown up.

Nevertheless Judge David Linn interrogated Larry, Toby (who broke into tears), and me, to inform himself of Joey's life during the three years he lived with Larry. He went into the circumstances leading to Joey's induction into the cult. It seemed to us, from the nature of his inquiry, that Linn's decision would be favorable.

It was delayed, however. A few days after the hearing, the court was notified by Legal Aid, a national free service for indigent litigants, that Miriam had asked for a new hearing. She requested that Larry pay her and Joey's transportation, to which he agreed. Then, a week later, Legal Aid bowed out, saying that Miriam had failed to cooperate in the preparation of her case. The court thereupon entered its order granting Larry permanent custody.

Among the findings of that order were the following:

"That on or about the 15th of November of 1972, the mother did voluntarily surrender the said custody of said child to the father...

"That on the last period of visitation in August of 1975, the child went to California where the mother is residing in a Hare Krishna commune, from which the child was not returned.

"That this permanent removal from the jurisdiction of this Court was without Order of the Court or consent of the father and without hearing as to whether said move is in his best interest.

"That personal efforts were made by the father to retrieve said child, which efforts were rebuffed by physical intimidation.

"That since the child has been in California, virtually all efforts to communicate with him have been fruitless and he has been isolated away from his father and family, failing even to call or respond to letters written to him.

"That in his present environment he is not attended to by his mother, but is separated from her and his rearing is left to members of the Hare Krishna Order.

"That he is not being educated in the traditional areas necessary for proper mental growth and existence in our society as it presently exists.

"That while the child resided with the father, his academic achievements were good, his health good except for allergy.

"That the mother has, by placing the child in this communal existence, abandoned her parental and custodial responsibility toward such child.

"That, as a result of all of the Court's prior findings, the Court further finds the mother, since she has abandoned her parental responsibility, is not fit to have the further care, custody, control, and education of said child and that it is in the child's best interest that his permanent custody...be changed from the mother...to the father..."

We breathed a sigh of relief; that hurdle was cleared. With this order, Larry was now able to get a California writ which, when served on Miriam and the Krishnas, would order them to bring Joey to court where Larry would receive him. We inquired among our friends for a Los Angeles attorney.

33

5

Joey Disappears

BERT ROGERS, THE LOS ANGELES ATTORNEY, GAVE us the immediate impression that he knew just what to do. He was a man in his fifties, recommended to us as one who taught the laws of child custody.

On Toby's insistence, I went with Larry to Los Angeles. Two heads were better than one, she said, since we didn't know what complications might arise. Besides, Toby and I had many friends in the city and, if needed for advice or help, I would be able to rally them more easily than Larry would.

On Monday, November 17, we met in Rogers' office with his assistant, Bryan Sachs, to lay out our course of action. To avoid the danger of Joey being spirited away, Rogers proposed an alternative to a writ of habeas corpus—a warrant to authorize the county sheriff to pick up Joey, without previous notification to Miriam and the cult. Sachs would go that day to the Superior Court for Los Angeles County to obtain the warrant. The sheriff would be instructed to go Tuesday morning to Palms Junior High, where Joey was now registered for school, and if he was not there, to the temple compound on Watseka Avenue. The sheriff would bring Joey to the court and we would be there to receive him. These blessed words fell on our ears like balm.

Rogers also suggested we file a damage suit against the cult for assaulting Larry and depriving him of his son. But that decision could wait until we had Joey.

The next day we arrived at court well before the appointed time. Taking a position on a bench outside Department Four, we waited. Anxiously, we peered down the aisles on either side to catch the first glimpse of our lost boy. After about two hours of this, Sachs arrived with the news. The deputy sheriff had gone to Palms School and been told that Joey had been absent for the last seven school days. While the deputy waited, the school principal phoned Miriam, who said Joey was being removed from school to be sent to Texas within a few days.

The deputy had not gone out to the temple since the sheriff's office had previous experience trying to execute warrants for lost children at the Krishna compound. As there were several residences scattered over a couple of blocks, it was impossible to find someone without the Krishnas' cooperation. In fact, the devotees had been known to shift a person from one residence to another when past searches had been carried out. In view of this, Rogers was filing a writ of habeas corpus in lieu of a warrant to order Miriam and the Krishnas to bring Joey to court. Hopefully, that should be ready for service Thursday, the morning of November 20.

We drove away in dejected silence. The principal's phone call must have alerted Miriam. Would she and the Krishnas defy the writ of habeas corpus?

We met again with our attorney on Wednesday, but this time the atmosphere was sober. Rogers confirmed that a writ of habeas corpus would be served the following morning and asked that we meet him at court. He again suggested we file a civil suit for damages against the Society, saying, "We should not let them get away without paying." He added that, because of the large backlog, it would take a couple of years before our case would be reached. The complaint he drafted charged that Larry had been attacked by Krishna members, that Joey had been kept from him causing mental anguish, and it asked for "exemplary and punitive damages."

And so, the next morning found us once more in the corridor outside Department Four. We observed the eddies of troubled humanity. The Department dealt with family disputes, and its petitioners could be seen along the walls of the wide aisles in anxious huddles with their lawyers. Near us, a man and a woman were arguing vehemently while two small children played peek-a-boo around them. Attorneys with briefcases under elbows strode by waving jovially at their friends.

Rogers arrived at 10:00 A.M. to inform us that the writ was being served at that moment, and that his secretary would have a report from the sheriff's office soon. We could phone her in an hour or so.

Larry and I were acutely aware that Miriam might at this moment be carrying out her threat to send Joey to another city, if she hadn't already done so. How could we stop her? Legally, we were doing what we could. Yet, other pressures could be brought to bear. If the cult felt the weight of public opinion, perhaps it might pause before circumventing the writ. Having made up our minds, we asked Rogers if he saw any objection to seeking publicity from the media. Surprisingly, he agreed that in our situation it might be helpful and offered to introduce us to a *Los Angeles Times* reporter, Myrna Oliver. We were lucky to find her in the Court's pressroom. She was bright and young, sharp with questions yet sympathetic to our plight. We told our story and the very first newspaper account of our search appeared the next morning. Its headline read, "Krishna Group Sued for $7.6 Million" and beneath, "Man says he was beaten and son taken from him." The sum, I noticed, took precedence over the human tragedy.

Rogers left us for a court appointment and, when we were through with Ms. Oliver, it was time to call Bonnie, Rogers' secretary. Her report encouraged us. A deputy sheriff had served a copy of the writ at the temple office on Watseka Avenue, and had been directed to Miriam's place of work at the Society's Book Trust on nearby Washington Boulevard. There the deputy found Robert Sandvig (whose Krishna name was "Advaita," we learned later), manager of the shipping department, who told him that Miriam was out for the moment, but he would give her the writ on her return. The deputy accepted the offer, warning that Miriam must appear in court with Joey on Tuesday, November 25, 1975, or face arrest. Sandvig assured him she would be in court with an attorney, adding that he had been under the impression that she had legal custody of Joey.

Miriam, then, was still in town. In spite of our foreboding, things might still work out well. To place more pressure on the Krishnas, Larry and I phoned the TV stations to get our story on the air.

We were successful beyond our hopes. By coincidence, the cult had become national news. Two nights earlier Walter Cronkite had described an attempt by the Krishnas to buy an abandoned academy in Aledo, Illinois. (This was the new school for Lainie of which Miriam had spoken to Doris.) The newscast showed the local population at a mass meeting protesting the sale, and despite an appeal by the Society's regional director, Jagadisha

("Are you intolerant?" he asked the meeting), maintained its opposition. The CBS report had focused interest on the cult and opened the media to us.

A crew from Channel 5 met Larry and me in Culver City in front of the temple office on Thursday afternoon. Because of the rough treatment Larry had been subjected to on the earlier occasion, we asked the police to send a patrol car. When, after a long wait, none came, we entered the temple office and asked for Sandvig, the shipping manager and also the only person whose name we knew. The devotee did not recognize the name; nor did we then know Sandvig's Krishna name. Instead, we asked the young devotee to fetch whoever was in charge.

We went outside with the TV crew to wait on the sidewalk before the office. It adjoined the temple, a two-story structure painted pink with four white columns. Drawn by the activity, devotees began to gather from all sides, many from the three-story residences across the street. Some ignored us, simply pausing before the temple to kneel and put their brows to the ground before entering. Others, curious, milled around the camera crew. One slight, pimpled devotee in a yellow dhoti bristled at us when, after he announced himself to be the temple's public relations man, Larry asked if he knew either Miriam or Joey.

"We have three hundred people around," he replied angrily. "I can't know them all."

The TV reporter, seeing the first bit of action, ordered the camera man to focus on Larry and the public relations man. Meanwhile, I walked up to a group of Krishnas standing nearby. When I asked if anyone of them knew Joey or Miriam, all walked off without answering. Finally, a young man of about thirty, dressed in temple costume, introduced himself as Myron Josephs, secretary of the temple. He must be Jewish, I thought. When I told him we had an order for Joey's return, he replied civilly, "I'll get in touch with the temple president, Bhima das, and let him know you were here. Can I have your address?" I gave him Rogers' address and phone number.

By this time, the television people had taken pictures of the exterior of the temple and were ready to go. Feeling safer, we left with them in their white station wagon and were dropped off at our car parked several blocks away.

The next day at noon we were at the temple again, this time with a crew from Channel 2, CBS. Again we entered the temple office, but hearing voices through the door opposite the one we

37

had entered yesterday, we knocked and opened. Larry introduced himself and me to the three devotees we found seated there. We learned that the big man seated behind the desk was Bhima das, president of the temple.

"Where is Joey Yanoff?" Larry asked him.

"I don't know," Bhima replied. "The last time I saw him or Miriam must have been a couple of days ago. I'm not sure exactly." He spoke coolly. "I'm like a minister," he continued. "I attend to the spiritual needs of our members when they come, but I am not responsible when they don't. I can't keep track of them. We're like any church."

He spoke smoothly, without rancor. I wondered how many times he had repeated these words to other parents in search of their children. I asked Bhima for Joey's spiritual name. He did not know, and as for Miriam's, he could not remember it.

While the TV crew was allowed to film a ceremony then in progress, Larry and I found our way to the Book Trust, where we understood Miriam to work. We gave her name to the receptionist who, referring to a list, told us Miriam's spiritual name was Yasoda. Just as the receptionist was about to dial her number, Myron Josephs appeared. He informed us that Miriam did not work there and invited us to take off our shoes and inspect the premises. She worked, he said, at the Washington Boulevard office of the Book Trust some blocks away.

On the way back to the temple area, I stopped a young woman Krishna to ask if she knew Miriam, Yasoda. Without hesitation, she said she had seen her yesterday at lunch. A male devotee, to whom I had spoken earlier, overheard us. He took the young woman by the arm, remarking that Miriam had been gone for several days. The woman hastily excused herself saying she must have been mistaken.

Bhima had come out of his office and was talking to the TV reporter on the temple lawn. Asked by the reporter about the August 31 incident when Joey had been taken from Larry, Bhima said, "Mr. Yanoff grabbed Joey and tried forcibly to remove him. Joey was protesting. We asked Mr. Yanoff to let him go, and when he refused we took Joey from him."

I asked, "How come Larry found himself on the ground?"

"There was a scuffle," he replied, "and maybe Larry fell on one knee. I saw it all and I can get one hundred witnesses to testify."

That evening we had still another TV appearance, an interview by Elizabeth Coleman of Channel 7. She already had a tape of an

38

earlier conversation with Donald Sherman, a temple director. She did not play the tape for us but reported that his position was the same as Bhima's—that the temple was not responsible for what individual members did. Sherman told her that Joey was not fond of his father and that he had been taken out of Palms Junior High because the children picked on him.

In response, Larry noted the Krishnas were *not* like any other church where people come and go. Miriam worked in their book department; Joey slept in their dormitory. "If Joey came to school with shaven head and in Krishna costume what reaction could one expect from the children?"

At 10:00 P.M. that night, Rachel, Walter, Larry, and I listened to Channel 5's newscast. It opened with Larry reading to the Krishnas' public relations man the Illinois court order, asking if the Society would obey the law and return Joey. The man replied, "The Society does not mix into disputes between husband and wife." While the camera wandered over the scene of the devotees before the temple, the reporter described Larry's efforts to find Joey.

At 11:00 P.M. we listened to Channel 7. There was a segment inside the temple with dancing and chanting, then an interview with Larry, followed by one with Sherman. Ms. Coleman asked Sherman about the August 31 scuffle. Joey did not want to return home, Sherman told her flatly, and added "he did not have much feeling for his father." Asked about brainwashing, he replied, "We do no more than any school does, if that's brainwashing."

All in all, I was satisfied. We had put the Krishnas on the spot: a child was missing; his father was looking for him at the temple; the law had ordered his return. It placed the sect under a cloud. We hoped it would prompt the leaders to be prudent, not to invite more such publicity as they had received in the last two days.

My niece Carrie had seen Joey with a group of Krishnas on Hollywood Boulevard on a Saturday night. From others, we learned it was the sect's regular practice on Saturdays to dance and chant on that crowded street lined for several blocks with movie houses. Larry and I thought it would be a good idea, as part of our campaign of public exposure, to confront the Krishnas there. We prepared placards charging them with hiding Joey and a leaflet which told the story. It appealed to the reader to withhold contributions until Joey was returned.

Bonnie's young son volunteered to help and came to our meeting place with two of his high school friends. We walked up and down the Boulevard for an hour, had coffee, and by 9:00 P.M. were concluding the Krishnas were not coming when suddenly we heard the sound of chanting. We ran out to meet them.

There were two contingents of about forty on each side of the street, the men in saffron and white dhotis chanting and leaping, the women in saris following dignifiedly behind. Each group was accompanied by devotees distributing packets of goodies and literature; they asked for donations. Larry and I suspended the placards from our necks; he marched at the head of one group, I, alongside the other. As we kept pace with the dancers, we shouted, "Where is twelve-year-old Joey?" Our young volunteers handed our leaflets to passersby.

There were surprised looks on the devotees' faces but they did not interrupt their progress down the street. Warned to expect trouble, we had alerted two officers on the beat, though the well-lit, well-travelled boulevard, seemed safe. People were friendly to us and hostile remarks were thrown at the Krishnas. After twenty minutes they turned up a side street, boarded a temple bus, and disappeared. As we watched their departure, a friendly couple told us that the Krishnas had cut this trip short because of us. We felt good; we had struck back. We hoped this incident would serve as a warning to the sect that they would be in for trouble if they persisted in holding Joey.

Until now, Larry and I had been operating pretty much by ourselves except for legal assistance. Organizing experience taught me that we needed broader support, specifically, the help of community groups. No religious sect, not even a far-out cult like the Krishnas, can afford to alienate the community in which it functions and from which it draws financial sustenance. Not for long, anyway.

To whom should we go? Through a Chicago friend, I had received an introduction to a retired Jewish center-worker in North Hollywood. Through this contact, I was able to meet with Charles Posner, director of the Los Angeles Community Relations Committee. Posner made many suggestions, most of which we could not implement because we had to go back to Chicago. But I had a particular request: a rabbinical delegation to the

Krishna temple to demand Joey's return. For this, Posner introduced me to Rabbi Harry Essrig, executive vice president of the Board of Rabbis.

The rabbi, whose quick, warm response won me, said the Krishna temple was seeking affiliation to the City's Ecumenical Council, and our story would be of interest to it. He thought a mixed delegation of religious leaders would be preferable to a Jewish one; I agreed to brief the delegation.

I left him in good spirits, pleased with the reception I had received. In our long ordeal, it was sympathetic reactions such as these which sustained and gave us the courage to fight against an organization with resources far beyond ours.

Tuesday, November 25, arrived, the day of the hearing on our writ of habeas corpus ordering Miriam and the Krishnas to bring Joey to the court. In spite of the rebuffs we had met at the temple, we left my sister's Los Angeles home hoping that today we would at last be able to put our arms around Joey. We were even prepared to hear him say he wanted to stay in Krishna. After four months of absence, our overwhelming desire now was simply to see him again. We drove along the freeways, mostly in silence, each alone with his thoughts of what the day might bring.

We walked into a cluster of reporters and TV crews in the hall before Department Four's courtroom. Among them were three Krishnas, two men and a woman, their temple garb adding bright splashes of color.

The woman devotee graciously offered me a cookie. She wasn't the least perturbed to learn who I was, but continued smilingly to hold out a cookie. Not wishing to offend her, I took it.

"You have such a pretty smile," I said, my face and voice no doubt revealing my misery. "You're so nice; why are you doing this terrible thing? Where is our boy?" Still smiling, she turned away without a word, holding out a cookie to another.

It was time to go into the court. The three devotees sat up front to our left. Rogers was seated in a section reserved for lawyers. In this room large enough to seat two hundred people there was a buzz of conversation as the audience peered at the Krishnas and asked who they were. Our case did not come up for two hours; it was the last to be heard before a lunch recess. The judge, an imposing woman in her forties, appeared to be capable and fair.

The Krishnas were not represented by counsel. Bhima, their first witness, stated their attorney had told them to "just tell the truth." He was sworn in.

To the first question from the court, "Is Miriam Jefferson present?" Bhima answered, "No." To the next query, "Is the minor child, Joseph Yanoff, present?" Bhima responded. "Not to my knowledge."

So there it was. We had hoped against hope, but now had to face the bitter truth: They were going to hide Joey!

Four devotees testified under oath—Sandvig, who had accepted the writ on Miriam's behalf, was phoned to come to court. They all swore that Joey and Miriam had disappeared just before the writ was served. Bhima stated he had last seen them at the Sunday temple ceremony. Later, however, in front of the news cameras, he modified the day to Tuesday. (The writ had been served on Thursday, November 20.) Sandvig said he had last seen Miriam at work on Tuesday and that on that day Joey had visited her. The cookie woman had seen Miriam last on Monday. "Does your faith forbid lying?" Rogers asked Pandu, who gave his legal name as Donald Sherman. "The goal of our faith is to become pure," Pandu replied. "So lying is impurity, and we try to avoid it as a regular principle."

Bhima's testimony contradicted his assertion that he was like any church minister. He had told us and the media that people came to his temple and went; he did not keep track of them; he attended to their spiritual needs only if they came. How, then, could he be expected to know where Miriam and Joey were? His testimony in court, however, showed the control exercised by the sect, and by him as its chief officer, over the devotees. Members worked without pay, their needs taken care of by communal lodging and kitchens. Before Joey could visit the temple, Miriam asked Bhima's permission. He knew Joey had come for a short stay and had a return flight ticket to Chicago. He had been consulted, he said, before Joey was sent to public school and when he was withdrawn "because he was having difficulty of some kind." He was aware Lainie was at the Dallas school. The movement of devotees to other temples was usually made with his knowledge.

The picture drawn by his testimony was hardly that of a minister of the usual congregation. Instead, his was a religious commune of which he was the absolute head. Yet he testified that

Miriam and Joey had just walked off without his or anyone's knowledge. In the months to follow, the Krishnas would seek to justify wrestling Joey from Larry's arms to prevent "a stranger from snatching him." Bhima, however, acknowledged that he knew Larry as the father but because "the mother was going 'no'...some members removed the boy from the father's arms..."

We had no witnesses to prove the Krishnas were lying, that they were hiding Joey, and the court dismissed our writ.

Outside the courtroom, reporters were waiting. As he was being interviewed, Larry could not hide his pain; he made an effort at self-control and managed some answers. Inwardly, I wept with him. We were not going to see Joey, perhaps, for a long time.

Myrna Oliver headlined our story, "Four Krishnas in Court Deny Hiding Boy from Father." She quoted Rogers, "'There is no doubt in the world they know where the child is.' But he said he would press neither perjury or contempt charges against the Krishnas, because he could not prove anything..." She reported Sherman (Pandu) saying, "We can't lie. Our principles forbid it. We live by the principles of truthfulness, cleanliness, austerity, and mercy."

When the courtroom corridor had cleared and Larry and I were alone with Rogers, I asked him, "What do we do now?"

"We have the damage suit," he said. "It will act as a form of pressure against them. But I should tell you it won't come up for a long time, years."

"Is there anything else we can do legally?" Larry asked.

"Not unless we can prove they were lying." He had nothing else to suggest and, having to rush to another courtroom, left.

We felt desolate, unable to bolster each other with comforting words. Over cups of coffee, Larry said he wanted to get back to his classroom for the remaining three days of the week; he had lost seven working days. He could still make an evening flight. I said I would stay another day to talk to some of the people who might have some suggestions and to thank those who had been helpful.

Before dinner that evening, Rachel, Walter and I watched CBS Channel 2's newscast of the court scene. The reporter told of the Chicago teacher who had filed a seven million dollar suit against the Hare Krishnas alleging they were hiding his son. Interrogation of Bhima followed; he hadn't seen Joey since the previous Tuesday; then Larry, "They have lied to me on other occasions;

why should I believe them now?" Finally, the reporter noted that Rogers could not prove that the Krishnas connived to ship Joey to one of their thirty temples in the United States, and that the judge dismissed the writ.

"Morris, what are you going to do now?" Rachel asked. "Everytime I think of Joey among those kooks, it gives me the creeps."

She was worried not only for Joey, but for me. Rachel and I had a special relationship, she the youngest of four; I, the oldest. Although, for the last thirty years we had lived two thousand miles apart, whenever we met, the old tenderness resumed.

"I don't know what we'll do," I answered wearily.

"I hate to say this," Walter said, "but if you had taken our advice and used the VanNuys detective to pick up Joey, you would have him now."

I was too low to argue. "I suppose you're right, but we thought going through legal channels was better. Joey is no infant; he's twelve. Snatching and holding him by force might not have been the best way. We hoped a court order would get his cooperation."

Walter was not one to give up easily. "Once you had him, you could have handled it. How are you going to find him now?"

"I don't know, but we're not giving up. We'll find him somehow and get him back."

"I don't know what you have in mind," he said, "but you'd better be careful."

"What do you mean 'careful'?"

"You weren't there when they attacked Larry on the lawn. I tried to come to his help, but a couple of their bruisers kept me and Rachel away and pushed us around. From the way they acted, I thought they were going to beat us up. They're crazies."

It was on Walter's suggestion that we tried to get police protection at the temple; he had cautioned us to park our car several blocks away and make sure we were not followed.

"I assume," I said, "we'll be running some risks, but we're not going to pull punches on that account. We'll take precautions as far as we can."

"How many temples do they have?" Rachel asked.

"A hundred," I replied.

"A hundred?" she asked in dismay.

"All over the world, on all the continents including Australia. I know it's going to be tough to find Joey."

"Do you have any plans?" Rachel asked.

"We haven't thought about it. When I get home the family will discuss the situation and come up with something. My feeling is that more of the kind of publicity we got here will show them we're not giving up."

"It didn't help you get Joey—all that publicity," Walter said. "They still came to court and lied. You have to do something direct. You have to go after Joey."

"How do we do that?" I asked impatiently.

"I don't know," he admitted, "but publicity won't do it. People read about the case, or hear it on TV, and forget it a few minutes later."

"Who knows," I said trying to end the discussion, "maybe Joey will get bored with their routine and call us to get him. Or Miriam may change her mind, as she often does. Somewhere along the line, we'll get a break." As soon as I could, I pleaded tiredness and went to bed.

6

Confronting the Krishnas

I CAME HOME TO FIND THAT THE CHICAGO PAPERS, informed by wire service, had prominently carried our story. *The Daily News* opened with:

> Four saffron-robed Krishna cultists have denied in court that they are hiding a 12-year-old boy from his father who is a Chicago high-school teacher. But the boy's weeping father, Lawrence Yanoff, said the Krishnas lied, although he cannot prove it.

The *Chicago Tribune* quoted Krishna Donald Sherman:

> My notion is that she [Miriam] did not want any hassles and she and her son took off somewhere. I don't know where she went. I only know she is not around.

James Bowman, religion editor of the *Daily News*, had a full story in the weekend edition, headed: "Father Hunts for 'Lost' Son" and a sub-head, "Krishna Cult Sued for $7 Million." A photo Ronald had taken a year ago in Larry's living room showed me seated, Joey standing with his hand on my shoulder, and Larry next to him—an old fashioned picture of three generations. A watch-chain across Larry's vest and a turn-of-the-century pendulum clock on the wall over the fireplace completed the effect. It was taken by Ronald, an amateur photographer, as a gift to Toby on her sixty-third birthday. When Joey gave it to her, after the birthday cake, he had said, "I'm the first-born son of a first-born son, and Grandpa is the first-born son of a first-born son. That's four generations of first-borns."

"That makes you something special." Toby smiled as if hinting at a remarkable mystery.

Two days after my return, our sons joined us for the weekly Friday night family dinner. In spite of the ordeal we had been through, we were in good spirits. The week's work was over, there was good food on the table, and, most important of all, we were together. We knew we would not be daunted by the setback in Los Angeles. Larry reported that a professional family counselor had advised him we must try to continue our lives as before, not permit our tragedy to disrupt them.

"But we'll find time to do whatever is necessary to find Joey," Ronald said.

"Luckily, Dad is retired," Toby added. "The two of us can get a lot done."

Out of our discussion that evening came a campaign to call public attention to our case, charging the Krishnas with violation of law in hiding Joey, with defiance of a court order. We could be most effective in Chicago, our home town, but we hoped to reach the news media in other cities where there were temples. If our campaign was successful, we reasoned, it would bring the realization to the Society's hierarchy that concealing Joey was too costly. At that point, they would send him home.

A clear and simple enough plan, but could we get the media to respond to a degree that the cult would feel its public image tarnishing and donations reduced? It was a big order, considering that we were up against a world-wide organization with great resources of manpower and money. Could we make enough of a dent? On the other hand, how much of a dent was needed to secure the release of one individual? How much would be necessary to make them say, "He's causing us more trouble than he's worth." These were questions for which there were no answers. We knew our goal—compel the cult to disgorge Joey—and our means—publicity, but we could only dimly perceive the obstacles and the degree of pressure we had to develop.

While this was to be our main thrust, we would also undertake a direct search for Joey. We conceived a plan to visit the cult's thirty-six temples in the U.S. and Canada in the hope of finding one of the three: Joey, Lainie, or Miriam. True, the Society had one hundred temples throughout the world, but we felt there was

47

a good chance that, to avoid expense, it would send Joey to one on this continent in the expectation we would eventually give up our search. We hoped to muster relatives and friends who would visit Krishna temples in their cities on Sundays when the sect held open house.

We were aware that the media would not repeat a story; something new had to be added. We had to do things to make news. As a first step, we decided on a community delegation to the local Krishna temple to urge Joey's return. To lay a basis for the delegation, we wanted to get the story of Joey's disappearance in the neighborhood newspapers serving Chicago's North Side, and Evanston, the locale of the temple.

Paula, a reporter for one of the largest local papers, was the first of many who showed us enormous sympathy and also put their talents at our disposal. Her article, along with the "three generations" photo, occupied the front page of a pre-Christmas issue of our local paper. It was headed: "Joey Yanoff's Family Chants Anything but Joy."

Paula's long article sparked further media interest, a two-hour interview of Larry by Anne Keegan of the *Chicago Tribune*, the city's largest daily. Her feature, which appeared in the Sunday edition of the paper, was the most moving account yet written of Joey's disappearance:

> Has anyone seen Joey Yanoff?
>
> He's disappeared into another world. And so far, not his father, or his father's lawyers, or sheriff's deputies with warrants have been able to bring him back.
>
> Not that he's not around—somewhere. He was seen once, his head shaven, chanting on the street in Los Angeles. And again at a fair in San Diego.
>
> But his father, Lawrence Yanoff, can't find him. For Joey, his twelve-year-old son, has slipped worlds away from their quiet life together in Chicago—from trumpet lessons and Monopoly games, evening concerts at Indian Boundary Park and the bike rides to get there.
>
> Joey has disappeared into the world of Hare Krishna, and his father is trying to bring him back.

48

In addition to the "three generations" photo, the *Tribune* published the Balboa Park picture showing Joey, head shaven and japa beads around his neck, standing forlornly alongside Lainie and Miriam. Keegan told the full story in its tragic implications for our family, but concluded with Larry saying: "What we had going was very strong. Whatever they do to him...whatever they say to him...whatever they do to his brain...I still have hope. Because they never can erase it all."

The publication of the *Tribune* article gave a flying start to our campaign. Cults, especially the Krishnas and Moonies, were news, and a personal tragedy such as ours added to the human interest.

Two days after Keegan's story, NBC's Channel 5 sent a crew to Larry's school to interview him. It was a high moment for Toby and me to watch that evening's newscast as our story was told and Larry answered questions. The Balboa Park picture was flashed on the screen as the anchorman appealed to listeners with any information on Joey's whereabouts to contact the station.

That night we learned from Paula that the Krishnas had called a news conference for next morning at the Chicago Sheraton Hotel. We were exultant; our plan was working. Stung by the attention we were receiving, the Krishnas felt compelled to make a reply. We decided to confront them directly.

The hotel meeting room was already crowded with reporters, television personnel, and their equipment when Toby and I arrived. Slowed by her wheelchair, we were a little late. Larry already was up front; Mukunda, Evanston temple president, was reading from a prepared text. Facing the charged atmosphere of the crowd, he sat cross-legged on a raised platform decorated with the Swami's portrait, floral arrangements, and a large streamer bearing the Krishna mantra. All in temple dress, several devotees flanked Mukunda. In the rear of the room were the female Krishnas, also in temple dress.

Tilaka on nose bridge and forehead accentuating his ruddy good looks, Mukunda spoke fluently in a throaty voice. "Yanoff's charges are full of speculation and rash statements. The Krishna Consciousness movement cannot in any way be held responsible for actions of friends, volunteer workers, and congregation members. We are emphatically not aiding or hiding the boy now.

49

This is a quarrel between a divorced husband and wife over a child. We would not stoop to be involved in such petty feuds."

Larry broke in. "If you do not engage in petty family matters, why was my child torn from me and why was I thrown to the ground by Krishnas?"

"That was a natural reaction," Mukunda answered, "to anyone who would go into a temple in the midst of a religious festival and take a child out, particularly when that person was a stranger." This was the first time we heard Larry referred to as "a stranger." It was to become the sect's official explanation for the attack on the temple lawn, despite Bhima's earlier testimony that he had known who Larry was.

"You say you are not involved," I said, "yet the boy was withdrawn from public school because they didn't teach Krishna. What's more, he must get up at three in the morning, he may not eat meat, fish, or eggs."

"I don't think the mother or the boy are in a Krishna temple," Mukunda replied, modifying the unqualified denial first made, "but if they are, nutritionists have examined the Krishna diet and the boy will receive proper nourishment. He will get enough sleep and attend school without the influence of violence, dope, and illicit sex."

His last words prompted broad smiles and chuckles from the reporters. A woman reporter asked Mukunda if he would make a plea through the media for the mother to come forward with the boy. "If I made such an appeal," he said, "it would imply that we are involved." But under prodding he conceded, "It would not be unreasonable for the mother to make some communication with the father and the grandparents to relieve them of anxiety."

With the formal part of the news conference over, Larry was interviewed by the newspeople. After that, Mukunda also came over to have a few polite words with him. As they were talking, women devotees in saris went around the room offering cakes and "nectar." When we left, the devotees had formed a circle, dancing and chanting, oblivious to all else.

That night the event appeared on two major channels and the next morning was reported in the principal newspapers. Many thousands of Chicagoans now knew of Joey's disappearance into the cult. They had heard two sides—which would they believe? Perhaps that would depend on what they already knew about the Krishnas, how they associated them with other far-out cults. More important to us was how the Krishnas saw it. Did they think the publicity cast a cloud of suspicion over the Society? Our hopes for success depended on it.

Two days later we had another confrontation with Mukunda, this time at the temple. For several days we had been putting together a delegation of civic and community leaders to urge the Evanston temple to find Joey. Our delegation was headed by a young rabbi, director of the Hillel Club on the Evanston campus of Northwestern University. He was tall, good-looking with a shock of chestnut hair, and quite eloquent. He had heard the whole story from us, offering to help in any way he could.

On December 12 at 10:30 in the morning, we arrived to keep the appointment I had made with Mukunda. In addition to the rabbi, there were two state representatives, a member of our Congressman's staff, a board member of a neighborhood organization, and a tall, stately Zen Buddhist minister who came to "correct the distorted image given Eastern religions by the far-out cults." Two reporters from the local press, a photographer, and I completed the delegation. Larry had to be at school.

Mukunda led us into a small, bare room with a couch and a few chairs. Some of us sat on the floor; Mukunda occupied a chair in the far corner of the room facing the delegation and a male devotee sat crosslegged on the floor next to him.

After the introductions, one of the state representatives asked Mukunda to arrange for Joey's return. He replied that he did not know where Joey was; that he did not think he was in any of the thirty temples in the U.S.

"Do you know the mother's spiritual name?" the rabbi asked. We had briefed him. When Mukunda shook his head, the rabbi reminded him, "It's Yasoda."

"Oh, yes," Mukunda said, "someone told me that."

"I believe," the rabbi continued, "that she is not given a spiritual name until she has been an initiate for some time and only after she accepts your discipline. She worked for your Society as a volunteer and her only means of support came from it. She lived in a dormitory for women. The boy, when last seen, was shaven and in Krishna dress, indicating that he has been inducted. There is also a little girl who was last known to have been enrolled in your Dallas school. Is it likely then that they would just disappear, separate themselves completely from your Society?" The rabbi paused to allow Mukunda to respond but

51

when he remained silent, continued. "We are convinced that she remains in your Society with her two children. We believe you can start the process by which she and the boy can be found."

"Whatever happened," Mukunda said, "happened in Los Angeles, not here. Why should our temple be put in the middle? Why should publicity be leveled at us?"

"Your sect is a national—international—organization," the second state representative said. "You are, I believe, governed by the same leader and the same rules."

"We cannot be responsible," Mukunda said, "for what individual devotees may do."

"You can contact the head of your organization," the legislator continued, "explain the situation you are faced with here in Evanston, and ask his help in locating the child. I'm sure he could exert pressure on the particular devotees who may be responsible."

Mukunda seemed lost in thought; we waited. "Our temple is autonomous," he said.

"Do we address you as Mr. Mukunda?" asked the first state representative.

"No, just Mukunda."

"A new sect like yours Mukunda, comes into a community and, as is generally the case, will be viewed with suspicion. That suspicion becomes justified by cases such as Joey's. You will want to dispel it by helping restore the boy to his father."

"Let me tell you of another case," Mukunda said. He drew himself up in the chair and spoke more forcefully. "This was a case in which I was directly involved, but which took place in another city. A young woman joined our Society and after a while she wanted to bring her four-year-old son. The grandmother, who had been taking care of the child, objected, and there was a court fight over custody. The court ruled in the grandmother's favor, allowing the mother visitation rights. The mother, naturally, was very upset. She wanted the child with her in Krishna. I advised her to respect the law and make no attmept to violate the decision of the court."

"You did right," the neighborhood representative, a mother of two, said. "We respect you for it. But if you obeyed the law in that instance, why not in this one?"

"I told you," Mukunda replied, "I, and my temple, had nothing to do with the boy's disappearance."

The rabbi made another attempt. "We need your help to find the child. Since the Krishna community is all over the country, the action of one temple reflects on all. The religious community has a common basis in trust. Children come into churches all the time; sometimes alone, sometimes with a parent. The church may not leave itself open to the charge of child-snatching otherwise the community becomes alarmed. When it does, it will react, sometimes in ways which don't bear directly on the particular case."

For the first time, Mukunda looked disturbed. I could guess why. One of our Evanston friends had filled us in on the temple's long-pending case before the City Council for a "special use permit" to allow it to continue at the present address. The sect had moved into the former YMCA building four years ago. It used it as a church, seminary, and residence, in violation of the zoning code for the area. In October 1972, the temple filed an application for the permit arguing that others on the street had received similar exceptions. The "special use permit" was granted, but on condition that violations of fire safety and sanitary standards were corrected and off-street parking provided. The temple agreed to the conditions, but after months passed without the corrections, the permit was revoked. The temple filed a new application, made a few corrections, and promised to make others. The second application was pending before the Council's planning and development committee. If the permit were denied, the temple would have to move at great expense. Understandably, Mukunda was sensitive to any comment bearing on the matter.

There was a long pause after the rabbi's remarks. Mukunda sat looking into his lap. Was he meditating? The shaven, gaunt-faced devotee sitting on the floor at his right looked somberly at the opposite wall.

"I'll see what I can do," Mukunda said finally. "If I find out anything I'll get in touch."

"Will you call me?" the rabbi requested. "How much time will you need?"

"About two weeks," Mukunda said.

"Call me when you have any news, but call me in any event at the end of two weeks. O.K.?" Mukunda nodded coldly.

I was pleased with the delegation, feeling we had made a strong impression and that there were grounds for hope. I felt Mukunda would convey to his superiors the Evanston temple's vulnerable position.

Would it be sufficient to move them? While it was far from clear that our case would influence the City Council, Mukunda might think so, and that would be most important when he reported to his home office.

Our family had considered Mukunda's situation. We believed it was in his interest, as head of the local temple receiving the burden of bad publicity, to work for an amicable solution. We tried to be friendly to him as much as the strained circumstances permitted. Anticipating the difficulties he faced convincing his superiors, we assured him that we had no wish to punish anyone for violation of law, or perjury. We just wanted Joey.

The headlines reporting the meeting were an interesting contrast. The *Evanston Review's* read: "Krishnas Say They'll Help Find Joey." The *Lerner Newspapers*, "Krishnas Confronted." One emphasized the promise, the other, the conflict.

7

"Write to the Swami..."

A FEW EVENINGS LATER I RECEIVED AN UNEXPECT-
ed phone call. Would I accept collect charges from Los Angeles?
the operator asked. "Who's calling?" "Joe Williams," the operator
replied.

Williams had phoned me once before in Los Angeles after the
court hearing. He was a member of a volunteer watch patrol
organized to keep down crime in the Culver City area where the
temple was located. Having read the newspaper accounts about
Joey, he offered to keep a look-out when he made his rounds in the
temple area. Since I was then at a low point after our court fiasco,
his proposal did more to raise my spirits than my hopes. Still,
upon return to Chicago, I did mail him the Balboa Park photo.

So now, in excited expectation, I told the operator to put the call
through. Joe reported that he had seen all three—Joey, Miriam,
and Lainie—at different times, not together, walking out of an
apartment house on the 10100 block of Venice Boulevard, a few
streets from the temple. They were dressed as devotees and, on
some occasions, Miriam had been in the company of a black man.

Toby, from my face and voice, knew something important was
being said. She looked at me inquiringly, but I motioned her not
to interrupt. I instructed Joe to do nothing more than continue to
observe, and that our attorneys in Los Angeles would be in touch
with him. I called Rogers, who wasn't in, and so spoke to Bonnie,
his secretary. I urged her to act quickly. When we still hadn't
heard from Rogers after a few days time, I was burning with
impatience. Tired of waiting, I called Joe Williams to learn of any
further news. By this time, however, his story had changed. The

location from which Miriam left was now a different address on Venice Boulevard, just around the corner from the temple. The black child she had with her was a baby, the white boy, about seven or eight. The woman had long, stringy hair; Miriam's was curly.

There was no doubt about Williams' sincere desire to help, but it was clear his detective work could not be totally counted upon. What was most exasperating was our inability to check things out for ourselves. Our attorney, Rogers, was not really set up for it either.

It was about this time, too, that a call came through from the City Desk of the *Chicago Tribune*. The paper had received a phone call from a "government informant" who said Joey had been seen at the Hare Krishna center at Third Street on New York's Lower East Side. The City Desk staffer offered to get the *Tribune's* New York correspondent to check out the information, but only if we couldn't do it for ourselves.

Though it was late, and an hour later in New York, Toby and I phoned her cousins in New York, begging them to track down the tip immediately. They did, and called us the next evening to say they could not find a Krishna center at the address. A conversation with the local police disclosed that while there had been one, it had long ago moved to Brooklyn.

These two incidents posed a real problem: how were we to handle leads? We could neither chase out to distant parts of the country simply on the strength of a phone call nor could we totally rely on the good intentions of others. It remained a dilemma.

Nevertheless, we had gotten underway an ambitious plan to monitor the thirty-six Krishna temples in the U.S. and Canada, whose locations were listed in *Back to Godhead*, the sect's monthly magazine. The plan was simple; the problem was to find enough people to carry it out.

To those who volunteered, we sent a letter of instructions and the Balboa Park photo. We asked them to visit the temple in their city on a Sunday afternoon when the Krishnas had open house. If our volunteer saw any one of the three—Joey, Miriam, or Lainie—they were to phone us.

Members of our family, if located in cities with a Krishna temple, would agree to our request. Similarly with old friends. We found, however, that these covered but a few cities. Thus, we resorted to asking friends to ask their friends, and, while we received many names, few acquiesced. Their reluctance was understandable. Unless a matter touches one directly, most people tend to shy away from involvement. Perhaps some also were fearful of being drawn into a controversy with a strange cult.

Yet, several people we had never met acted on our appeal. A retired Chicago social worker monitored the Honolulu temple; a college professor monitored the one in Boston; a retired airline pilot checked in Washington, D.C.; a retired gentleman helped out in Laguna Beach, California; and vacationing friends gave us a hand in Mexico City. Along the way, I even discovered a lost cousin who visited the Phoenix temple for us.

After much letter writing and phone calling, less than half the temples were visited. We knew, of course, that even if Joey lived in one of them, to avoid exposure he could be instructed to stay away during open house. We hoped, however, that as time passed the Krishnas would relax their guard.

Our campaign included newspaper publicity in other cities where there were Krishna temples. Even if we got our story to three or four cities, we had to show the cult that our influence extended beyond Chicago. I prepared a release which opened as follows:

> A 12-year-old child has been taken from his father and is believed to be hidden in one of the 30 Hare Krishna temples in the United States. The men Krishnas are known by shaven heads and saffron-colored robes.

It closed with a statement by Larry:

> "The ironic thing," said Yanoff "is that the Hare Krishna sect receives much of its money in donations from an unsuspecting American public at airports and downtown centers." Yanoff alleged that there are many other minors being kept without parental consent. "I am not the first parent fighting the Krishnas to find my child. I am afraid this will happen again."

Along with the release went a black-and-white glossy picture of Joey with his trumpet. It was taken at our home in the spring of 1975. He had just started lessons and surprised us by choosing the trumpet, an instrument neither of our sons played although between them they knew clarinet, guitar, recorder, banjo, and others. Perhaps it was a sign of Joey's independence.

In sending out the release I was confronted by the problem of monitoring its publication. The central library took in the newspapers of large cities; but to go through thirty newspapers without knowing the exact date our release appeared was beyond my capacity. I decided to select six cities for a first mailing and see what happened. A week after I made the mailing I went to the library to scan the six newspapers. I spent three hours flipping hundreds of pages covering issues of the three days which I thought had the highest probability. I soon realized that some papers had more than one daily edition and our article could appear in one and not another, that it could be held for a filler to appear later, and so on. I decided I had to think the matter through more carefully.

In the meantime I sent the release to a few Jewish periodicals in cities with temples and had the satisfaction of seeing it in three of them; it may well have appeared in others.

In 1950, when my union merged with another, I had returned to private industry. Before my retirement I had managed the real estate desk of a large personal care products company. Now, a former colleague put me in touch with Samuel Lerner, the father of a devotee "high up in the Krishna hierarchy" and reputed to be Prabhupada's financial expert. Being a brilliant student at an Eastern university, great things were expected of the young man by his family. Instead he wound up in the sect. Curiously, Lerner's disappointment was mixed with a strong dash of pride because his son had "made it to the top" in the Krishna movement.

The boy kept in touch with his family, and occasionally returned from India for visits. I had hoped Lerner would suggest that his son intercede with Prabhupada on our behalf; instead, he told me to write to the Swami: "He's a businessman with a lot of common sense. If he knew what was happening—all this bad publicity for his movement—he would put an end to it. Write him."

Disappointed that Lerner would do no more, I followed his advice. Before writing the Swami, I studied his portrait in *Back to Godhead* to imagine the kind of man I was dealing with. In the direct gaze of the hooded eyes and the firm set of the large, thick-lipped mouth over a square jaw, I judged he was accustomed to command. There was no touch of softness or humility in the old man's face. I decided to appeal to his practical side, state the facts, be respectful but firm.

From Mukunda I got the Swami's address in Bombay and wrote describing events from the time Joey was sent for a visit to the Los Angeles temple to Bhima's testimony that he had disappeared. My letter closed, "We appeal to you, sir, to check into the facts and we trust that through your good offices our grandson will be returned to his father." I enclosed Anne Keegan's *Tribune* article to illustrate press criticism. In the hope that Lerner might change his mind and ask his son to help, I sent a copy of the letter to him.

Every now and then a friend would ask, "Why don't you bring the law down on them? It's a kidnapping, isn't it? What about the police, the FBI?"

We had checked the law. Our Chicago attorney, who had acted for Larry in winning custody, advised him that he could proceed with contempt charges against Miriam and put her in jail until she returned Joey. But how would Miriam be served with a court order when we couldn't find her? And to proceed against the Krishnas in the absence of proof of their complicity would put us in the same position we had been at the Los Angeles hearing.

Still, a child was missing. There must be some agency charged with responsibility for finding missing children. We contacted our local police who sent Youth Officer Walston to interview us. The result? Joey's disappearance would be reported and his picture filed. If we had a lead, they would check it out, but only if it was in the Chicago area. If we wanted the police in other cities to cooperate, we would have to get a writ of habeas corpus in an Illinois court which would permit our local sheriff to contact his counterpart in another city, provided once again that we had a specific lead in that city.

Could the police help find Joey? Officer Walston sighed: "Do you folks have any idea how many missing and runaway children there are? Your photo will be filed with thousands of others and that will be the end of it unless you can give us a definite lead where he might be."

That left the FBI. Larry made an appointment with the Chicago office. There was no encouragement from the officer he

59

spoke to. Because one parent was involved in the disappearance, the FBI man viewed it as a "domestic dispute." But suppose, Larry asked, the cult was hiding Joey in one of their temples? The FBI officer promised to send a report to the Justice Department. On that meagre hope, we wrote our senators and congressmen asking them to intercede with the Department.

Our hearts were filled with longing for Joey. On December 21, some five months since we had seen our grandson, I wrote in my diary:

> The worst thing to bear is not to receive a word from him, not to hear his voice, the voice which I love, simply because it is Joey's.
>
> I wonder what is keeping him from calling us? What fears were put into his mind by his mother and the Krishnas? What lies have been told about us? That we don't write him? That we don't want him?
>
> It is only in my dreams that the call comes. I pick up the phone. 'Grandpa?' (Oh, that wonderful word I haven't heard for so long.) 'It's me, Joey.'
>
> I say, 'Joey! Where are you?' He tells me and I go and fetch him. That dream takes many forms, but always the opening words are, 'Grandpa? It's me, Joey.' As if I wouldn't know his voice.
>
> If I suffer so, what must Toby be feeling, and Larry? Until recently Ronald could not even bring himself to visit the Krishna temple. Larry told me that Ronald had nightmares after that visit. I can imagine why: he pictures Joey as a frenetic dancer with wild eye and straining throat.
>
> And Larry? Not only were they father and son, but also comrades. It was a lovely sight to see them leaving our home on their bikes, Larry following to keep an eye on him.
>
> How many times in the past have I sat Joey in my lap to read to him? I delighted in his young mind opening thirstily to new knowledge. How I loved his questions!
>
> And just to see his fresh, beautiful face across the dinner table was such a joy to me and Toby. We would silently exchange admiring glances, not wishing the boy to see. Yet he knew our feelings. It was evident when Toby kissed him goodbye. He would wipe his

cheek ruefully as if to say, "Bubbie, how mushy you are," but the twinkle in his eye told us that he loved to be doted on. And dote on him we did, our only, our dear grandson. Where is he now, at this moment? What kind of life is he living? What fears hold him hostage?"

8

Assailed by Doubts

MORE THAN TWO WEEKS HAD PASSED SINCE OUR
delegation had visited the Evanston temple, but Mukunda had
not phoned the rabbi. On the morning of January 8, I found in my
mail a letter postmarked from Culver City, California, and giving
"Bhaktivedanta Book Trust" as the return address. Was this the
sect's response to our campaign? I shouted to Toby, "We have
something from the Krishnas." As I read the letter and the enclosure, she watched my face. "I'm not sure what it means. It's from
Prabhupada in answer to my letter," I said, handing the two
pieces to her.

The Swami's letter read:

> It is not our policy to play hide and seek. We are a
> spiritual institution, so everyone is welcome to join. It is
> not compulsory, there is no attempt to keep people
> against their will. If someone joins and the parents
> object, we do not try to keep anyone by force.
>
> I do not think that your grandson is in any one of our
> temples. However, since you have written me express-
> ing your concern, I am immediately sending out a
> notice to all temple presidents, a copy of which is
> enclosed herewith.

The enclosure, addressed to temple presidents with the nota-
tion that copies were being sent to "All temples," read:

> Please accept my blessings. I have received one letter
> from a Mr. Morris Yanoff with a newspaper clipping

explaining the disappearance of his grandson Joey
Yanoff, age 12 years. Mr. Yanoff is very anxious about
the whereabouts of his grandson and he has asked me to
help locate him. If this boy is in your temple, please
contact the following address.

My address followed. The Swami's letter dated December 18
from Bombay was mailed from Culver City on January 6. Why
this roundabout transmission and the delay—exactly one month?
Was it possible that Mukanda's report to his superiors had
released the letter?

I phoned Sam Lerner, on whose suggestion I had originally
written the Swami, and read the letter to him.

"That's it!" he said. "If your grandson is in one of the temples,
you will be contacted. Prabhupada's instructions are like God's to
the devotees."

Two others who had considerable knowledge of the sect also
shared Lerner's optimism. There was Freddy Loewe, a thirty-
year-old engineer, the nephew of a friend who introduced us. It
was not clear to me whether he had once been a devotee, but it was
evident he had spent a lot of time in the Boston temple during the
cult's early days. He thought the movement had deteriorated
since then.

Wanting to learn more about the Krishnas from Freddy's positive point of view and still hoping to make contact with Krishna
leaders, we spent several hours talking with him one Sunday
afternoon.

"Those who joined in 1969 and 1970," he said, "were mostly
intellectual, idealistic. They were disillusioned with the country,
especially our failure to get out of Vietnam. They had taken part
in campus teach-ins, anti-war marches, draft card burnings, and
nothing happened. In disgust with the whole scene, they dropped
out. Some tried dope, the counter-culture bit. Joining the
Krishnas was a logical development. That was when George
Harrison of the Beatles joined."

Freddy Loewe spoke eloquently of his experiences. For the
first time in his life he knew God. It came through chanting; he
would join the devotees at 3:30 A.M. and chant for two hours. He
had seen the face of Krishna, had felt a personal relationship with
God. "Anyone who goes all the way," he said, "has a beautiful
experience."

Recalling the wild dance scene I had witnessed at the Evanston temple, I asked, "How does it differ from the holy rollers?"

"Krishna is a whole culture," he replied, "a complete life, not ups and downs like the holy rollers, but sustained, controlled."

When we recited in detail what had happened with Joey and showed Freddy the *Los Angeles Times* stories of the events around the habeas corpus writ, he took strong objection to Larry's charge of "brainwashing and hypnosis."

"That's a hateful attitude and totally unjustified," he said. "Krishna is not like that at all. Even a child of twelve, especially coming out of an environment like yours, could have a religious experience." He was about to finish a novel based on cult life and hinted that the Society might assist in its publication. "Within Krishna all answers are given. Devotees are in a state of bliss from chanting, dancing, rituals, eating prasadam. That's enough. It's hard for people like you to understand, coming as you do from a different culture in which you think of 'becoming' rather than 'being.' You think of shaping things, events, to your desires, to your needs, of finding new ways of doing things. For Krishnas, all has been discovered; the devotee has only to learn what is already known and practice what is taught by the Spiritual Master."

"But if these practices are out of step with modern society?" Toby interjected.

"What, for example?"

"Well, their attitude toward women, for one. I read in *Harper's* magazine, an article by Judith Wax, who visited the Dallas school, that the girls are being trained to be subservient to men, that marriages are arranged by Prabhupada without the consent of either party, and girls of fifteen are considered at the ideal age for marriage to men of twenty-five. Wax asked one of the teachers, a woman, 'Suppose a girl objects?' She replied, 'Krishna-consciousness girls are completely submissive.'"

Loewe was unperturbed. "I can only say that from what I observed at the Boston temple, the women are treated with consideration and respect."

"I hope," I said, "you won't mind our raising such questions. We would like very much to understand what kind of movement it is. What we have experienced has antagonized us and what we have read raised fears for Joey's education. But we'd like to listen to your views."

"As I said, my experience has been good. It's true their literature reflects a backwardness characteristic of ancient religions. But what religion doesn't? The Jewish?"

"I visited the Evanston temple," I said. "I watched men prostrate themselves before a picture of Prabhupada. It embarrassed me to see such abject submission to another human."

"You have to understand the devotees attitude toward Prabhupada. Many consider him God's representative on earth, even God himself taken human form, an avatar of Krishna. If Christ returned, don't you think Christians would prostrate themselves before him?"

"To be candid," I replied, "I've been educated in a scientific, rational tradition, and we have brought up our sons that way. We hope Joey will follow in our footsteps."

"O.K.," Loewe said, "you have your preconceived notions of what you want for Joey; his mother and the Krishnas have theirs. Either way, the kid will be raised to someone else's ideas, not his own."

I was on the point of retorting that our approach to education was open-ended, a readiness to entertain other views, whereas the cult taught that the Truth with a capital "T" issued from Prabhupada, but I held back. We needed Loewe's help.

"Do you still visit a temple?" I asked.

"No, I've been out of touch, but I still chant." He was one of those rare individuals, he said, who can have one foot in Krishna and the other in the material world, living comfortably in both.

"How does the Society govern itself," I asked.

"It's like the Communist Party," he said. "Orders go from the top down. But for the most part members know what they have to do: chant, practice the rituals, study, and "sankirtan," proselytise. Leadership comes naturally when members recognize the superior qualities of an individual."

We showed him the letter I had sent to Prabhupada and asked what sense it made to hold on to Joey in defiance of a court order and in the face of hostile public opinion. He agreed it made no sense and that someone should be reached to correct the situation. He offered to make contact with an old friend, Janaka, who was high in the organization, second perhaps only to Prabhupada. "That's assuming that Joey is indeed being hidden by them. It may be that he is with his mother on the periphery of the movement. They may visit a temple but live elsewhere. There may

65

even be individual devotees who, on their own, are cooperating with her. The temple president may know nothing about it. There are all these possibilities."

"Still," I said, "if Miriam and Joey come to a temple several times, the president is bound to notice and talk to them. There aren't that many people visiting."

We urged him to reach Janaka quickly. Loewe hadn't seen his friend for some years; he would have to locate him. He thought Janaka would be concerned about Joey's transition back to his previous life and referred to the shock effect of Ted Patrick's methods of deprogramming. We too expressed concern that no mental damage be inflicted on Joey and welcomed help toward that end. He then brought up the danger of the legal risks the sect would suffer if Joey gave evidence. We assured him we had no intention of punishing anyone if we received the Society's cooperation.

He left with the promise to begin at once to locate Janaka. His parting words surprised us, "The Krishnas are not like gypsies, you know; they don't steal children."

Toby and I were cheered by his visit. The fact that Loewe had dealt with the mechanics of Joey's return gave us the feeling he was serious and knew what he was doing. A week later he phoned to inform us Janaka was touring the universities lecturing and selling books. Loewe was trying to catch up with him. Several days later, when we received Prabhupada's letter, we phoned to let him know. He was certain it would be obeyed by responsible Krishnas; if Joey were being hidden, it could only be surreptitiously. (So Prabhupada's voice was not God's to every devotee.)

Some days later Freddy Loewe called again to say he had reached Janaka in Houston and had given him a complete report of our conversations. Janaka promised to get in touch with the Los Angeles center, but from Loewe's report we could not judge Janaka's attitude.

Another week passed without word from Loewe, and so we phoned him. He had not heard from Janaka and did not know what to make of it. "You have Prabhupada," he said, "you can rely on him. Anyhow, it's your best bet."

About the same time, we spoke with another Krishna-wise person. Phyllis Feller's son, now twenty, had for the last three years been a devotee. It was a tragedy to her and her husband, an executive of a large company, but one, she said, she "had learned to live with." Like Lerner, she kept in touch with her son. He had been to India and was now in Dallas. When she read Joey's story in the *Tribune*, she asked her son whether he had seen them. He hadn't.

Since we thought Joey, at some point, might have visited the Dallas gurukula (the guru's school) to see his sister, she offered to check with a devotee who had recently taught there; Bhakta was his name. She had met him through her son and regarded him highly as a "man of character." She was as good as her word and relayed to us what she had learned from Bhakta: Joey had never been to Dallas. It would have been, he said, a "very unintelligent thing" to admit him to the Dallas gurukula after his disappearance. Bhakta had gone to the trouble of conferring with the Los Angeles devotees who had told him the mother and the boy had indeed vanished. "They would not lie to me," Bhakta said. "Prabhupada's letter was going out to all the temples in the world, and, if Joey was in any one of them, he would be surrendered."

To this report, Phyllis Feller added her own estimate. For their own protection the Krishnas would not harbor the two. "As a rule, they do not lie, and in this case their self-interest dictated they not be implicated in the violation of a court order." She too thought the Swami's word was law and that he was considered like God to the devotees. She confirmed that Janaka was in the leadership.

These conversations with Loewe and Feller, whose intelligence and opinions we respected, posed uncomfortable thoughts. Were we unjustly accusing the Krishnas? Had Miriam bolted the cult and now was in hiding with Joey? Was Lainie with her, and not in Dallas? If so, how could she support herself and two children? We had checked the California welfare rolls. Without means, how could she travel? Could she keep Joey out of school? If she enrolled him in a public school, we would hear from the Chicago school when his transcript was requested.

If she wasn't in Krishna, why would she want to keep the boy from his father? She hadn't before. Nor, as far as we could observe, was her attachment to Joey so strong that she must have him by her side. She had voluntarily surrendered him to his

67

father, and, during the next three years, except for the occasional visits he made to her, seldom communicated with him by phone or letter.

Our reasoning led us to the conviction that she wanted the boy for Krishna. Joey had been at the temple ten days when she told us happily, "Joey has his own mantra." She had pulled him out of public school because "they didn't teach Krishna." She endured separation from her five-year-old daughter to give her a Krishna education. In our two phone conversations she showed complete devotion to the cult, even urging us to read the *Bhagavad Gita* and insisting that only the Swami's text was authentic. She told Rachel, and later Doris in Balboa Park, that she was happy in Krishna and that "for the first time in his life, Joey is too." The cult had become her life. If she was not connected with it, and supported by it, then the events of the last five months made no sense.

We surmised that Miriam had arranged with Bhima to indoctrinate Joey quickly so that before the month's visit was up, he would be induced to stay. That was why he did not reside with his mother, but with the devotees in the men's dormitory, the only child among them. That was why, even though he was there but a month, he attended temple classes, chanted with the devotees, took part in their ceremonies, wore temple dress, and accompanied them for street dancing. It explained why Rachel and Walter were discouraged from seeing him and why he was prevented from going with them to Disneyland. That was the reason our phone calls did not get through to him and why we had no response to our letters. His isolation was a necesary part of the scheme to make him completely dependent on the cult.

The process was aided by 3:30 A.M. risings, several rituals a day, two-hour chantings daily of the Krishna mantra, a complete diet change, separation from his peers, sports, television news, and the hundred and one things which connect a child, a person, to his family, friends, community.

The Krishnas objected to any charge of brainwashing, no doubt because of its ugly association with the horrors of the Korean prisoner of war camps, in which prisoners' beliefs and values were manipulated through reward and punishment. I refrained from so characterizing Krishna methods because, from my observation, devotees were not forced to join and were physically, if not mentally, free to leave. But whatever phrase fit the description of what happened to Joey, the fact was that within three weeks he was changed from a typical city boy to something entirely different. Such things do not happen in the ordinary course of events. It was frightening to us who loved him, and our fright was intensified by being cut off completely from sight of him, his voice, and his written word.

9

We Hire Detectives

SWAMI PRABHUPADA'S LETTER, ENIGMATIC AS IT was, became the focus of our renewed hopes. It overshadowed even the work that had been done for us by Sammy Dale.

Dale was a former Chicago police officer turned private investigator, who had read about Joey and offered his services. In December he had phoned to say he was driving to Los Angeles where for a few days he would handle a private matter; after that, he would like to find Joey. We would not be obligated to pay anything, not even expenses, since they were already covered, unless he returned the boy to us. In that event he would want a finder's fee of $300 plus expenses such as plane fare for Joey's return, but not to exceed another $300. He sounded business-like but pleasant.

We had only one other encounter with a detective agency, the one in Van Nuys which Rachel had recommended in October. Larry had turned down its proposal to snatch his son for fear of the shock effect. Yet friends continued to urge us to hire a reputable agency. They argued that the search was a job for professionals, not amateurs like us. Some offered to help raise funds for this purpose; the cost was known to be from $150 to $200 a day. We had resisted because we were not comfortable with the idea of detectives; we tended to link them with the underworld. The costs too were prohibitive; it wasn't going to be a three or four day investigation. Moreover, we believed in our strategy of public pressure.

70

In any event, the suggestions of our friends and a nagging feeling that we might have made a mistake in not using the Van Nuys agency opened us to a positive response to Sammy Dale.

Two evenings later our family met with him. Tall, good-looking, and about thirty-three years old, Dale won our confidence with his frank, easy manner. His stint with the police as a youth officer dealing with runaways, some of them cult members, was further good recommendation. What's more, he had a friend in the Los Angeles sheriff's office who could be helpful. If Joey was in Los Angeles, Dale asserted, he would find him.

After drawing up and signing a letter of agreement, we told him Joey's story in detail, turning over photos and legal documents that would be needed should he find Joey.

We had not long to wait before Dale phoned us from Los Angeles at the end of December. He and his female aide had spoken to our attorney and to Joe Williams of the neighborhood watch. He had checked for Joey at the men's dorm of the temple, and his aide had inquired for Miriam in the women's dorm. He had visited the nearby hospital on Venice Boulevard on the chance there was a record of Joey's allergy shots.

Back in Chicago once more, Dale phoned to say that though he had not found Joey or Miriam, he had turned up a valuable lead. Toby, Larry, Ron, and I met with him next night in our living room.

Dale had been not only to Los Angeles, but had visited the temples at Laguna Beach, San Diego, Dallas, Phoenix, and Denver. He was sure neither Joey nor Miriam were now in Los Angeles. They had left about the time we served the writ, returned a week later, and then left again, Dale surmised. But the most important thing he had discovered was that Lainie was at the Dallas gurukula. He described her wearing a granny dress, heavy rimmed glasses, and hair somewhat shorter than on the Balboa Park photo.

If Lainie was in the Dallas school, then, that meant Miriam and Joey were still in Krishna, just as we had thought. Our anger flared anew at the cult's deception.

We asked Dale what he would now recommend. He hesitated to offer his services further because success was problematical and the effort would be costly. We urged him to be specific. He thought he should join the cult, giving himself three months to find his way into the traveling temple caravans. Through them he could visit all the principal temples and by winning the confidence of the devotees, hope to get a lead on Joey's whereabouts. He estimated the cost for the three months at about $5,000.

What about Lainie leading us to Miriam? we asked. Dale advised us against putting a watch on the Dallas temple. Miriam might not visit it for a long time, and then, Lainie might be sent to her without Miriam ever coming to the temple.

We told Dale we would have to give his proposal careful thought; it was a big commitment for us. We separated with cordial handshakes; he had given us a greater respect for his profession.

After he left, the four of us discussed his proposal. We trusted Dale, but felt he was new to the profession and had no other resources but himself. We thought, too, that his plan would take more than three months. To join, win the confidence of the Krishnas, be permitted to move freely around the temples, interrogate individuals, all without arousing suspicion, seemed to us unlikely of accomplishment in so short a time. We broke up without resolving our course of action. The next day we received Prabhupada's offer of assistance and we put Dale's suggestion on the shelf.

Several days passed without any response from temple presidents to the Swami's circular letter. If it had gone out directly from Bombay, then more than a month had elapsed. We began to have our doubts about the power of the Swami over his temples. Though we had no way of knowing whether the Swami was sincere or not, it still seemed that the devotees were making their own decisions. The "voice of God" seemed to grow faint as it crossed the distance between Bombay and Dallas, for instance. How else explain Sammy Dale's report that Lainie was in the gurukula there? Mukunda had once tried to explain such inconsistency: "Not all devotees are on the same plane of Krishna consciousness."

For my part, I was begining to think some devotees might have gone out on a limb in order to conceal Joey and were now not about to cut it off.

While still waiting and hoping that somehow the Swami's letter would bear fruit, we received a call from Phyllis Feller which hit our family like a bombshell. "Through Los Angeles," she had heard a rumor that Joey had been sent to India—to Mayapur where ISKCON had a temple and a school. Her informant (Was it her son?) thought Joey had departed some two months ago.

I was stunned—India! The other side of the world! "But why would Prabhupada send a letter to temple presidents if Joey was in India," I asked her. "Wouldn't he know?"

"He may not. Remember, it's only a rumor. As a matter of fact, I hesitated relaying it to you. But since the Swami has written you and offered his cooperation, why not ask him to check it out?"

I told Toby the dreadful news and phoned Larry, catching him between classes at school. "Not India." he groaned. "Two months ago? That would make it the first half of November. Joey didn't disappear until the third week of November. Maybe it's a mistake."

"It could even be planted," I said, "to make us give up. But just to think of the kid by himself in India gives me the shivers. What if he gets sick?" I was thinking of the frequency of malaria and dysentery among visitors to India.

Following Phyllis Feller's suggestion, I wrote Prabhupada the next day thanking him for his cooperation and requesting that he run down the rumor. "Will the temple presidents know Joey?" I wrote. "He may go by his spiritual name." I sent the Balboa Park photo and added a verbal description.

We continued our efforts to obtain FBI assistance. Its entry into our case would bring the cooperation of INTERPOL, the International Police Organization. If Joey were abroad, its help would be indispensable. We felt, perhaps over-optimistically, that the FBI's mere expression of interest, a letter of inquiry to ISKCON, would be enough to flush out Joey. We thought the cult would want to avoid FBI investigation.

A flood of correspondence and phone calls went to our senators and congressman asking them to intercede with the FBI; many of our friends also wrote. Toby and I, old campaigners, knew that busy legislators often responded in proportion to the "hue and cry." We built up fat files of our letters and their replies.

One of our Washington friends, a young attorney, took great pains to prepare a brief complete with copies of letters and news clippings. He met with Department of Justice officials to argue its acceptance of our case.

The result—nil. The federal kidnapping statute did not apply where one parent was involved in a child's disappearance, even though the other parent had legal custody.

The fact, pointed out in our correspondence with the Department of Justice, that Miriam could not have abducted the boy without the Krishnas providing the means, made no difference. Clarence Kelley, FBI director, suggested that we might "obtain relief through local authorities."

We had already turned to our local authorities. Our police could help us only if we could tell them where Joey might be. In the meantime they filed his photo among a thousand others of lost or strayed children. We could go to an Illinois court and secure a contempt citation against Miriam, but where could we find her? We were on a merry-go-round: where one agency, the FBI, could help, they wouldn't; where another would, our local police, they couldn't because Joey was in another state, or another country. We wanted to shout from the rooftops, "The law has awarded custody to the father. Let the law act to give us our child!" But the law said it had done all it could.

Out of this exercise in futility came the realization, shared by many friends, that a change in the federal kidnapping law was necessary. Larry joined with the Children's Rights, Inc., a national organization seeking to alter the federal law to include child-snatching by one parent.

The principal result of our experience with the FBI was the conviction that we would have to rely more on what we ourselves could do directly in the situation. It was good that our legislators and the public knew of the outrage; it was fine that we had their sympathy and readiness to help, but we ourselves had to make an impact on the Krishnas if Joey were ever to be rescued.

The weeks continued to pass without any results from Prabhupada's circular letter. Once again we turned toward professional help when a friend recommended to us Peter Scarlatt, a detective highly successful at finding lost children. Larry thought there would be no harm in meeting with Scarlatt to learn how he worked, but I suggested we find out first through our friends in the legal community what was known about him. Since Larry was busy teaching and attending night school for his Master of Arts degree, I undertook the task. I turned up only one attorney who recognized the name, and while he had never employed Scarlatt, he had a favorable impression of his record.

We made an appointment to meet Scarlatt in his office, hoping in person to better assess his abilities. He was over an hour late and while Larry and I waited, his secretary gave us an album of news clippings of Scarlatt's successes. I couldn't help but notice most of the clips related to a single case and that the items went back only two years. Was Scarlatt new to the profession?

When finally he arrived, the detective apologized, explaining that he had been tied up in court giving expert testimony. He was a big, jowly, highly nervous man; about forty-five I guessed.

Before beginning the conference, he asked permission to tape it, saying that it helped him to go over the details whenever he needed to refer to them later. But he appeared in a hurry. We had hardly begun our story when he came down to business details. Evidently, he had no intention of wasting time on exploratory conversation. He wanted a $5,000 retainer to be paid at once toward expenses. His fee would be on top of that, anywhere from $2,500 to $5,000, depending on the time he spent.

Larry and I were negatively impressed and must have shown it. We began to ask questions, but didn't get far before he interrupted to say, "I feel so sure of finding Joey, I will give you a proposal you can't refuse, one I've made to only one other party before this. It will cost you nothing unless I find the boy."

It was a surprising offer and Larry asked him to explain.

"Here it is. You give me a retainer immediately of $5,000. If I don't find Joey within one year, I will return the $5,000. If I find him within that time, you will give me an additional fee."

"How much additional?" Larry asked.

"That depends on how much work I have to put in."

We wanted the fee pinned down to a maximum; he said he'd think about it. "Are you ready to sign the agreement tonight?" he asked.

"No," Larry said. "We must have a little time to think it over. We've never before hired a detective. We also have to think about getting the money together. It's a large sum to us."

Scarlatt showed his impatience. "I have a hundred percent record finding missing persons. I feel confident I will find your son, that's why I'm making the offer. But you'll have to act quickly."

We continued to insist on having time to discuss it with the family.

"Okay," he said. "I'm going to Washington. I'll be gone two days. Come back on Thursday but I want the money then or else the deal is off."

"Suppose," Larry asked, "Joey is being hidden in a foreign country?"

"It's tougher in a foreign country," he replied. "I once had to go to Turkey, but we found the guy."

Driving home in Larry's Volkswagon, we discussed the strange proposal. On the one hand we were turned off by Scarlatt's brashness; on the other, we were attracted by the guarantee to find Joey or else no fee. It gave credibility to his boast of a perfect-find record. He was willing to risk it; what did we have to lose? Still there was something that didn't meet the eye, that made us uneasy.

"You know what I think it is?" Larry said. "He's anxious to get our case for its publicity value. The $5,000 is nothing compared to the business he would get if he found Joey. It would be all over television and the newspapers. He would cash in on all the publicity the case has already received; he would be a hero."

"You're right," I said thinking of the album in his waiting room. "There are thousands of people with lost children. They'd beat a path to his door. But that's O.K. with us, isn't it? We want Joey; he wants the publicity. He's entitled to it if he can find the kid."

We drove along in silence for a while heading north along the lake. The setting sun, the panorama of sky and water put us in a reflective mood. We felt at ease; we liked each other. Not that we hadn't had our differences, particularly when after two years Larry dropped college to become a beatnik in Venice, a Los Angeles suburb. During the year in California he never asked for financial help. He earned what he needed for an austere life from night shifts as an elevator operator and from coins tossed into a hat when he read his poetry at a local bistro. My sister, Rachel, on a visit to his "pad" was horrified that his bed had no sheets. When Toby, at his description of the life he had led, looked pained, he laughed: "Actually, I was living it up, doing just what I wanted. The night job gave me all the time to read and write." While it had angered us that he quit college, it had not disturbed our underlying relationship—the flow of affection ran as strong as ever. Our respect for him grew when on his return from service he resumed schooling while working nights and weekends to support Miriam and Joey.

"How is your M.A. coming along?" I asked.

"O.K. Some of the stuff I have to learn is irrelevant to what I'm teaching, just something to plow through." Larry taught emotionally disturbed high school children. "My prof asked me to lecture the class on my teaching experiences."

"How much longer before you finish and get your degree?"

"That depends on how much of a load I want to carry. At the rate I'm going now, it will take another two years."

Despite Scarlatt's assurances my common sense dictated that I try to learn more of his record. Unable to reach anyone who could help me on this score, as a last resort I called Scarlatt to ask for names of some of the people he had helped. I expected, of course, he would give me those from whom he would get good marks, but still, something might be learned—sometimes people let down their hair. Scarlatt was out and his secretary promised to report my request to him.

When he called a few days later, he was boiling with indignation that I should require references. My explanation that in business it was common did little to mollify him. He was offended that I questioned his reputation, had no confidence. In anger, he withdrew his offer. If we wanted him to work for us now, we would have to go back to the first proposal he made. Our discussion, heated most of the time, must have continued for half an hour before he cooled down. In the end, he gave me several references and restored the last offer. At my request, he promised to submit the same evening a draft of the contract he proposed.

The former clients Scarlatt referred me to gave him good marks, making his reluctance even more mystifying. What had he feared?

The only change we made in his draft contract was to provide that, in the event we found Joey by our own efforts, or, he came back on his own, our liability would be limited to the retainer of $5,000. If he found Joey within a year, he would receive an additional $5,000. Otherwise, the retainer would be refunded to us.

The formalities were completed at our next meeting and a working session followed at which we gave Scarlatt the full story and turned over our leads, documents, photos, handwriting samples, and all the other details he required. Seeing him so thorough and efficient lifted the doubts raised by some of our previous exchanges, and hope took wing once more.

10

Passport to India

AT TIMES EVEN OUR GRIM SEARCH REVEALED A lighter side. Among the totally new experiences of the first month of 1976 was a phone call from a Dave Helmsted from Personal Consulting and Psychic Healing. He offered, without charge, to have the next meeting of a group of psychics with whom he worked direct itself to locating Joey. There were a dozen in the group, he said, and he was confident that if they concentrated their attention on one subject, they would come up with the location of Joey's hiding place.

A similar proposal was suggested to me by a Russian defector whom I met during a brief visit to London in June 1976. He recalled the Dutch psychic who had successfully located the bodies of three New York civil rights workers who had been murdered and hidden in a Mississippi field. On my return, I mentioned the incident to a friend whose opinion I hold in high regard. Her face lit up; she remembered the case and urged me to contact the Dutchman.

"What have you got to lose?" she said.

"My self-respect," I answered. "Larry and I discussed it, and he feels the same way."

"You may not believe in it," she insisted, "but it has worked for others; it may for you."

All of which made me remember a story about Enrico Fermi, the nuclear physicist. While in Chicago working on the first atomic device, he was visited by friends who, on entering, saw a horseshoe nailed over the door.

"Enrico," one exclaimed, "don't tell us you believe horseshoes bring luck!"

78

"Of course I don't believe in such nonsense," he said. "But they say, whether or not you believe, it works."

Another strange incident occurred during my stay in London. I was in the apartment of two Chicago friends who suggested on the Sunday morning of my arrival that we go to Trafalgar Square. When we came up from the "underground," we heard distant chanting. It sounded familiar, yet…As we came into the huge square, we saw a devotee with a loudspeaker leading the crowd in chanting the Hare Krishna mantra at the foot of the Lord Nelson monument. It was the day the London temple had chosen for its Lord Jagganatha celebration; a smallish "juggernaut" cart stood near one of the crouching lions.

Topping off my surprise, I recognized Bhima, president of the Los Angeles temple, taking part in the ceremonies. To make certain, I queried one of the Krishnas at the food tables. He said Bhima had been recently transferred from Los Angeles. I wondered if the shift had anything to do with the events surrounding Joey.

Coincidences popped up often during our search. I had been corresponding with Bella Johnson, an artist-teacher I had met in 1930 while on a summer job in Wingdale, New York. Although we had not met in forty years, Bella and I had a common interest in Mark Rothko, a painter whom I had also known at Wingdale. When I wrote her about Joey, she immediately responded:

> One of our close friends has a son in that sect. The son, his wife, and their two small sons, are living an apparently useful life somewhere in Virginia, operating an incense business. I'm wondering whether he, the son, could help in this situation? If you think so, let me know. Our friend is a doctor, and though he's most unsympathetic to his son's philosophy, he visits him occasionally, or is in touch with him.

My next letter suggested that her doctor friend look around for Joey on the next visit to his son. I enclosed a photo. When I again heard from Bella, she reported:

> My doctor friend spoke to his son, who is now located somewhere in Pennsylvania, managing a very large farm for the sect. He gave him information regarding your grandson. According to the son's view, they do not

79

hide people; in fact they don't favor harboring children;
thinks Miriam may not be in one of their places at all.
The son would see what he could learn about their
whereabouts.

The doctor's son held an opinion common among sincere devotees: the Society would not violate the law. Confronted by our
case, devotees generally fell into three classifications: a) those
who, like the doctor's son, could not believe that the sect would
willfully hide Joey, and that our persistence in making that claim
was either mistaken or had malicious intent; b) those who felt
that if Joey was, in fact, in the sect—fine, he was well-off—they
cared nothing about the legal or moral implications of inducting
a twelve-year-old without the consent of his father; and c) those
who understood the implications and its dangers for the Society
and deliberately sought to conceal its culpability. These were the
guardians of the gate.

One Sunday afternoon Larry, two friends, and I were handing
out our leaflets to visitors entering the Evanston temple when a
young woman devotee stopped to talk with us. Harani listened
sympathetically to our story, but said she could not believe the
Society would deliberately hide a child from his legal parent.
There must be some misunderstanding which, with a little effort,
could be cleared up.

"Prabhupada is in Detroit," she said. "Go see him. He will help
you."

"We have written the Swami," I told her, "and asked for an
appointment to present our evidence, but he has not replied."

"There must be some mix-up," she said. "I'll give you the name
and address of a friend of mine, a devotee who knows the Swami
intimately. Send him the facts; he will reach Prabhupada." We
were warmed by her directness and goodwill.

My letter to her friend brought no reply. When after two weeks
I phoned Harani hoping she would have other suggestions, her
attitude had changed. Why, she wanted to know, were we hounding the Evanston temple? After all, the incident had occurred in
Los Angeles. Was not the matter a personal dispute between
husband and wife? Why were we making the Krishnas scape-
goats for Larry's marriage failure?

It was evident that the devotees of the third classification had
set Harani straight. Like a "true believer," she fell into line. In

anger at her blindness and disappointed by her refusal to make an independent assessment of the facts which I offered to present to her, I used some vigorous language. Her last words were, "You're sick; you should see a psychiatrist."

I had a long phone conversation with another devotee of the first kind. He answered my call to the Evanston temple, and, Mukunda being out, spoke to me frankly and freely. We had been told that Joey and his mother might be in one of the travelling caravans which visited the temples and colleges, and we were concerned that Prabhupada's letter would not reach them. He explained how the travelling temples were organized, their routes, the number of buses, the names of the responsible heads, and the place, Phoenix, from which they were directed. He told me that Miriam could not be among them because no women were permitted; the buses were used as men's sleeping quarters, and moreover, they were celibates. He thought Miriam could be in an apartment near a temple, perhaps with a devotee family. He was emphatic that Prabhupada's order would be carried out: "If Joey is in any temple, anywhere in the world, his order will be complied with."

Much as I wanted to, I could not risk asking him to explain Lainie's presence at the gurukula, since Scarlatt would want to guard that information as a lead. Instead, I pointed out to him that Joey might not be recognized if he was under another name.

The second kind of devotee—and they were the most numerous of those we encountered—took the view that if indeed Joey was with the Krishnas, he was well off. One devotee even proposed I join the cult in order to find and be with him. Perhaps typical of this group was Bali, president of one of the temples in India, a young man of Jewish descent who had once considered studying for the rabbinate. I got his name from the mother of a girl he had once dated; the girl had been a student at a Sunday school when I was its director. Bali sent a prompt reply to my appeal for help in finding Joey:

> If it is a fact that Joey is a devotee, we think that he may be very happy. In the International Society for Krishna Consciousness we never use force; we only accept students who voluntarily want to become devotees. Therefore if Joey has actually become a devotee, we trust that he has chosen a life that he likes. Otherwise, he is free to

81

leave at any time. Thus we request you not be unduly
anxious about your grandson.

The last sentence, in particular, angered me. At the time I
wrote Bali, we had not had word of Joey in months—we were sick
with worry—a fact my letter made clear to him. How could he be
so callous to our feelings? I met with a similar attitude among so
many of the devotees. Was it part of their training in "non-
attachment to the material world?" Nor did Bali, an officer of
ISKCON, appear concerned that the Society would be in violation
of the law if Joey were in one of its temples. And what did the
pious words "he is free to leave at any time" mean in the case of a
twelve-year-old, particularly if he had been sent to a foreign
country?

The third group of Krishnas were few in number, but were
high in the leadership. These people seemed well aware of the
legal aspects around the case of Joey and took steps to minimize
the cult's exposure to public opinion and to prosecution. They did
the cover-ups. They wrote the official letters to us and to the
inquiring public. They gave the press interviews.

Typical was Advaita (Sandvig), who wrote from ISKCON's
national offices in Los Angeles in reply to an inquiry from one of
our friends:

> While Joey and his mother were staying here in Los
> Angeles, they attended the temple functions and par-
> ticipated in the activities of ISKCON. However, they
> both lived outside of the temple and were completely
> free to do as they pleased...

To the contrary, the two had lived right there in the temple's
dormitories. Advaita had accepted service for Miriam of the writ
of habeas corpus, promising the deputy sheriff she would be sure
to appear in court. Yet, in court he swore under oath that she and
Joey had disappeared two days before. Advaita had since then
risen in the hierarchy.

On January 20, Larry phoned from school, his voice giving
away a deep misery. "Dad, a passport was taken out for Joey to
send him to India."

"How do you know?"

"I wrote the U.S. Passport Office after we got that rumor from Phyllis Feller. I just received the reply giving the number of Joey's passport and a copy of his application; it's stamped 'Los Angeles.'"

"So it wasn't just a rumor."

"Here's another thing. The application is dated November 20. Wasn't that the day when the writ was served?"

A glance into my legal folder confirmed the date. "That's right, Thursday, November 20. God! Those bastards!"

"Dad, Joey was sent by himself." Larry sounded really low.

"She sent him by himself to India?"

"The passport application reads that in case of accident Miriam Jefferson is to be notified, and it gives her address as '3764 Watseka,' the temple's address."

"Oh boy," I sighed. "Poor kid. How the hell can she do a thing like that? What could she be thinking of? Bad enough to send Lainie to Dallas, but India..."

"What do you think we ought to do?"

"I think we should blast them in the press; show them up for the liars they are. Make it hot for them." I was furious.

"That's the way I feel, but what about Scarlatt?"

"Scarlatt...I guess we should tell him first what we plan."

As I hung up I recalled Miriam's words to Doris, "They can send us to any one of thirty cities, or even to India."

Even as I boiled with new indignation at the Krishnas' perfidy, I was amazed at the lengths they were going to keep one child—opening themselves to charges of perjury, suffering bad press. It foreshadowed a long, difficult struggle to get Joey back. Would we be able to sustain that kind of effort—Toby in a wheelchair; I, sixty-eight, arthritic; Larry, and Ronald occupied with making a living? Where would we find the strength, the time itself, to continue a campaign that demanded so much?

Two days later we were in Scarlatt's office. Larry brought out the contents of the envelope from the Passport Office. Joey's passport photo showed a shaved skull and large ears, and it hurt me to look at it.

"Notice that the application is stamped 'Urgent,'" Scarlatt pointed out. "They wanted it in a hurry. Usually there's a wait of a few days, but for an extra fee you can get the passport the same day."

We proposed using the information to attack the cult and charge it with complicity in Joey's abduction. But Scarlatt instructed us not to do anything.

"Let's first establish if Joey actually went to India. The application gives his scheduled flight time, November 22, 1975, 8:45 P.M., and the airline, Pan-Am; his destination, New Delhi. I'll check it out through my contacts. Give me a week. I'm going to make it hot for them. I've a lot of stuff I'm going to unload on them."

His self-assurance was impressive and, though we wanted to ask for details, we refrained because he had made it plain at the start of our association that he would tell us only what he deemed necessary. "I run my business the way I have to; it's that kind of business. Some things you're better off not knowing."

He promised to devote himself entirely to our case the whole of next week. "Be ready," he warned Larry. "We may have to go to India."

During the next two weeks, however, Scarlatt was unable to ascertain if Joey had gone to India; Pan-American could not confirm that he was on the scheduled flight. "I'm working through Ambassador Saxbe and the Indian Embassy," he said. "It'll take a little time."

11

Child-Snatching

THE PUBLICITY AROUND OUR CASE BROUGHT LET-
ters from other victim families, some of whom lost children to the
Krishnas in circumstances similar to ours. The first, November
28, 1975, over the signature "a desperate grandmother," was sent
to the *Los Angeles Times* in response to the two articles by Myrna
Oliver. The letter in part said:

> These people [Krishnas] along with my son came and
> literally kidnapped my six-year-old grandson and put
> him on a plane for their center in Dallas, Texas,
> although my daughter-in-law screamed her disapprov-
> al. She was talked into or threatened into going with
> the husband and the child back to Dallas where he was
> placed in this school....My daughter-in-law was told
> that these people and my son could move this child so
> fast that we could never find him and this is the reason
> she went along with their plans.

The grandmother's letter ended with the heartrending question, "How can we protect these innocent children?"
While the letter had no name or address—she feared reprisal—
it did have her phone number. Our common misery drew us
together, and we quickly established a warm relationship with
Mrs. Celia Norton. This happened again and again when we
communicated with victim families—strangers one moment,
friends the next, as we discussed our tragedies and their common
source.
We inquired if her daughter-in-law Julia, now living near the
Dallas temple, could let us know if she saw Joey, Lainie, or

85

Miriam. She was uncertain if Julia would be willing, but promised to ask Julia's mother. Mrs. Norton wished to help us, but was in dread that her son and grandson might be sent to India or some distant country and she would never see them again. While they were in Dallas, occasional visits kept hope alive that there would someday be a change in her son.

Julia proved partially receptive to our request. She passed word along that Joey was not at the gurukula and that Prabhupada's letter had been posted. But she made no reference to Lainie. Did it mean that Lainie was no longer there, or that Dale had been mistaken in his identification, or simply that Julia was loath to tell?

Another letter came from a small Midwest town:

> My husband was given permanent custody of his daughter, Linda, by a former marriage. My husband is in the Army and is on assignment out of the country.
>
> Linda was enrolled in the first grade and doing well. Her natural mother, who is a Hare Krishna, came to the school and captured her.

Piecing the story together from correspondence and phone conversations, it appeared that at first the mother had been given custody of Linda at the time of the divorce. When the father, during visits with Linda, learned that she was being raised a cultist and kept from school, he sued for custody. He was warned that unless he dropped the suit, Linda would be sent out of the country. He was not deterred by the threat; he reported it to the judge who awarded him custody.

The last letter we received carried the tragic news that the cult had carried out its threat: "I wrote to Washington at the Passport Agency and found out that a passport was issued for Linda.....I have just written Ambassador Saxbe in India..."

Another grandmother, Marion Jones, wrote us:

> It is my five-year-old granddaughter, Mary, I am trying to locate. My daughter, Rita, 25, is also in the movement and has been for a year or more.
>
> On February 10, Rita picked up Mary for the weekend and never brought her back. I am sure that they hid in

the San Diego temple but they disappeared. Mary's
father, Daniel, is traveling across the U.S. looking at
the Hare Krishna farms for Mary. Daniel and I went to
the district attorney and got him to issue a warrant of
child stealing. The San Diego police went to the temple
in San Diego but they did not find them and have since
returned the photos.

So that is where we are now, with Mary in the Hare
Krishna movement somewhere. Her father, step-
mother, paternal grandparents, great maternal grandparents, aunts and uncles…are all concerned about her
whereabouts.

Daniel gave up his job, bought a travel van, and with his second
wife visited Krishna temples and farms in search of the little girl.
They have had no word, even indirectly, to calm their anxiety for
the child's welfare.

Throughout our long battle to recover Joey, this particular
practice of the Krishnas provoked our greatest anger: failure to
communicate with the bereft family to assure it of the child's
well-being. It was a needless cruelty. I understood their fear of
discovery but a letter from the child, posted from a city other than
the one she was in, would have shown a measure of compassion
one expects from a religious movement.

Many a time I awoke in the early hours of the morning when it
was still dark outside my window, and lying in the silence,
thought of our grandson. These were the worst moments, when I
could not control frightening thoughts of what might have happened to him. Larry once expressed his fears to a neighbor, "I
don't know if Joey is alive or dead." His words, revealing the
depths of his suffering, haunted me. I would turn on the radio at
my bedside, or pick up a book, hoping that daylight would bring
relief to my fears. At such times I wondered if there wasn't
someone in the Krishna hierarchy who could understand this and
bring an end to the senseless suffering imposed on the victim
families—at least, in this regard. Even the rules of war provide
for the avoidance of unnecessary pain.

These letters described cases analagous to ours: child-snatching
by one parent with the Society's assistance. But there were
instances where children were concealed over the objections of
both parents, as in the case of the Delgados. They wrote:

87

Our son, Ralph, got gulped into the Hare Krishnas
when he was fifteen and a half during summer school
vacation when he stayed in the Hare Krishna temple in
Culver City, California. He was supposed to have been
picked up by our daughter, Elizabeth, while we were
out of town on vacation. Ralph himself called her to
pick him up, but when she did, the President said he
had disappeared....We went to the temple and tried to
get information from the President, who was very
evasive and claimed he did not know where our son
was. We went to the police in Culver City...but got no
response: "Just a runaway kid," they said.

Two years passed, but the Delgados persisted in their efforts to
find their son. When at last they did so, he had undergone a
drastic change. His sister wrote:

My brother was normally a very gentle person who
loved animals and plants and never harmed anyone,
yet a month ago when my parents tried to talk him out
of the Hare Krishna cult...he threatened to "slit" the
throat of my mother.

I love my brother Ralph; and just now I don't know if I
will ever be allowed to see him again. We don't know
where he is or even if he is still in the United States.

A case which drew considerable publicity in Los Angeles was
that of fifteen-year-old Robin George, who had accompanied a
friend to the Laguna Beach temple. Attracted to the sect, she
made repeated visits and while still living at home arose at 3:00
A.M. to chant the Hare Krishna mantra. The following account of
an interview with Robin is from the *Los Angeles Times*, April 7,
1976:

Finally, she decided her home life and Krishna Consciousness were not compatible.

"They (Krishna devotees) made it seem like it was
sinful to live with your parents. They convinced me
that my parents were a bad influence."

She left home with a promise from the officials at the
Laguna Beach temple that she would be sent where no
one would find her, she said.

So began an odyssey which led from temple to temple
in the effort to conceal her from her parents and the
police who were searching for her.

The parents sought help from temple officials in Los
Angeles and Laguna Beach, but were told Robin could
not be located.

While Robin was at the New Orleans temple, Mrs. George
called several times, "but each time was told her daughter was
not among the devotees."

Finally apprehended on the streets of New Orleans, she was
returned home but three weeks later ran away again.

This time, she said, the devotees at the Laguna Beach
temple made arrangements to send her to a temple in
Ottawa, Canada. She said she boarded a plane to Buf-
falo disguised as a pregnant woman and was met there
by devotees who drove her across the border.

Jayatirtha, whose office is located in Los Angeles, said
he sent letters inquiring about Robin to other temples,
but received no response.

The last reference made me wince as I recalled the hope
aroused in us by Prabhupada's letter to temple presidents.
Jayatirtha was the Swami's representative in the U.S.

Eventually, public pressure and threats of legal action forced
the cult to send Robin home.

When she arrived in Los Angeles, she said, she was
kept under close watch for several days while devotees
tried to convince her to help protect the Krishna leaders from prosecution.

There was a tragic postscript to the story in the *Laguna News-
Post*, September 22, 1976: "Robin, 16, attributes her father's

death on September 4 to a stroke caused partly by pressure and anger from a year-long ordeal..."

During a phone conversation with Mukunda, when once again he charged that the Society was being put in the middle of a dispute between Larry and Miriam, I brought up the Robin George case: "*Both* parents objected to their child being hidden by the Society, yet you did not voluntarily return her."

"The *Los Angeles Times*," he said, "distorted the story. Robin was running away from home. Would it have been better to leave a young girl to the dangers of the street, or shelter her in a temple devoted to God?"

A letter from Annette Klein appeared in the *Evanston Review* (December 18, 1975) expressing "anger and resentment for a group which, in the guise of religion, is really a threat to our community." It accused the Krishnas of kidnapping and concealing Joey and asked the *Review* to investigate the cult.

Two months later a reply signed by Carlotta Lamb and Carl Lippman urged Klein not to feel "anger and resentment for a religous group she obviously knows little about." The writers had visited the temple numerous times and knew that the movement "is doing nothing more than trying to turn people's hearts toward God." It asked readers to examine the Krishna movement for themselves.

Impressed by the letter's sincerity and hoping to enlist support, we invited the two writers to visit us. They accepted and turned out to be very young people—he, sixteen, and she, eighteen. Carl, it chanced, was the son of a friend, a talented artist we had known for twenty-five years. This was the first time we met her son. He said he had dropped out of school "because I wasn't learning anything relevant," and was investigating various cults and disciplines, including yoga systems. He was employed by a health food cooperative where he baked bread from organic grains and seeds, he explained the process to us at length. For a sixteen-year-old he was highly articulate and self-assured.

Carl was Jewish; Carlotta, Catholic. She had left the church because "it no longer meant anything to me." She was searching for a meaningful religion, for peace of mind, for a spiritual community. Both she and Carl had been visiting the Krishna temple and liked the experience. He spoke familiarly of Mukunda.

They were attractive, earnest, not opinionated, just searching. Toby and I warmed to them, feeling affectionate, even on so short an acquaintance. Carl and Carlotta said they had written the letter in opposition to what they conceived to be anti-Krishna prejudice. "Though their dress and ritual may be different from ours," they wrote, "it is their own path to peace, and we must each have our own."

Toby agreed with them, "Prejudice is often an element in people's reaction to a strange religion. We have tried to steer clear of it. We have told the press again and again that we accord any adult the right to choose the Krishnas if that is his preference. That's not a new position for us; we have held it all our lives. We are civil libertarians, members of the ACLU."

The young people nodded their approval and became more at ease now that we had met the main point of their concern.

"What is behind your fight against them?" Carl asked.

We told them of the circumstances of Joey's disappearance, of the four Krishnas who swore that he had suddenly vanished, of the passport to India issued on the same day the writ was served, of the discovery of Joey's sister in the Dallas gurukula and of cases similar to ours in which children were secreted by the cult. We showed them the exchange of letters, the news clippings, and let them judge for themselves. We won their sympathy, although at no point did they pass judgment or say a word in condemnation of the cult. They had no theories to offer nor suggestions. They reacted humanly to our bereavement and we were grateful.

When taking leave, Carl invited us to visit him at his bakeshop and Carlotta, a waitress, asked us to try her restaurant in downtown Evanston. It was late and, since they had come by public transportation, I offered to drive them home. I dropped off Carlotta first and when we reached Carl's home, he asked me to wait a moment. He soon returned with two loaves of his bread; they felt weighty and, even in their wrappings, smelt delicious

12

False Hopes

PRABHUPADA'S REPLY TO MY LETTER ASKING HIM to check out the rumor that Joey was in India did not come for a month. It was terse, nearly a dismissal. He had forwarded my letter to his "West Coast Secretary, Drupada, at Berkeley, California, for necessary action." What did the last two words mean? He did not confirm or deny that Joey was in India.

We waited ten days for word from Drupada; then tried to phone him; finally we wrote again asking he phone us. Two weeks later we heard from him. Joey was not in Mayapur, he wrote:

> I can appreciate your concern about the whereabouts of your grandson and am sorry that we cannot be more helpful in locating his whereabouts. I must say, however, that from the beginning, your handling of this matter has been regrettable. Frankly, I think the matter is between husband and wife and should be worked out on that basis rather than involving the national media, lawsuits, etc. Although I am sure you are well-meaning, my feeling is that your goal is more likely accomplishable if you were to moderate your tone and approach to the matter. I am sure that Miriam and Joey, wherever they are, would feel much more comfortable about contacting you if they thought your position was more negotiable.

I interpreted this as an invitation to negotiate Joey's return and could not restrain a surge of hope. I was even able to convince Toby out of her doubts. Still, if negotiations were to begin, the letter gave no indication how. Larry took a dim view when he heard the letter over the phone, but Toby and I decided to phone Mukunda anyway.

Mukunda, however, could add nothing to the letter's content, but suggested we might open negotiations with Miriam by having a message posted in the Los Angeles temple assuring her she would not be prosecuted if she got in touch with us.

"Suppose she is not in L.A.," I said.

"Someone who may be in contact with her may read it and send word along to her."

It sounded unsure. "Would a direct appeal asking Drupada to help get negotiations underway be worthwhile?"

"It might," he replied. "I can't say for sure."

"We have tried to reach him, without success. Would you be willing to phone him and convey our willingness to negotiate?" I offered to pay the cost, and he agreed to phone in the evening when night rates prevailed.

The next day Mukunda phoned to tell us Drupada did not want to speak to us; he felt we should moderate our position; he had nothing to add to his letter—nothing about negotiations. When we pressed Mukunda further, he suggested a letter to Bhima. We said we had no faith in Bhima, considering his part in the hearing. He then offered to take a letter from us to Mayapur where Drupada, Bhima, and other leaders would be gathering for their annual pilgrimage. He promised to show the letter around and write us from Mayapur. He said, too, he would look for Joey and Miriam just in case they were in India. Toby and I were pleased; he seemed sincerely trying to help.

Larry drafted the reply to Drupada's letter, sent a copy to the Los Angeles office of ISKCON, and delivered the original to Mukunda. It read in part:

> We are certainly willing to discuss and negotiate the terms of Joey's return if Miriam is willing to return him on a voluntary basis, and, we are prepared to consider, under such circumstances, not proceeding with the criminal and civil remedies...

I kept hoping that somewhere, somehow, we would find the person in ISKCON who would have the sense to see our affair as bad business and bring it to an end. I could not understand how an enterprise of this magnitude—one hundred temples, five to ten thousand members, millions in assets—would permit itself to be held up to public condemnation, more, face possible criminal charges and a civil suit for more than $7 million, to hold on to one member, a child at that.

Toby's answer was, "They're fanatics; you credit them with logic. They don't think the way we do."

"How can they run an organization without business heads?" I argued. "There must be those who read a balance sheet and a profit and loss statement. Somebody minds the store and meets the bills. They couldn't continue to exist otherwise."

My quest took me back to Prabhupada. Lerner said he was a business man; in fact he had managed a chemical firm in India before he became Swami Prabhupada. Perhaps the Swami was being insulated from the real state of affairs and my letters had not been enough to alert him. If there were some way to forcefully call his attention to our case, matters could be turned around. Having started on this train of thought, I recalled that one of my former business associates had a powerful, wealthy friend in Bombay; Naipul was his name. They visited each other (I had been introduced during one visit) and entered into joint business ventures. If Naipul, at the request of my friend, could be persuaded to see the Swami, it would be an impressive display of our influence. But more important, armed with the arguments we would supply and speaking as one businessman to another, Naipul might convince Prabhupada that, for the good of his organization, he should rid it of Joey. As the one who had righted an injustice, the Swami could come out smelling like a rose. We, on our part, would publicly thank him and acknowledge his help.

My former associate, while skeptical, yielded to my urging. He asked me to draft the letter to Naipul, promising to forward it with an accompanying letter from him. He then leaned back and said:

"Can I give you a piece of advice? It's for your son more than for you. You have yourself a can of worms. The boy's mother is in the cult with him and if he had wanted out—he's old enough—he would have gotten in touch with his father in some way. Sure the law is on your side; she and the cult are hiding him unlawfully. So, what will the law do about it? You've seen how little it *can* do. It's not likely you'll find him; they can hide him in a hundred temples in God knows how many countries. You'll knock yourself

94

out looking, spend your time and money. And, if by remote chance you do find him, what will you have then? The same can of worms. They will have brainwashed him. Tell your son to forget it. Tell him to get married again and raise a new family. He's still a young man."

I was too shocked to say anything. Then again, what could I say? How to convey the depth of our feelings for Joey, our deep aversion for the life he had been thrust into? My friend simply had not experienced our sense of loss nor did he know what we knew about the Krishnas. If we followed his advice, we would be dooming a child who had still not tasted of life, who was still not ready to choose, to a sterile existence, withdrawn from family, friends, school, society—from everything but the cult. We would be betraying what we held most dear—our love and our convictions.

Naipul acknowledged receipt of my letter three weeks later, writing my friend: "I am investigating and will write to you as soon as I get some information of the whereabouts of the boy."

Eventually, the report from Naipul came. He had sent two of his most trusted men to the Bombay ISKCON center where they met with "Hari Das and Gopalkrishnadas Adhikari, secretary of ISKCON...whose statements could be relied on." The visitors were told, "There are six centers in India...and this boy is not anywhere in India." The Swami "has written personal letters to all the centers all over the world and has received no reply so far. It was not their policy to hide information...and also not to register any member without the written consent of his/her parents or the guardian."

And then came this significant assessment by Naipul:

> This may be a true and a fair statement so far as policy of the center is concerned, but there is always the possibility of there being exceptions to the general rule and policies not being followed strictly. According to me, efforts should be intensified in USA and Europe, if possible.

The last paragraph gave me cause for thought. Was Naipul delicately conveying to me what had been told him off the record? Even before this we had sensed the inner politics in ISKCON. Was this another instance? Were we being given a signal by

95

insiders who felt our affair had been mishandled by fellow Krishnas? If so, it confirmed my feeling that there were indeed people in the organization who had the sense to want to close out a costly mistake. It was clear, too, they were not calling the shots— as yet.

There still remained the most important lead of all: the fact that Lainie resided in the Dallas gurukula. Yet Scarlatt was doing nothing about it. We did not press him on the issue because, frankly, we were intimidated by him. Then, too, we were uncertain whether Lainie was still there. Julia Norton, whose child had been placed in the gurukula by her devotee husband, made no mention of Lainie. Yet, she had supplied us the information that Joey had not visited Dallas and that the Swami's circular letter had been posted. Had she withheld news of Lainie out of fear (expressed to us by her mother-in-law) that her own child might be sent to a distant temple?

On February 29 our doubts were resovled. A Dallas friend and his wife who had volunteered to visit the temple wrote that they had identified Lainie from the Balboa photo we had sent them.

So Sammy Dale had been right back in December. Lainie had been at the gurukula all along, proof that Miriam had never left the sect. She and Joey were somewhere in the movement when the circular letter was received by temple presidents. The Society's protests of innocence, its assertions of being dragged unjustly into a dispute between husband and wife, were that much hypocrisy. My indignation boiled over.

Our Dallas friends also wrote that the gurukula was being closed because it could not meet the State's standards for health and safety, and the children dispersed to other of the Society's schools. We now became concerned that Lainie might be picked up by Miriam, or that she might be sent away before we could act. Larry gave Scarlatt the news and proposed that he, Larry, go to Dallas. Since Lainie knew him, she might mention where Miriam was and when she had last seen her. Hopefully, too, on the basis of Prabhupada's letter, Larry would attempt to have the temple president put him in touch with Miriam, or convey a message to her that he was prepared to discuss the terms of Joey's return. Scarlatt, however, was opposed to the idea and instructed Larry to leave matters to him; if there were to be any conversations with temple officers, he would have them.

The next day brought a news clipping confirming Lainie's presence at the gurukula. It was from the *Dallas Times Herald*, headed: "Krishna sect India-bound," and opened as follows:

> The Hare Krishna Gurukula in Dallas...has gone to a better location in Vrindaban, India...
> About 30 or 40 children...are already in India, and from now on all will be sent there as soon as they become 8 years old. So "they can have a more austere, spiritual upbringing without interference."
> Swami Janaka said children under 8 will go to Krishna schools in Vancouver, B.C., Pennsylvania and Los Angeles.

A photo showed Sukadeva, president of the temple, kneeling and washing Janaka's feet. Looking on from the background, were a group of small children; among them, big as life, stood Lainie in Afro hairdo and large glasses!

Janaka was Freddy Loewe's friend, the higher-up who promised to help us. Was it conceivable that he did not know Lainie's relation to Miriam and Joey? If his promise of help to Loewe had been sincere, wouldn't he have questioned the Dallas temple president?

As the days passed with no word from Scarlatt, we became apprehensive that the opportunity would be lost to follow Lainie as a lead to Miriam. Larry checked with his Chicago attorney whether it was possible to get a court order to be left with the temple president for Miriam. The attorney thought it futile; it would be ignored. He suggested that, instead, Larry write the president requesting his cooperation, in line with Prabhupada's circular letter. Larry drafted a letter to Sukadeva but before sending it, tried for three days to reach Scarlatt for his approval. When at last he was contacted, he asked Larry to hold the letter for another three days because he might soon receive word of Miriam's whereabouts. We placed little hope on that possibility. Three days later, Larry sent the letter—registered, return receipt requested. It referred to the Swami's letter of cooperation and repeated our offer to negotiate Joey's return:

> We know from reports in the *Dallas Times Herald* that Elaine Jefferson, Joey's half-sister, is at your school and in view of its closing, that she is waiting to be

picked up by her mother, or, perhaps, to receive instructions from her mother where she is to be sent. In any of these events, I request that in keeping with the expressions of cooperation cited above, that you inform me when Miriam is expected, or, when she comes, or, when you receive word from her, so that I can make contact with her.

Sukadeva did not reply. Soon after, information came to us from a reliable source that Miriam had removed Lainie on April 9 to a destination which the administrator of the school refused to divulge because "Larry was looking for her."

So much for the tenders of cooperation. Our only lead to Miriam and Joey was gone; we were back on square one. Scarlatt had been of no help. But we established something important: if Lainie was in the gurukula, then Miriam and Joey were in the cult during the months the Krishnas were claiming they had disappeared. We would make effective use of this to publicly expose their duplicity.

13

Mukunda Drops a Clue

MUKUNDA DID NOT KEEP HIS PROMISE TO WRITE from Mayapur, nor for four days after his return did he phone. Finally, Larry and I met with him by appointment at the temple. Six weeks had elapsed since Larry had passed on to Mukunda the letter for Drupada. For the Krishnas, on familiar terms with eternity, what were six weeks? For us it was an agony of waiting for word of our lost one.

Before Mukunda came out to meet us in the reception lounge, a small boy of four with shaven head and mischievous eyes asked who we were. We told him our names and he asked Larry, "What do you do?"

"I'm a teacher."

"Where do you teach?" he demanded to know.

"In a high school not far from here; big boys and girls."

"Do you teach them nonsense?" It was a surprising question from a child, yet it echoed the frequent use in Krishna literature of "nonsense" to describe non-Vedic knowledge.

Larry had just begun his explanation to the child when Mukunda appeared. The boy lunged gleefully at his leg and held on with all fours. "That's my son," Mukunda said, as he disentangled the boy and showed us into the small meeting room off the lounge. The boy clung to his father and let out a howl when he was firmly placed outside the door. He made an attempt to come in but Mukunda went outside to suggest to him that he play elsewhere. After a few words between them, the child left. The incident brought us closer; we were all fathers.

Mukunda sat, as on the occasion when the delegation visited him, in the corner chair. His head had sprouted a fuzz; the white clay tilaka ran from the hair line to the bridge of his nose. His white dhoti did not quite cover muscular legs; his feet were bare. It seemed strange that English in familiar accents should come from this exotic figure.

"Well, I know you want news of what happened on my trip to India. I'm sorry, but I was never able to give Drupada your letter. I was very busy and I forgot; and when I remembered and looked for him, he was gone. He was given a new assignment to England. So I don't have an answer for you about your letter."

We were numbed by the news. The misery in Larry's face must have mirrored my own. We had hoped that perhaps our offer of a negotiated solution would be taken up. We had counted on those in the Krishna command who would want an end to the notoriety the case had brought them. Mukunda, we had reasoned, would be an effective spokesman for this view since his temple bore the brunt of our efforts. Were we wrong again?

"I did get to talk to Bhima, though," he continued. "I asked him if he knew where Joey and Miriam were." Then followed a report incredible more for the manner of its telling than its content. "Bhima said, 'I don't know where they are.'" With this, Mukunda imitated Bhima's speech and cryptic smile, conveying that what Bhima had really been saying was: "I know, but I'm not telling."

We were positive Mukunda was tipping us off. But why? Was he exasperated with the failure of his leaders to accept our offer and close the affair? Did he, perhaps, in good conscience, resent being drawn into the deception?

He went on to tell us that he had checked the temples in India for Joey—Calcutta, New Delhi, Vrindavan, and Mayapur—but the boy was not there.

We showed him the *Dallas Times Herald* article and the picture of Lainie and read the letter Larry sent to Sukadeva. "Why," Larry asked, "didn't Sukadeva cooperate with us as Prabhupada had instructed?"

Mukunda did not answer directly but went into an explanation about the character of the movement, the gist of which was that not all devotees were on the same "platform of Krishna consciousness."

"But we also informed Prabhupada of Lainie's presence at the gurukula. He could have instructed Sukadeva to put us in touch with Miriam." Larry's voice rose in anger.

Mukunda made no reply to the direct charge against the Swami. Instead, he said, "Sukadeva is a former resident of the

100

Evanston temple. I'll get in touch with him, if you wish, and ask him what happened."

We grabbed at that straw, as Mukunda promised to call within three days and let us know the outcome.

But, as so often in the past, he did not phone; after a few days I called him. Yes, he had reached Sukadeva who told him that shortly after the news article appeared, Miriam had arrived without warning and taken Lainie away. Since it was her child, Sukadeva felt he had no right to refuse. Further, until that moment, they had not heard from Miriam in months and she had stopped paying tuition for Lainie. But why hadn't Sukadeva replied to our letter, or phoned us so we could attempt to talk to Miriam? To these questions, Mukunda had no answer. It was evident that Sukadeva had concocted a cover-up story and Mukunda now repeated it. Was Mukunda a dupe or part of the plot? We were never quite sure.

It may well have been that he himself was in conflict, reacting at times to our pressure, at others to the cult's need for a cover-up. We dealt with him on the premise that he could best serve the Society by bringing the ugly situation to an end. All we could do was keep applying the pressure and in that way furnish Mukunda with arguments for convincing whoever had to be convinced that the Yanoff situation could be resolved in only one way—by Joey's return.

It was clear after our last meeting with Mukunda that the cult had no intention of returning Joey. Publicly, they maintained their original position: "We don't know the whereabouts of either Miriam or Joey." A letter from the Governing Body Commission (GBC) in Los Angeles said that since there had been no reply to Prabhupada's circular letter this "is evidence that they are not being sheltered anywhere within our residential facilities..."

Yet, there was Lainie at the gurukula and Mukunda's hint that Bhima knew more than he would tell. Could the operative words in the GBC letter be "within our residential facilities?" Was it possible they were being kept in some place loosely connected with the cult? We had heard there were Krishna communes in cities without temples, and devotees traveled to the nearest temple for important observances. Were Joey and Miriam in one of these?

We were keenly aware that in a perverse way our public efforts and our legal suit for damages worked against us. It made it dangerous to the sect to allow Joey to return to tell his story to a waiting press and a courtroom. Was Scarlatt's strategy correct then? "Drop everything. Let them think you have given up; they will come out of hiding and I will nab them."

Our confidence in him had been shaken. His failure to do anything while Lainie was at the gurukula disappointed us. Though he was required to make regular reports to Larry, these were very few and inconsistent. He hinted of being on Miriam's track in Florida, and then we heard nothing more. Or he reported she had been arrested on a traffic charge—he didn't say where—and again, nothing more. He failed to respond to phone messages. We got the feeling his was a strategy of marking time. We conjectured he had spread Joey's picture among a network of informers, had notified his pipeline to Social Security in case Miriam should find work, and to the welfare agencies should she file for aid, and was waiting for these to bring him a lead. But suppose she and Joey were out of the country—what then?

It was at this time that we learned through our congressman that efforts to locate Joey in India had failed. Our ambassador wrote to the Indian Ministry of Home Affairs which replied that "it has not been possible to confirm his arrival in India." Did this mean he had not arrived, or that records were such that no confirmation was possible? Our Embassy at New Delhi wrote to the temples at Calcutta and Vrindavan:

> We have been requested by the Department of State to
> ascertain the whereabouts of Mr. Joseph Yanoff, a U.S.
> citizen holding U.S. passport NO. 1941936...

They wrote back that Joey was not in their temples. The other four temples were not contacted. Suppose Joey *was* in one of the Indian temples—would they admit it? Our embassy had no means for compelling a truthful reply; we hoped, however, that the inquiries would act as pressure for his return.

The most important consequence of these inquiries was to bring into the open what we had kept hidden until then: that we knew Joey had been issued a passport for India. Scarlatt's instructions, contrary to our wishes, were to keep the passport information secret. Now there was no reason to. We decided on another community delegation to the Evanston temple to confront Mukunda with the passport application, hoping it would shake the cult into action; if not we would take it to the press.

Toby went to work to organize the delegation. Our congressman and state legislators consented to come or be represented,
and our friend, the young rabbi, agreed to lead it. New to the
delegation was the head of the Evanston Church Council representing all the denominations in the City. This time Larry
accompanied us—it was after school hours on May 21. Mukunda
sat in his customary place facing the delegation.

After the introductions, Larry opened with the assertion that
the evidence secured since our last meeting showed that Joey was
in Krishna. He told of the discovery of Lainie at the gurukula and
our unsuccessful efforts to get the cult's cooperation in contacting
Miriam. He didn't, at this point, refer to the passport. Mukunda
made no attempt at a refutation, saying only that the Evanston
temple was not responsible for Joey's disappearance and that he
had done all he could in the matter.

I pointed to his failure to deliver the letter to Drupada and to
write from Mayapur as he had promised. The rabbi charged him
with not keeping a promise to let him know the results of his
effort to locate Joey: "You yourself told me that you did not
believe your people in Los Angeles were telling the whole truth."

Mukunda still made no reply; the look on his face seemed to say,
"Why pick on me?"

I asked him a direct question, "How does a child get to go to
India?"

"What do you mean?"

"Suppose a child is sent to one of your schools in India; how is it
arranged?"

He replied, "With the consent of the parents and with our
agreement."

"I have here a copy of a passport application showing that Joey
was issued a passport on November 20, 1975, at Los Angeles. His
destination is given as New Delhi; the purpose of the visit—
school. In the place which asks who shall be notified in case of
accident, Miriam Jefferson's name appears and her address is
that of the Watseka Avenue temple. November 20 is the same day
on which the writ of habeas corpus was served on the L.A. temple
officers. How do you explain it?"

Mukunda tried to look composed but had no reply. Larry asked,
"Could Joey be sent to India without the consent of the temple
officers?" Mukunda kept silent. One of the members of the
delegation made an effort to get an explanation but the only

103

Where Is Joey?

result was some comments about the purposes of the movement—
to bring people to God, to chant the holy name of God. The state
representative impatiently exclaimed, "We are wasting our time
here. These people are not going to cooperate." The board
member of the neighborhood organization angrily accused
Mukunda of acting in bad faith: "We will have to deal with you in
terms which you can understand."

Mukunda flushed. "Go ahead, if that's what you want to do."

Someone added, "We may have to close you down."

Mukunda angrily retorted, "You can't do that. God won't let it
happen."

There was an uncomfortable moment until someone got up and
started a movement to the door. Larry and I lingered to ask
Mukunda about Prabhupada's visit to the States, rumors of
which had reached us. Mukunda did not know his itinerary but
said that the Evanston temple was trying to get him for their
annual parade in downtown Chicago on June 26.

I made a last effort to get through to him: "Why do you want to
let yourself in for all this. Why won't your people help us find
Joey?"

He replied, still angry: "Do you think we have nothing more
important to do than look for him? This is a small thing with us."

I was stung by the reply; this was the first time he had lost his
cool with us. "You just said it," I retorted. "It's a small thing to
you. Well, we're going to make it a big thing."

"Only when it gets too big for you," Larry added, "will we get
Joey."

14

Picketing the Temple

THAT FRIDAY EVENING LARRY, RONALD, TOBY, AND I discussed our next steps. It was at these Friday night family dinners we felt Joey's absence most keenly, but we could waste little time grieving. Though we missed the boy—his lively curiosity and our teasing banter with him—our attentions were absorbed in the campaign to bring him home. Right now we felt the main issue was how best to publicize the passport information. We doubted we could get much play from the newspapers because the passport incident had occurred too long ago to be considered news. We felt too that TV reporters wouldn't be much attracted either since there was nothing to photograph. We considered a press conference and a challenge to the Krishnas to answer our charges. But here again we felt that the item of news was insufficient in itself to bring down reporters, much less TV crews.

Eventually we came up with an idea drawn from our union experience: a picketline in front of the Evanston temple. We would picket on a Sunday afternoon between 5:00 P.M. and 6:00 P.M. when the temple had its open house, catching visitors as they walked in. We would hand them and the press a leaflet telling of Joey's disappearance, highlighting the passport information. One side of the leaflet would have two photos of Joey: one with his trumpet, taken at our home before he left for Los Angeles, the other at Balboa Park with shaven head. The headline would read: "My 12-year-old son missing since visit with the Krishnas." The

105

other side of the leaflet, which told his story, would be headed, "Help me get my son back!"

We visualized the event as a happening likely to attract the news media—a picketline for a lost child in front of the gaudy temple with exotically clad devotees looking on. Our picket signs would read: "Krishnas, where is 12-year-old Joey?"

Another consideration favored the picketline. The hearings on the temple's application for a "special use" permit were coming to a head. While the sect's failure to correct building code violations was at issue, the climate of public opinion could effect the City Council. Mukunda at least seemed to think so, judging from his angry reaction at our delegation meetings. I imagined him phoning the GBC in Los Angeles, pleading to be rid of the Yanoff issue before the City's decision was made.

Our picketline would also coincide with the start of Prabhupada's tour of the United States. He was to begin from Los Angeles the very week of our picketline. We would ask Doris, Joey's San Diego aunt, to organize a line on the same Sunday at the Los Angeles temple, hopefully while the Swami was there. We could count on relatives and friends to help us, and possibly the Citizens Freedom Foundation, an anti-cult group.

We could launch a petition drive at the picketline urging the Illinois legislature to investigate the Krishna practice of inducting minors without the consent of parents. Some time ago we had spoken to our State Representative who told us that there was a standing committee empowered to look into anything requiring new laws. Whether it would act in our situation, he did not know, but would make inquiries. The petition would support his efforts.

Still another decision taken that evening was to write Prabhupada at ISKCON's Los Angeles office requesting a meeting "to present additional evidence that Joey was within the Krishna movement." Perhaps we would get to meet the Swami.

Finally we agreed we had to confront the Krishnas at their annual parade downtown on Saturday, June 26. Our plan was to bring out picket signs and distribute the leaflet to parade participants and onlookers. We thought this action might be more important than the picketline since it would occur in downtown Chicago and be more likely to attract news coverage.

We were excited as we broke up our conference. If the Krishnas thought we would fade away, they would soon learn we were only getting our second wind.

Next morning, Toby began to mobilize our friends for the picketline. Many were from our union days in the forties when I was regional director for my union; others, from a Jewish Sunday school our boys had attended and where I taught. Toby had kept touch with people she had known during her many years in the PTA. We were both active in our neighborhood as members of an independent voters organization. Then too, there were all Larry's and Ronald's friends. Combined, these were a legion to be reckoned with.

The picket line was a great success. About one hundred and fifty joined it during the hour we were at the temple. Toby, from her wheelchair, greeted people she had not seen in months, even years, while meeting our sons' friends as well. The Zen Buddhist minister, who had been on our first delegation, was on the line, an imposing figure in his long, black robe. With him were his wife and members of his congregation.

Going round and round, the line filled the narrow sidewalk and spilled into the street. From across the street, residents of a senior citizens' building came over to find out what it was about, and their expressions of sympathy were followed by complaints over the Krishnas' noisy chanting in the early morning hours. Passing drivers stopped out of curiosity. One of our pickets gave them leaflets, saying to me over his shoulder, "Let the Evanstonians know the kind of neighbors they have."

At about 5:30 P.M. temple visitors, mostly Hindus, began arriving. Standing at the foot of the steps, Larry handed them leaflets. A few, after reading, asked him questions. Some looked puzzled, others really disturbed. I hoped they would question the devotees when they got inside.

Devotees' faces appeared at the windows, and Mukunda came out on the steps to look at the crowd. From where I stood I could not make out the expression on his face, but he could not help but be impressed—and, I hoped, alarmed. A young woman with audio equipment slung over her shoulder and a microphone in her hand interviewed him. Afterwards, she came up to Larry. She said she was from WBBM, our Chicago news station. She reported that the TV crews were all down on the city's south side where a riot over black-white housing integration was taking place in the Marquette Park area. Speaking into the tape recorder, she told Larry that Mukunda said that the Society was being dragged into a controversy between husband and wife over custody of a child. "If so," Larry replied, "why did the devotees forcibly take Joey from me on the lawn of the Los Angeles temple?" He went on to describe the passport information. "He may be in one of the Krishna schools in India. We don't know for sure and they won't tell us where he is."

Learning that Joey's grandmother was in the crowd, the WBBM reporter asked her, "Why are you picketing the temple?"

"We are here for only one reason," Toby said into the mike, "to secure my grandson's return. We believe he is being hidden by the Krishnas."

"Are you opposed to Krishna beliefs?"

"Any person has a right to believe as he chooses. But they have no right to hide my twelve-year-old grandson from his father. We wish to bring public attention to our case."

Meanwhile our petition to the State legislature was circulated among the pickets; many took extras with them. We had footnoted the petition with an appeal to "help us distribute Joey's story at the annual Krishna parade. Saturday, June 26, in the Loop."

At six o'clock Larry and I mounted the steps at the west end of the temple and the pickets, stacking signs against the wall, gathered around us. Looking down at the mass of upturned faces, I felt we could continue fighting indefinitely. Many had come from distant parts of the city, giving up their Sunday afternoon to be with us. They had come out of friendship to help us in our time of need. Some saw it as a wider issue affecting any child who found himself in Joey's circumstances.

Larry spoke first. Thanking the pickets for their response to our appeal, he went on to describe several similar disappearances of children younger than Joey. A woman with two daughters—all three had been on the line—spoke up from the crowd, "It could have happened to my daughter."

"Right at this moment," Larry said, "another line is in front of the Los Angeles temple. Swami Prabhupada, the founder of the Krishnas, is starting a national tour from there. When he sees our line and hears about the one we've had here, we hope he will see the light and order Joey's return." There were cheers from the crowd.

When I spoke, I stressed the importance of the Krishna parade. "It's our chance to let thousands know our story, particularly if

108

the television cameras are there. We aim to show the Krishnas they will have no peace, that we will confront them again and again until they return Joey."

After the meeting, we gathered up our signs with the bold black and red letters, "Krishnas, where is 12-year-old Joey?" and loaded them into our car for use at the parade.

That night our niece, Laura, phoned from Los Angeles, her voice reflecting the excitement of the day's events. There had been a tussle before the temple; the police had been called.

Thirty people had picketed the temple, she reported, half from the Citizens Freedom Foundation, the others, our relatives and friends. Doris came in from San Diego; Jason Beech, a union colleague of the thirties, took charge when the Krishnas tried to break up the line. A devotee grabbed a sign from one of the pickets and in the fight over it, Doris' eyeglasses were broken. Another fetched a wrench, twisted the sprinkler heads toward the sidewalk and turned the water on the pickets. Jason sent Laura for the police while he held the line together in spite of the drenching. When the police arrived they ordered the sprinklers turned off, and the line continued until six. A lawn festival for devotees and visitors to mark the kick-off of Prabhupada's national tour was cancelled.

"The Krishnas were terribly upset," Laura concluded her report. "They were running every which way." She had not seen Prabhupada; they had kept him out of sight.

On June 9 we received a reply to our letter for a meeting. It came, not from the Swami, but from Pandu, his personal secretary "in charge of overseeing the temples in the Western United States." The two page letter dealt with some of our charges, but failed to respond to our request for a meeting.

Pandu (one of the four who testified that Joey had disappeared) wrote that the arrangements to send Joey to India were done without the Society's knowledge and approval. Miriam's removal of Lainie on April 9 was a surprise to everyone. He did not explain, however, Dallas' refusal to put us in contact with Miriam. The letter concluded with the charge that we were involving ISKCON in a family dispute and "scandalizing" the Society.

Coming after our picketlines, the letter was disappointing; there wasn't a hint of a desire to come to terms. Larry wrote to

109

Pandu reciting the evidence that convinced us that Joey was in Krishna, and again offered to meet to negotiate a mutually acceptable solution.

"Go to Detroit and talk to Prabhupada; he's easy to talk to," an Evanston devotee had urged. On a sudden impulse I picked up the phone and made a direct call to the Detroit temple. In a long conversation with the Swami's secretary, I was told that yes, Prabhupada had received our May 30 letter asking for a meeting and had seen our leaflet passed out before the Detroit temple. (The local chapter of the Citizens Freedom Foundation had made the distribution.) Pushoc (his name as it sounded to me) insisted this was a domestic quarrel and made the startling statement, "Joey and Miriam were beaten by Larry; that's why they left him." That charge had first been made by Bhima in a TV interview, but he had confined the beatings to Joey.

I asked him to explain why a passport to send Joey to India was applied for on the day the Krishnas were served with a writ of habeas corpus.

He evaded a direct answer. "Prabhupada sent a letter to all temple presidents. If Joey was in a temple, you would have heard."

"His sister was in the Dallas temple. Why didn't we hear from Sukadeva, the temple president?"

"I can only surmise that Sukadeva did not know her relation to Joey."

"Then why, after we informed him, didn't he cooperate, or even reply to our letter?"

"Mr. Yanoff, you are embroiling us in a personal matter between husband and wife." Pushoc had fallen back on his original defense line.

"Very well; then tell me why, when both parents want the return of their child, the Society fails to comply?"

"When did that happen?"

"In the case of Robin George."

His reply came quickly: "She ran away from home. What were we to do, let her be raped on the streets or give her the protection of the temple?"

"You could have called her parents or the authorities."

"The press distorted the facts," he said.

"We would like to meet with the Swami," I persisted.

"No, it's not possible. He is busy all the time writing, translating Vedic literature. He had only four hours of sleep last night."

"Could I speak to the Swami himself."

"Impossible," he replied.

15

The Juggernaut

OUR PLANS FOR THE JUNE 26 COUNTER-DEMON-
stration to the Krishna's downtown parade went ahead. We ordered
additional leaflets, prepared more signs, and made up lapel cards
to distinguish our friends in the crowd; they read, "Where is
Joey?" A letter to all who had signed the petition was ready with
instructions when and where to gather. Then the blow fell.

Scarlatt phoned Toby in a fit of anger. He told her our public
activities had blown his chance to get Joey from the Krishna
farm-school in West Virginia to which he had tracked the boy.
Toby asked if Joey had actually been seen there, but Scarlatt
simply ignored her question. He charged we were in violation of
our contract, which in paragraph three required our cooperation.
We had failed to follow instructions to keep a low profile and let
him find Joey. Larry couldn't be reached at school; Scarlatt
demanded I phone him.

No sooner did I do so than he exploded into a tirade. He had
been two days away from getting Joey at the farm-school. A black
man had come into the farm waving copies of our leaflet and
demanding Joey be turned over to him. That man, Scarlatt said,
claimed to represent us and was going to collect on the reward
offered in the leaflet. When I denied we ever issued such a leaflet,
he brushed it aside.

"I worked hard to find him," he shouted, "and you blew it. You
are in violation of our agreement. As of now, the contract is
cancelled." He hung up.

When Larry went downtown to see Scarlatt two days later, the
detective repeated what he had told me, adding even more
details. Just when he had been making preparations with the

local police to pick up Joey, a black man with paint on his forehead appeared at the farm with our leaflet, asking for Joey. By now, he said, Joey must have been sent away.

"Can I see the leaflet offering the reward?" Larry asked.

"I don't have it—not yet, anyhow. I trust my informants to tell me the truth."

Larry explained that we were not seeking to duplicate his work, but, rather, to put pressure on the Krishnas to release Joey. If we succeeded, Scarlatt would still earn the initial fee. He replied that our activities were futile, the cult did not respond to publicity. We had gone against his orders to leave it to him. All we were succeeding in doing was to keep Joey under wraps and make it more difficult for him. Larry tried to debate the point, but Scarlatt wouldn't listen. Informed of the temple picketline and of our plans for June 26, he ordered Larry to call them off or face cancellation of the contract and forfeit of our fee. His lawyer, he said, told him to drop the case; it was his concern for Joey which made him hesitate.

He told Larry that the plan to send children to school in India had not worked and the Krishnas were opening four schools in the U.S. Joey would be sent to either Pennsylvania or Mississippi. Impressed by Scarlatt's detailed knowledge of the cult's plans and convinced the man was indeed on Joey's trail, Larry agreed to call off our June 26 action.

After his meeting with Scarlatt, Larry called to report. As Toby and I listened, my heart sank.

"Do you believe Scarlatt?" I asked.

"Yes, I do," Larry replied. "If you had heard all he told me, you would've too. I think he does have contacts inside the cult. He showed me a lot of stuff."

I felt Larry had been wrong to promise to call off our downtown action without consulting us. But I could also understand his fear of losing Scarlatt and inviting a suit over the contract.

"I guess we'll have to go along with him," I said. "At least, for now."

"You don't believe him?" Larry asked.

"Let's say I'm skeptical. But if you're convinced, O.K."

Later, Toby asked me, "What would Scarlatt gain by concocting such an elaborate story?"

"He wants to find Joey on his own so he can get the extra fee; more important, he wants the publicity. It would be a big thing for him. It would make his fortune."

"Still he gave Larry a detailed description of what happend on the farm."

"He didn't have the leaflet he claims offered a reward for Joey."

"It's possible his informant heard wrong, or maybe the black man who asked for Joey thought he would get a reward even if not promised in the leaflet—something like that."

"I guess it comes down to a lack of confidence in Scarlatt. I don't trust him anymore."

"Then it's a good thing Larry went by himself to see him," Toby said. "You would have shown your distrust and made things worse."

Alone, I tried to sort out my feelings and thoughts. I wrote in my diary of the time:

> I am still boiling over Scarlatt's demand that we give up our public activities against the Krishnas. Perhaps we should tell him to go to hell and take our own chances. I don't think he is doing very much. In any event, he can do nothing if Joey has been sent abroad.
>
> My own inclination is to refuse to comply and continue our campaign augmented by a new tactic: cut into their contributions at the airport and elsewhere. I am afraid if we go along with Scarlatt, we will find ourselves at the end of his contract year, January 1977, without Joey and having to build a public campaign from scratch.
>
> Scarlatt argues that he knows of only one case— Robin George—where the cult caved in to public pressure. Why, he asks, haven't there been others? We found out about Robin only because a West Coast friend sent us the clipping. There may have been other cases about which we simply haven't heard. Then, again, there are few families with the experience, friends, and means to undertake a campaign such as ours.
>
> I think they got themselves into this mess because they did not expect a fight from us—not the kind we're putting up. Now they're stuck and don't quite know how to get out unscathed.
>
> The campaign has been a great drain on our energies, especially Larry's. He is living under great emotional stress.

Devotees had come from St. Louis and Minneapolis to take part in the Krishna's June 26 parade. There must have been about a hundred cult members, but they were outnumbered by Chicago Hindus who came to observe an ancient tradition. Along the crowded sidewalks, men and women devotees were distributing sweets and selling literature.

I went to the Krishna parade for two reasons: to see it for myself, and to intercept any of our friends who had not heard of the cancellation of our plans. When I got to the rally point at State and Quincy alongside the new glass and steel Federal Building, there were about two hundred people milling around a huge juggernaut, two stories high, on wheels the height of a man. Its platform was topped by a tent-like structure in bright reds and yellows. "Juggernaut" derives from Jagganatha, "Lord of the Universe," one of Krishnas' incarnations. Each year the deity is paraded in this fashion as part of a festival called Ratha-Yatra, "The Festival of the Chariots." From newsreels of my childhood, I recollected images of fanatically devout Hindus throwing themselves under its wheels.

A young man, bearded and with head-hair, but in the cult's costume, offered me his food in a little plastic bag. I asked his name.

"Larry Lerman."

"You're Jewish," I said. He nodded. "So'm I. What's your home town?"

"Minneapolis."

"You're not a devotee," I said looking at his head hair.

"No, not yet."

I thought I would test Lerman. An interview with Prabhupada in the *Los Angeles Times* reported that the Swami refused to believe there had been moon landings. How could there be, he had said, when the moon is more than a million miles further than the sun. For proof he offered the days of the week, Sunday came before Monday (Moonday). I described the interview to Lerman, asking, "What do you think?"

"It doesn't matter," he replied.

"The truth doesn't matter? What is more important than truth?"

"Bliss."

"Bliss?" I asked, puzzled.

"Yep; bliss that comes from chanting Hare Krishna." With that he left me abruptly.

Soon after, a small, redhaired girl in a sari offered me a little bag of candy. I took it, told her my name and asked hers. She gave

115

me her Krishna name but at my request added her real name, Terri McPherson. She had come from St. Louis to join the Evanston temple. She had been born and raised in Iowa.

"You look kind of young," I said.

"I'm seventeen."

"How long have you been in the movement?"

"Two years."

"What did your folks think of your joining the Krishnas and leaving home at fifteen?"

"My mother let me go."

She seemed to want to talk, to tell about herself. "Suppose she hadn't, would you have gone anyway?"

"That's hard to say," she equivocated.

I asked her about the Swami's assertion there were no moon landings. "That's right," she replied. "The astronauts landed on another planet—Raju, I think it's called, something like that."

I told her I was Joey Yanoff's grandfather, did she know where he might be. She didn't, but said he would be happy in Krishna.

"But he's only twelve," I protested, "and hasn't had a chance to see what the world's like."

"The world is dying," she said. "Only in Krishna there is life. The body is dying all the time; only the spirit lives."

"Are you in touch with your mother?" I asked.

"If my mother knew where I was she would come and try to get me to go home." She had forgotten what she had said earlier. I watched her leave with mixed feelings—pity, exasperation, and anger toward the sect for having taken a runaway child, another Robin George.

By 1:30 P.M. the parade had started. Scores of devotees and Hindus picked up the heavy ropes and moved the juggernaut slowly north on State Street. At the head of the column chanting, dancing, beating drums and clashing little cymbals was a group of twenty devotees led by Mukunda. I had never seen him as I saw him then. Banging a large, jugshaped drum hung from his shoulders, his shaven head thrown back, his ruddy face dripping sweat, he was shouting at the top of his lungs, leaping, whirling, laughing. He was in ecstasy, completely unlike the Mukunda sitting in the corner of the temple meeting room composedly answering questions and expounding Krishna policy.

The juggernaut rolled its way a few blocks up State, turned west on Randolph and pulled to a stop in the Civic Plaza.

Mukunda and several devotees mounted a temporary platform and through a loudspeaker asked the crowd to join in chanting the Hare Krishna mantra. A hundred feet away was a display of cult literature. Ronald, who had been taking pictures of the parade, showed up at my elbow and together we looked over the tables. I selected two items: *Easy Journey to Other Planets* and the *Scientific Basis of Krishna Consciousness.* The chanting was still going on when we left the Plaza.

16

Making of a Cult

IN MAY I WROTE TO PHYLLIS FELLER OF OUR DIS-
covery of Lainie in the gurukula and our failure to get the
Society's cooperation in contacting Miriam. I asked if she had any
more suggestions. She phoned a month later, having just returned from travelling abroad.

She could not understand why we had not received the help of
the Dallas temple officers. "If through my contacts I should hear
any news of Joey, I'll get in touch at once," she promised.

I asked after her son. "He's on his way to India." She sounded
depressed. "This time he'll be gone for several years." Then on a
note of resignation, "He has found what is satisfying to him; who
am I to say different? I have had to learn this is something I can do
nothing about. I can't live his life for him."

"You're not giving up?" I asked.

"What else can we do? We had hoped he would now be doing
graduate work, for which he is eminently qualified. He chose
another course; perhaps his way is better. Maybe this is the wave
of the future and, like others which started out unpopular, will
prove to be correct. I don't know. I had to make up my mind either
to be driven crazy with worry or to learn to live with it. After all, I
have my own life to live."

It was obvious she had gone through a bad time. She must have
fought with her son against his going to India and now had to live
with the fact she would not see him for a long time. I thought of
our own loss and the years she had lived with hers. Yet, I was
vexed that she could entertain the thought that her son's choice
might have merit. I wanted to fight off what I considered

defeatism—or worse, rationalization—that the cult might represent a new dawn for mankind. I suppose, too, I was struggling to conquer my own fears that we might not get Joey back, that even if we found him, his heart would belong to the Krishnas, as was the case with Phyllis' son.

I argued against her mood of surrender. I told her what I had learned of the sect: that it worshipped Prabhupada as a god; that its members were taught to avoid relations with non-members and to separate themselves from family and friends; to limit conversation to the teaching of Krishna consciousness; to shun what they termed "frivolous"—games, sports, TV—anything which diverted attention from Krishna.

"I think of Joey," I said, "forbidden to listen to Beethoven, barred from picking up a tennis racket, growing up to believe that women have half the brains of men. We mustn't, by our inaction, doom him to that kind of life."

"My traditions," she said, "are the same as yours. But there is always that grain of skepticism which permits us to look tolerantly at other forms of coping. Krishna is one way."

"Have you seen the Bronowski series on Channel 11, the *Ascent of Man?* In the last program, he warned against the loss of nerve, of defeatism in the face of problems brought by the industrial revolution, by new technology, by overpopluation." My voice had become strident; I was lost in the heat of argument. "Bronowski warned against turning for solution to magic, of the search for the Absolute, or uniting with the Infinite. In that direction lies disaster, a futile attempt to escape from problems."

"You're not telling me anything I don't already know." There was an edge to her voice. "You don't understand the position from which we view the Krishnas. Our son was on drugs before he joined them. Once he was in a padded cell because of a bad trip. When our phone rang, we were afraid to pick it up; it might be news of disaster. We were thankful he made it from one birthday to the next. O.K., so now he's in Krishna. But he doesn't take drugs; he lives a clean though bare life, and he's reasonably healthy. Best of all, we know he's safe. I wish he'd found another way out, but I can live with this one. Anyway, it's his life, and I respect his choice."

Her words pulled me up short. For the first time, I realized that from her standpoint the sect had saved her son. Still, I couldn't accept what I considered a namby-pamby liberalism that viewed

119

the sect as a possible "wave of the future." I began once more to explain my position when she cut me short.

"I should tell you this," she said coldly. "Frankly, your methods of finding Joey are wrong. It was wrong for Larry to barge into the temple during a ritual and grab Joey. The devotees saw a stranger taking one of their children. (She had accepted the Society's explanation.) Their reaction was only natural. There was no conspiracy to abduct him."

"Then why don't they return him?" I asked brusquely. "Or tell us where Miriam is so we can talk to her? Or, at the very least, permit him to send a letter to let us know he is well?"

She didn't respond; I had turned her off. She had been helpful, kind to us, making long distance calls to get us information, relaying the rumor that Joey had been sent to India. I felt sorry to have come on strong. "Perhaps," I said softly, "you have better ways to go about it?"

"Well, you have Prabhupada's cooperation; why don't you develop it further?"

"We tried to meet him when he was here, but got turned down."

"I still think that's your best hope," she said flatly.

I don't know what prompted me to say it, but I knew before I finished I would get a negative response. "We were thinking of going to O'Hare Airport to ask people to refuse to contribute to the Krishnas until they return Joey."

"That would be awful," was her swift reaction. "It would mean the end of their cooperation. I can't see how it will help Joey if the devotees and their children are deprived of funds to live on."

"It would be a form of pressure," I argued.

"It will only antagonize them more," she said.

After that, our conversation lapsed, but before she hung up she assured me that she would continue to make inquiries after Joey whenever she was in contact with Krishnas. She offered, too, to let us know, when she found out, where the new gurukulas would be located.

I remained agitated after the call, the argument still continuing in my mind. I felt I had muffed it; I hadn't convinced her; worse, I had antagonized her. I wondered if we would hear from her again.

In July 1976, I was introduced to a scholar of religions who became a rich source of information. John Lake also became a friend with whom I could freely discuss our situation. I sometimes disagreed with one or another of his views on the cults, but so much did I respect his judgment, I felt compelled to re-examine my own.

He thought New Vrindavan, West Virginia, where the cult had a farm, school and temple, would be the most likely place to look for Joey.

"Write the president of the temple," he suggested. "Tell him that, if Joey is there, he is acting in loco parentis for Miriam and hence responsible for him. Since Miriam is in violation of a court order, the president could be guilty of complicity in hiding him and subject to criminal charges."

The idea interested me very much; none of my attorney friends had thought of it. "Suppose we write and Joey is there. How will we know, if the temple president keeps quiet?"

"The president would be put on the spot if he is harboring him. It might pressure the cult to return him." I looked doubtful. "If you fail to hear from the president, you could send the boy's picture to the local sheriff and ask him to search the temple. The sheriff would be more likely to respond if you got our local police to contact him."

I thought of Robin George, of how they shifted her from temple to temple. "It's more likely they'll ship Joey out if he's there."

"Possibly," Lake said, "but in that event what have you lost? You would be in the same position you are now."

True, I thought, except that Scarlatt would be on our necks if he found out.

Lake, who was in touch with all kinds of people interested in the cults, suggested names of search experts. One of them, Gene Austin, worked out of compassion, asking only for out-of-pocket expenses; he had been written up in the *Wall St. Journal*.

Lake had little regard for Ted Patrick, the noted "deprogrammer," nicknamed, Black Lightning. He thought him an adventurer; that when he was successful it was only because the subject was ready to come out anyway. He cited instances where Patrick claimed success, but the subject feigning cooperation, once freed, returned to the cult. In one such case, for which Patrick received national attention, Lake thought the parents should have allowed the girl to remain in the cult, Love Israel.

"She was happy in it," he said, "and would have become a mental case if she had not returned to it."

Lake was a man in his late fifties, quite tall, mild of manner, and very articulate. His library was crammed with books about the cults, and listening to him giving names, dates, places, facts of all kinds, made me wonder if he forgot anything he read. I liked his commonsense approach to a subject usually shrouded in mystery.

How did the Krishnas make converts? I wanted to know. "How could they take my grandson, an average city boy who liked junk food, TV, movies, games, the whole bit, and in three weeks have him writing home that he wants to stay? What of the charge of brainwashing and hypnotism?"

"Nothing of the kind," he said. "It's by a process of withdrawal from society. The act of shaving the head is also an act of separation. Taking a Sanskrit name, leaving school or job, dressing differently, eating a special diet, all this deepens the separation and fosters dependence on the cult. It makes it extremely difficult to leave."

"Doesn't the constant repetition of the Hare Krishna mantra have an hypnotic effect?"

"No more than Gregorian chants. Chanting strengthens communal feeling and increases devotion to Krishna. Sort of wears grooves in the brain by repetition of his name."

He recited the history of the movement. "It goes back hundreds of years to the split in Hinduism between followers of Shiva and Vishnu. The Krishnas stem from the latter and are referred to as Vaishnavas—followers of Vishnu—considered by them an avatar of Krishna. It was a small minority movement until about five hundred years ago when it was revived by Chaitanya whose most noteworthy contribution was to promote public chanting of the name of Krishna. Chaitanya's disciples considered him an avatar of Krishna; perhaps Krishna himself.

"The Vaishnavas themselves split and at the end of the nineteenth century one branch formed the Gaudiya Vaishnavas in Bengal. In the early nineteen hundreds its head was Bhakti Siddhanta, Prabhupada's spiritual master."

"On page twenty-nine," I said interrupting his account, "of the *Bhagavad-gita As It Is*, Prabhupada claims to be thirty-second in direct succession from Krishna himself. Was he anointed by his spiritual master and conferred the mantle of leader?"

"As a matter of fact, there is a dispute over that and a court case in India—still pending, I believe. Prabhupada claims he was given the mission by Siddhanta to spread Chaitanya's teaching to the Western world. But after Siddhanta's death in 1936, controversy arose over the succession. Prabhupada did not devote himself to the movement until his retirement in 1954. Until then he was the manager of a chemical firm and known as Abhay Charan de. He still retains the first two initials in his present name. At any rate, nothing succeeds like success, and when the Swami established ISKCON in New York in 1965 and it rapidly spread, he came back to India to open temples there. However, few Hindus joined; his Indian temples are manned mostly by Americans. All the money comes from the States."

"How do you explain his success in the U.S.? How could young Americans go for a far-out Hindu cult?" I asked Lake.

"I won't go into the complex reasons for the spread of cultism among the young; that relates to the whole American scene. Prabhupada added two ingredients to the Hindu religion to make it congenial to Americans: congregationalism (communal living) and evangelism (proselytizing)."

"What do you think of the cult looking on him as Krishna's representative on earth."

"You have to understand the Hindu attitude to the divine and the mundane," he replied. "We in the West make a sharp separation; they don't. They believe the divine is present in the worldly. So when devotees look on him as godlike it doesn't have the powerful meaning of a Second Coming of Christ or of the Messiah."

I came back to our search for Joey. I described our strategy of using publicity to pressure the Krishnas. He didn't think it would work because "publicity has a momentary effect; the public quickly forgets." I told him of our suit for damages and our fear that the Krishnas might continue to hold Joey to prevent him being a witness against them.

"We have indicated to them," I added, "that we would be willing to compromise, to make concessions to get him back."

He suggested an academic person close to the Krishnas who might help us in that regard—perhaps as an intermediary. He referred to him as one who had entry to the hierarchy and felt that if we made our proposal for compromise through him, it would receive a respectful hearing.

I left with two books from his vast collection: Faye Levine's *The Strange World of the Hare Krishnas* and J. Stillson Judah's *Hare Krishna and the Counterculture*.

17

The Intermediary

WE WERE ASKED BY FRIENDS, "DID YOU KNOW THE Krishnas collect money at O'Hare?" One Sunday, Ronald drove to the airport to observe them. He reported that several young men and women solicitors dressed in street clothes pinned flowers on travellers and sold books. What importance could that have to us? From time to time, especially after a dashed hope, I chewed on that bone. Suppose, as a form of economic pressure, we intervened? How would we go about it? Would the airport permit it? How would the Krishnas react? Could we be effective?

Such questions were not new to me. I had been an organizer for a CIO union for thirteen years; Toby, too, had been a member, active in its affairs. We had encountered many situations which had required novel solutions. Once we won a strike against a credit information bureau by keeping its phones so busy its customers could not get through. (That was when it cost a nickel for a call.) During a strike against a wholesale drug company in 1937, I had gone from pharmacy to pharmacy asking druggists to boycott the company's products until it bargained collectively with its employees.

True, our dispute with the Society was not a union-employer situation, yet, if it sold books, people could be urged not to buy. The boycott was a powerful tool, but could it work against the Krishnas?

That public solicitations were important to the Society became increasingly apparent. News articles now and again voiced criticism of the Krishnas for the emphasis placed on airport collections. A San Francisco journal wrote, "Every day—seven days a week—the temple sends a group of devotees to the San Francisco Airport to sell books.... Each day these devotees 'sell' approximately one hundred books. Even at $5 each, that's $500 a day." Randy Sacks, a former Krishna interviewed by the *Chicago Tribune*, said, "We learned how to rip people off. We actually had classes in book distribution—with lines galore ('Help feed the needy children,' 'Cure the drug addicts')." A letter in the *Tribune* from another ex-devotee, Barry Stewart of Marietta, Georgia, said, "It's funny Krishna is not a business! It's exempt. Prabhupada...had every member out distributing books for money. Some bring home up to $700 a day."

When we learned that ISKCON was suing the Chicago police for interfering with its solicitors at O'Hare, we thought it would be an opportunity to look more closely into this phase of the cult's activities. I attended the hearing which was presided over by Judge Hubert F. Will of the U.S. District Court. ISKCON based its case on a two-year-old ruling by Judge Will enjoining the police from interfering with its parades on State Street. It now asked for an order to set aside the airport's regulations governing the solicitation of funds, claiming they were arbitrary and unnecessarily restrictive. The City Attorney, representing both the airport and the police, argued that the regulations were vital for the orderly management of the airport and its heavy flow of passenger traffic. For example, the rules prohibited solicitation in certain areas—ticket lines, loading zones, restaurants—to prevent harassment of travelers while they were standing in line or eating. Required, too, was daily registration by solicitors who were given permits for display so that complainants noting the permit number could report abuses.

Judge Will ruled that ISKCON's complaint was not covered by the two-year-old injunction. At that time, he said, the sect was performing religious acts on State Street—chanting and dancing. Now it was distributing books and flowers at the airport. "You may have a basis for another lawsuit," he ruled, "but not under the previous injunction."

Afterward I told the City Attorney of my interest in the Krishnas and gave him a copy of Anne Keegan's *Tribune* story. I asked if there were any law or airport regulation to prevent us from handing copies of Keegan's story to would-be contributors.

"You have the same rights as they," he said, "to approach people at O'Hare."

Evidently the Krishnas' attorneys took the advice of Judge Will and filed a new complaint. There were delays and the case did not come to a hearing until August 27, 1976. This time ISKCON was represented by two attorneys: a Chicagoan, Al Cohen, red-bearded and wild-haired, and William Gordon, who had flown in from Los Angeles for this case. O'Hare fund-raising was obviously of great importance to the cult.

ISKCON asked for summary judgment to enjoin the commissioner of the airport from arbitrarily posting regulations for solicitation by religious groups. Referring to the municipal code, Gordon argued that, while the airport had the right to manage, it failed to set standards for the regulations in question. The procedure did not allow for due process, for the right of those affected to take exception; hence it was arbitrary. He also charged that the requirements were overdrawn, more than was necessary for keeping order and efficiency. For these reasons, he concluded, the regulations were an infringement on ISKCON's First Amendment rights of freedom of religion. He cited several cases to support his position.

The presiding judge, George Leighton, asked if both sides agreed that ISKCON had a constitutional right to be in the airport. The City Attorney conceded it did; the only question at issue was the regulations under which religious groups could solicit the public. The law under which the airport authority was established, he said, gave management sole responsibility to operate in the most efficient manner and, accordingly, it had set up the regulations.

When both sides had concluded arguments, the judge announced he would make his ruling on September 28 and gave the attorneys ten days to file briefs. The court then recessed for lunch.

While I had come to listen, to keep up with events connected with the cult, I was looking for an opportunity to advance our cause. I could have spoken to the press (I saw two reporters taking notes), but I was inhibited by Scarlatt's demand to keep out of the news. I had nothing more to say to the City Attorney, so I approached Cohen. My intention was to feel him out as a possible intermediary with the Krishnas. We had a mutual friend in a former Chicago labor leader, and I used his name when I introduced myself.

"I've heard about your case," he said brusquely, "but no more than I've read in the papers. I handle only civil liberties cases for the Krishnas." It was a brush-off.

Just then an old friend of my union days threw his arms around me—we hadn't met in two years. He was in court for a case which arose out of the Marquette Park riot of June 6; he was one of the pro-integration leaders. Cohen was their attorney. My friend introduced me to him in a manner to get a more receptive response.

Hearing my first words, Cohen interrupted to say he could not help me but that he would introduce me to one who had the trust of the sect's officers and was in an excellent position to act as intermediary if he would agree to do so. Cohen kept his word; he introduced me to Peter Braun, who indeed had a pipeline to the cult's hierarchy.

I met Peter Braun only once; thereafter, our communications were by letter and phone. A man in his thirties, of middle height, deliberate of speech, the first question he asked was, "How do you know your grandson is in ISKCON?"

"We think our evidence is pretty convincing," I replied, and then launched into an account from the time we sent Joey to Los Angeles for a month's visit up to the present moment. Braun was already aware of many of the things I described: the passport, the Evanston zoning case, the picketing, and even that Doris had picketed the West Coast temple. But he had no knowledge of the exchange of correspondence with ISKCON officials. Nor did he know of our efforts to get the intervention of the Justice Department and Internal Revenue Service. He pooh-poohed the latter until I quoted from Senator Adlai Stevenson's letter that the IRS would probably review ISKCON's tax-exempt status because of the Yanoff case. He wanted a copy of that letter as well as Drupada's suggestion we stay out of the news.

There was no mistaking Braun's reaction when I told him of our plans to go to O'Hare to ask people not to contribute to the Krishnas until Joey was returned. "Oh boy," he said softly.

"Listen," he said. "I know you've made your impact felt." I was stirred by these words; our labors had not been in vain. "I'm willing to see what I can do. I think there is a chance to do something in the situation."

I could have thrown my arms around him and kissed him. "Need I tell you how grateful we would be? We love our little boy; we miss him terribly. We haven't had a word in a year."

"I know how you must feel. I'm a father too. What I would like from you is a letter dealing with two things: what you plan to do to get Joey back; what assurances you can give if Joey is returned." The stick and the carrot, I thought. He wants to show the Krishnas what they would be in for if they held on to Joey.

"What do you mean by assurances?" I asked guardedly.

"Well, for one thing, the Society will want to be assured that you will not exploit Joey's return—you know they would leave themselves wide open. I am assuming that he is really in."

"It's not our intention to blast the Krishnas, if that's what you mean."

"Something more concrete would be needed to assure them."

"Well," I said, "suppose we sent a letter to Prabhupada thanking him for his cooperation. It would tie in with his circular letter."

He thought it would be worth considering. "Another thing," he said. "You know Joey has been in for a year now; he won't be the same child you knew."

My heart sank; here it comes I thought. "What do you mean?"

"I'm assuming from what you told me that he must be part of Krishna. How are you going to meet that problem?"

"We don't know at this point whether he does or doesn't want to be in. We will have to see him and talk to him, judge his condition to know how to handle it."

"But suppose he is sold on Krishna?" he insisted. "Pulling him out just like that could be a terribly traumatic experience. Have you thought about that?"

"Yes, I can see that," I said. "We don't want to hurt the boy. We'll do what has to be done even if he has to remain in some kind of contact with the local temple."

"If you can give assurances on that," Braun said, "it would help impress the Krishnas and make it easier for me."

"I'll have to talk to my son."

Braun went on to discuss the damage suit. "I don't think it has any merit but it is a nuisance to the Krishnas."

"I think we would be willing, if everything else is worked out, to withdraw it."

"Are you speaking for your son, too?"

"I think so," I said, "but I'll have to talk to him now in more concrete terms."

"You will also have to talk to your L.A. attorney. Call me after you've had your discussions." He gave me his card.

"You know," he said, "I got involved in the Robin George case. I helped resolve that. The papers garbled the story. But she had become more trouble to the Society than she was worth."

My hopes soared. Had we become more trouble than Joey was worth? Was Braun already aware that the cult wanted out? Maybe this, at long last, was the break we had been looking for!

As if reading my thoughts, Braun said, "You know the Krishnas are not the wild fanatics some people make them out to be. They can be talked to. They're reasonable."

"I truly hope so. You will find us reasonable too, and let me assure you we will keep our word on any promise we make."

Braun hurried off to make a plane, and I for home, imagining the scene when I broke the news to the family.

Everyone was as joyful as I. Perhaps the end of our search was near. Braun's presumed connection with the Society was such that we had good grounds for thinking so, and his role in the Robin George case was evidence he knew the right people. He would not have undertaken our mission, we reasoned, unless he had good expectations of being successful.

Larry raised one point of difference over my assurances to Braun: we should not drop our damage suit without reimbursement for our expenses. I did not try to argue him out of his position.

But we did have to persuade Larry that for Joey's sake, not alone as a concession to the Society, we would have to think of his present religious beliefs and make provision for a transition period. Larry, to the contrary, felt it would be best to separate him completely from the cult as a first step to normalcy. Ronald sided with him.

We had all read about and discussed forcible deprogramming where the devotee is locked in a room and verbally hammered at until he discards his beliefs. John Lake had expressed himself strongly against Ted Patrick's methods. Others were harsher in their judgment, calling it "brainwashing in reverse." None of us could see ourselves doing this to Joey. Larry had turned down a Van Nuys detective's offer to snatch Joey precisely for that reason: its shock effect. Neither had we arrived at any other process by which he would be restored to everyday life. We had tacitly agreed not to try to meet that problem until we had Joey back and observed his condition. Now we had to meet Braun's question, "Would we respect Joey's religious convictions?"

In the give and take of argument, we eventually worked out a flexible position: not to close any avenue by which Joey could be brought back. We could promise Braun that we were prepared to do whatever was best for Joey's welfare including, if necessary, maintenance of his contact with the Krishnas. Once Joey was back with the family, with his friends and in school, time favored his reintegration. We were confident we could cope with any new problem as long as he was where he could again receive our love and care.

A long distance call by Larry to Bert Rogers, our Los Angeles attorney, secured his consent to our negotiations. The suit, he said, should not stand in the way of getting Joey back.

I had met with Braun on Friday, August 27. The weekend intervened, and when I called on Monday, he was out of town. It wasn't until Wednesday that I spoke to him. I reported that we were all in general agreement with the points developed at our meeting. Predicated on Joey's prompt return, we would agree to drop the law suit, but Larry wanted reimbursement for his expenses. Braun thought that might be a sticking point.

As to publicizing the circumstances of Joey's return, I repeated the suggestion made at our meeting, that we would be willing to reply to Prabhupada's circular letter to thank him for his good offices in effecting Joey's return. He thought it a good idea.

He asked if we would continue our activities against the cult after Joey's return; he referred, too, to Doris's efforts in the San Diego area. I replied that our interest was to secure Joey's return, not to carry on a vendetta. As to Joey's transition period, we wanted to cause him no anguish that a sudden withdrawal might bring, and, depending on his condition, his frame of mind, his attachment to the sect, we would agree to make whatever provision was indicated to ease his return including contact with the local temple. Our first concern was his mental and physical well-being.

Braun thought we had laid a sound basis for him to approach the Krishnas and that he would get back to me at the end of the next week. If he did not call, I should call him.

One can imagine the anxiety and hope with which we waited to hear from Braun. Had he been in touch with the sect's leaders during the interval between our meeting and our phone conversation? Did he already know that they were prepared to negotiate, and did the nature of our conversation, the attention to details, indicate that the proposals we made were acceptable? Or, could we be wrong, that he was a brash, young man who overestimated his influence? He didn't strike me as such, but who knew? While I was talking to Braun, I was confident of his ability to help us; in the intervals between, I was beset with doubts. And the doubts increased with the passing days.

Ten days passed without a call from Braun. What did it mean? Filled with misgivings, I phoned him at the end of the second week. He had been "running around putting out fires," he said, and hadn't had time to attend to our business. My God, I thought, here we are biting our finger nails, waiting for *the* phone call which might end our long agony and he has done nothing in all that time.

"I've read the material you sent," he said, "and it supports my hunch that something can be done." I cheered up. I had sent him clippings to describe the circumstances of Joey's disappearance and copies of letters from ISKCON officials. "Pandu is away for a few days; he will be back the first of the week. I'll speak to him then." So he does have contacts at the top, I thought. Pandu was the representative in Los Angeles of the governing body Commission (GBC), the highest authority in the Society.

I was anxious to get some acknowledgment that Joey was in Krishna and that he was all right. I asked, "Have you made any contact at all?"

"Just with lower echelons. They don't have any information, or, at least, no recent information. If Joey is in the Society, it will take pressure from the higher-ups to bring him out from where he is."

I took the bull by the horns. "Have you received an impression of any kind that Joey is safe and sound? We are terribly anxious for him."

There was hesitation. "I have no impression at all. I understand and sympathize with your feelings. I'm a father, too. You will hear from me as soon as I know something."

That was disappointing. "Do you think our proposals fit the needs of the situation?"

"I think they do, but we'll have to see."

He promised to call after speaking to Pandu. I urged him to call even if the first meeting was inconclusive, just to get a progress report.

During the days which followed, every time the phone rang, we jumped to answer. Friends who phoned must have sensed a note of disappointment in our greeting. Five days after our last conversation, Braun phoned to say that Pandu was in Australia and not expected back for a week. My hopes sank. What did these delays mean? If they wanted us off their backs, they seemed to be in no hurry.

"However," Braun went on, "Drupada is coming in from London. He stopped over in Chicago for a couple of days and is due in L.A. today." Drupada, now assigned to England, had been GBC representative when Joey "vanished."

If Drupada had been in Chicago, it must have been at the time the Evanston council voted to turn down the temple's application for a "special use permit". Could he have been one of the two devotees sitting up front with Mukunda? They had attracted attention—shaven heads, white and saffron robes, and Mukunda wearing a lei of white and red carnations. During the debate, one of the three aldermen who sided with the temple charged "that the group's different looks, religious practices and the Yanoff case was behind this." *This* referred to the unanimous recommendation of the Planning and Development Committee to deny the permit. In the final vote, thirteen of the sixteen alderman voted to accept the recommendation. I hoped Drupada had been impressed by the far-reaching effects of our case.

I told Braun of the Council vote. "Although Drupada is in London," he said, "he is well aware of what's been happening. It's a good thing he's coming in." Did this mean Drupada would be more inclined to settle our affair? Braun was niggardly with words and I was loath to press him. Before hanging up, he promised to call again as soon as he had something definite.

18

The Vigil Begins

ALMOST THREE WEEKS HAD GONE BY SINCE MY
August 27 conversation with Braun. I had the impression from
our conversations, and the delays between calls, that the cult was
in no hurry to settle. We had brought them grief, of that there was
no doubt, but it was not of such compelling force that they were
ready to return Joey. They must be debating the issue. I could
imagine Mukunda urging a conclusion, but beyond that I could
not guess at the inner politicking. Pandu had testified that Joey
had disappeared; Drupada, in Los Angeles at the time, might
have been consulted on the plan to send Joey to India. Wouldn't
these two try to sweat it out rather than admit they had made a
costly error? I guessed they were teetering in our direction, but
unless there was more pressure, they could come down on the
wait-and-see side. We had to throw something more onto the
scales, and it had to be done while they were debating. My own
thinking had crystallized; that "something" was O'Hare.

The next Friday I proposed it at the dinner table. Larry was
reluctant. We had not given Braun enough time, he argued.
Braun seemed sincere; we might alienate him if we went to the
airport. Then there was Scarlatt, we had promised him to stay
out of the public eye.

"*You* promised," I said to Larry. "His contract is with you, not
with us. You had best stay away from the airport. If Scarlatt
complains, blame us. As for alienating Braun, that's a chance
we'll have to take. We may be strengthening his hand. He'll be
able to say to the brass, 'Better settle with the Yanoffs before you
lose a lot of money.'" We didn't convince Larry that night but
decided to go ahead anyway.

The O'Hare vigil, as we came to call it, was not adequately prepared although we had talked about it off and on for weeks. The pressure of recent events seemed to be calling for powerful action, and O'Hare was on the back-burner. Perhaps it was just as well we had not thought it through completely. The difficulties were so great that too much foresight might have discouraged us.

I knew that "direct action" often led to unfortunate developments— violence, for example. Mrs. Kallin, one mother who had rescued her child from the Krishnas, thought the sect capable of it. The attacks on Larry and on our Los Angeles picketline bore out her fears. Also, some Krishnas had recently been charged with attacking some children who were collecting for muscular dystrophy at the San Diego zoo. As the zoo represented one of their prime collection points, the Krishnas must have resented the competition. Based on these incidents we couldn't be sure what the devotees would do when a principal money source was threatened.

On the other hand, we would be in a busy airport with travelers, employees, and security police all about. Premeditated violence shuns witnesses. I felt we could minimize the danger by warning our people to avoid provocation, to tolerate non-violent reactions such as insults. We would stick to the issue—Joey's disappearance into the cult—and under no circumstances allow ourselves to be drawn into personal disputes. Our quarrel was with the Society, not with its individual members. We were going to call public attention to our case and let contributors decide to donate or not.

A major risk was that our vigil could quickly fade and die if our friends did not respond. The hundred and fifty who came out for our Evanston picketline showed they cared, but the commitment we now asked was of a different order. How many were prepared to confront the Krishnas on their own turf—busy O'Hare where the sect had been collecting for three years? Moreover, the demand on their time would be not for an hour but for three or more; not a one-time event on a Sunday, but a daily stint. And, instead of being part of a group, the vigilers would have to act individually, one on one. To ask so much from our friends took a boldness combined with great tact. The job fell to Toby.

I had no ambitious ideas of cutting off the cult's income from the airport, only to reduce it a little—just enough to tip the scales of GBC deliberations. Nor did I envision a long-range action. We would play it by ear, meeting each day's demands as best we could. We would ask our retired friends to join us on weekday mornings and supplement them with our sons' friends on weekends. We planned to start Sunday afternoon, September 19, when Ronald was available.

The Friday evening we came to our decision, Toby immediately began phoning people. With those who showed willingness but were busy on Sunday, she asked for Monday, Tuesday, or Wednesday. For the moment we did not schedule beyond that. To make it easier to accept, we offered transportation.

As Ronald had spent one Sunday afternoon observing the Krishna solicitors at the airport, he and I now discussed the logistics of our vigil. The Krishnas grouped where traffic was heaviest, in front of the entrances to the loading concourses of the two main terminals.

"Depending on how many people we have," he said, "we can either concentrate at one terminal, or split up and cover both."

"Since people will be new to it," I mused, "perhaps we ought to stay together on our first try."

"That might be the right idea, but we can judge better when we see how our people take it."

"In case of trouble, one of us should be uninvolved and ready to call the police." Ronald would be that person.

"To make our people comfortable," Ronald suggested, "I think they should watch you and learn how to go about it. When they feel confident, they can pitch in at their own pace. Another thing; if they have something in their hands to show, it acts as a support, makes it easier to approach strangers with our message."

"I've thought of that, too," I said. "Let's mount Keegan's story on paperboard and hold it up to prospective contributors to read. The headline is an eye-catcher."

"The article is too long for people to read right there. We should have copies to give away."

Ronald, who was good at layouts, prepared the article for the printer. It displayed the *Chicago Tribune* logo on top. In the lower righthand corner, I typed in:

> It was not until much later that Yanoff learned from the U.S. Passport Office that a passport had been taken out for Joey on November 20, 1975, the same day the writ was served—destination, India, Krishna headquarters.

As we made our preparations for the vigil, my excitement mounted. It was like the old days, forty years ago, on the eve of a strike. I was keyed up, a little apprehensive, but I knew that would go away the moment the action started.

Five of us rode the Kennedy Expressway to O'Hare in my old Chevy. Besides Ronald, there were Sylvia and Rose, sisters, both retired social workers, and Esther, a retired public school teacher. Esther, after a lifetime of curbing unruly students, was articulate and self-assured. Sylvia was a widow; her husband had been our dentist. Rose was Toby's closest co-worker during their PTA days. The sisters were models of good manners but beneath was a steel firmness. Their voices and distinct enunciation were so alike that over the phone I had to guess who was who. The three were well chosen for our first sortie.

En route, we briefed our friends. "The Krishnas will accost many people," I said, "but only a few will stop to listen. When they've caught someone's attention, that's the time to step up and say, 'Before you make a donation, please read the story of Joey Yanoff.' Hold up the *Tribune* article so they can see the headline. They won't be able to read much of the article then and there. If anyone asks, we have extra copies. Don't get into arguments with the devotees. Address your remarks to the prospective contributor. If they ask who you are—you are friends of the family helping to call attention to its plight and asking for public support."

"Suppose," Esther asked, "the devotee says we're lying; Joey is with his mother somewhere, that they're not hiding him."

"Read the whole of Keegan's article. It has all the main facts to support our position. I've added a footnote that a passport was taken out for Joey. If he's not in Krishna, why would they send him to India?"

"There are both men and women devotees at the airport," Ronald added. "The men wear wigs and white or blue shirts; the women granny dresses. The women pin flowers; the men distribute books. Both ask for donations."

"Should we concentrate on the women?" Sylvia asked.

"Whatever is most comfortable for you," Ron suggested.

"Suppose they try to push us out of their way?" Sylvia asked.

"Push them back," Esther urged.

"No, don't," I cautioned. "Don't allow yourselves to be provoked into a fight. Avoid it. If it gets bad, call Ron and he'll get an officer. We have as much right as they to be in the airport talking to people. I've checked that with a city attorney."

I parked my car in the open-air lot east of the American Airlines terminal, which I later learned was Building Three; Building Two housed United, among other airlines; Building One, the farthest west, served international lines. The three terminals, interconnected, formed a horseshoe.

We walked slowly toward Building Three, suiting our pace to that of Rose, who had recently had cataract surgery. We entered at the lower level, where baggage was picked up, and took the escalator up one flight to the main floor. Hundreds of travelers were standing at ticket counters or sitting in the waiting lounges. The terminal was the length of a city block, framed by high windows on both sides. On one side, passengers arrived in cars and taxis; through the windows of the opposite side we caught glimpses of planes at their loading ramps. Down the middle of the enormous building were the ticket counters. A passageway, some forty feet wide, connected the two halves of Building Three.

We found the Krishnas in that passageway. Departing passengers went through it to the security check-points and down a long concourse of boarding gates. Arriving passengers also came through this passage on their way to pick up baggage downstairs. On either side of the passage were restrooms. The Krishnas had shrewdly chosen the most congested area in the terminal.

There were four men and two women devotees today, all young. The women carried over their shoulders large plastic bags filled with red carnations and magazines—*Back to Godhead*. Two of the men wore pouches filled with books; two others wheeled grocery carts with books.

"Let's watch for a while," I said. The five of us stood in a corner of the washroom area and observed the devotees at work. Many travelers went through waving them aside or ignoring their approaches. A good-looking devotee with a tiny gold ring in one nostril pinned a carnation on an elderly man. There was a brief exchange of words, the man pulled out his wallet and handed her a bill. She thanked him and gave him one of the magazines from her pouch. Wasting no time, she turned next to accost a well-dressed woman. One of the cart-wheeling devotees extended his hand to a sunburned traveler who mechanically took it, a puzzled look on his face. The devotee spoke to him for a few moments then handed him a book. While the man looked on, the Krishna flipped its pages and made his pitch. We saw the man nod agreement, put the book under his arm and walk away. But, before he could take more than a few steps, the devotee stopped him, said something to make the man hesitate. After some discussion the man pulled out his wallet and gave the devotee some money.

I turned to our group. "I'm going to announce ourselves to the Krishnas. Stay close to me." I selected a tall male devotee with an aquiline nose and swiftly moving eyes. He might have been about twenty years old.

"May I talk to you for a minute?" I asked him. He looked at me with an automatic smile, taking me for another prospect. "I'm Joey Yanoff's grandfather, Morris Yanoff." I noticed a light of recognition but he said nothing, continuing to smile. "We are here," I continued, "with some friends," I turned to indicate them, "to tell people what happened to Joey. We want you to know we have nothing against you personally, or the other devotees. We want your Society to return Joey; that's the only reason we're here."

He said nothing but went over to another Krishna, a slightly older man who seemed to be their leader. As they talked, they looked in my direction. A few steps away, a devotee was talking to a middle-aged man who was holding one of their books. I motioned to my friends and walked over.

"Sir," I said, "before you make a contribution, would you please read this." The devotee, surprised, said nothing. The traveler read the headline on the card I held up to him. "Who are you?" he asked.

"I'm the grandfather of this little boy," and I pointed to Joey's picture on the *Tribune* article. "He was sent for a visit to their Los Angeles temple and was never returned. If, after reading his story, you still want to contribute, that's your privilege."

The man, puzzled, looked at me and at the devotee, handed the book to him and walked off. I couldn't tell if he understood me or simply used the interruption to get away. Having seen what happened, my friends wore broad smiles. The devotee went over to the other two, who had also watched the incident. They appeared disturbed.

Just then the ring-nosed devotee swung into my vision as she pinned a flower to a woman's coat lapel. "Lady," I said, walking over to them, "before you contribute, will you please look at this," and I held up the article to her eyes. She read, looked at me, said,

"I have no time," and hurried off. She made no contribution and walked away with the flower still pinned to her coat. Ring-nose gave me an angry look and she too joined the circle of devotees in the center of the washroom area. They were obviously upset; our friends, delighted.

Now Esther was ready to try her hand. She approached the second flowergirl, a brunette slightly older than the first, who was in the act of pinning an elderly man.

"Just a minute, sir," Esther said loudly. "These people are hiding this little boy," and she pointed to Joey's picture. "Don't give them anything until they return him." The man turned to her with a question I could not hear, and they got into a conversation. The devotee left.

By then, the huddled devotees had recovered and were back at work. Their leader headed toward a telephone. He's calling the temple, I thought.

I caught ring-nose smiling at a young man. Her smile, slightly crooked, was quite attractive. I ran up, calling, "Sir, before you make a contribution," but he was already giving her a bill and accepting the magazine. She did not give me a glance, but went for another prospect. Following her, I passed Rose and Sylvia listening as Esther talked to the elderly man.

I stopped another contribution to the ring-nosed devotee. For the first time I noticed she had an oblong tag on her sleeve. It had the date in one corner, a number in the other, and the name "Saci devi." Under the name she had written "World Relief." I had difficulty following her and, in the sudden rush of traffic from an arriving plane, lost her. When next I caught up with her, she had pinned a sailor and was smiling at him. The sailor, obviously embarrassed, was making no move to his pocket. When I got to him, Saci adroitly put herself between us, but I walked around to his other side saying, "I'm the grandfather of this boy," and held up the news clipping to him. I watched his eyes scan the headline. "Who's Krishna?" he asked. "It's a Hindu cult," I said, "and she is a member of it. Your money will go to it, to support their organization."

"She said it was to help the needy," the sailor said.

"Don't listen to him," Saci said to the sailor. In answer, the sailor began to fumble with the flower trying to get the pin out. "You can keep it," she said, and the sailor left. She turned on me furiously. "You're a demon. You're going to be smashed." For a moment I thought she was going to attack me and involuntarily drew back. Instead, she darted into a doorway. I followed, but running into two corridors going in separate directions, turned back.

I returned to the main passageway between the washrooms and seeing a tall, baby-faced devotee accosting a young man, I thought I would listen to his pitch from beginning to end. The name on his sleeve-tag was "Narada." The traveler, who wore a large, pearl-gray Stetson, had the weathered face of an outdoors man.

Narada: *(holding out his hand)* Hi, Buddy! *(The traveler automatically extends his, a look of cautious surprise on his face)* Visiting Chicago? *(Narada sees me nearby, but ignores me. If I made him nervous, he didn't show it.)*

Traveler: Yup.

Narada: For the first time?

Traveler: Yup.

Narada: Great! Welcome to Chicago. How long are you staying?

Traveler: Two weeks.

Narada: Wonderful. You'll like it. Where you from?

Traveler: Denver.

Narada: Denver! That's a beautiful city. I was there a couple of years ago—enjoyed it. *(Changing to a confiding tone)* We're giving away, free, this book today. *(Hands the book to traveler, who takes it hesitatingly.)* This is a five-thousand-year-old book. *(It is the yellow-jacketed short version of the Bhagavad Gita.)* It's all about God. *(Using another copy in his hand, he turns to pages of color pictures as the traveler looks on.)* You do believe in God, don't you?

Traveler: Oh, yes.

Narada: Fine. Well, it's all yours. Hope you enjoy it.

Traveler: Thanks. *(Starts to walk away.)*

Narada: Would you give us something to cover the cost of printing? We're doing the work of God; bringing more people to God.

Traveler: *(Doubtfully)* How much is it?

Narada: Most people give us ten dollars.

Traveler: I can't afford that. *(He offers the book back to Narada.)*

Narada: No, no. We want you to read it. Give me whatever you can afford. It's just that we want to have money to print more to give away.

140

Traveler: *(Ashamed now to return the book.)* Will five dollars be O.K.?

Narada: If that's what you can afford, sure *(taking the bill)*. Could you spare another dollar or two? *(He gets another dollar bill.)*

Narada: Thank you and God bless you. Hare Krishna. *(That is the sole indication of Narada's affiliation. The man walks away without any sign that he heard or, if he did, understood.)*

Our three friends were busy in the passageway. Esther seemed to be in her element. Her hearty, clear voice could be heard above the airport hum. When they heard it, people turned to look.

"That's no free book," she said to a woman holding a copy of the *Gita*. "He's going to ask you for money in a minute. I wouldn't give these Hare Krishnas a nickel. Ask them where they are hiding this little boy." She showed the picture and looked accusingly at the devotee. He hesitated in his sales pitch, looked uneasy, and the prospect, her attention diverted, walked off.

Rose had developed her own method. Shuffling slowly, peering through her thick-lensed glasses, she was particularly effective against the booksellers. The flower-girls were too fast for her, but the booksellers needed time to bring their prospects to the point of paying five dollars and up. She mutely held up the cardboard on which the *Tribune* article was mounted and when she saw the prospect's eyes drawn to it, she said in her deliberate manner, each word sharply enunciated, "We ask you not to contribute to the Krishnas until this boy is returned to his father."

Sylvia had followed Saci about fifty feet away from the passageway and was now earnestly urging a young soldier to refuse a contribution. I was pleased to see that our friends had taken the plunge quickly. Ron told me he was going to Building Two to see what was happening there.

While I was standing at a corner of the washroom area, one of the airport porters came up to me. "What are you passing out?" he asked. I gave him a copy of the reprint. "I'm the grandfather of this boy. We're trying to make the Krishnas return him. That's why we're doing this."

"I hope you get him," he said and walked over to where two other porters were watching the scene. The leaflet was passed among them. One of them came over to ask for several copies for his "buddies."

141

"I'm glad to see you here," he said with a distinct Irish flavor. He was a little man in his forties, with apple-red cheeks and merry eyes.

The airport identification shield on his brown blouse read "Kevin McNeil." "These bastards have been getting away with murder. I don't know why the airport doesn't throw them out on their butts. They stick the soldiers with their junk and the poor kids don't know how to refuse. We pick the books out of the garbage when the kids throw them away. The Krishnas try to buy them back from us for fifty cents apiece after they take the kids for five and ten bucks, maybe more. Ain't it a shame? Give me about ten of them sheets; I'll pass them around to the night-shift porters."

"How late do the Krishnas stay?"

"I don't know for sure. I think till six or seven. I quit at four. But I can find out for you."

"I wish you would. It will give us an idea of what we have to do."

"Do you want these books?" he asked.

"What do you do with them?"

"Rip 'em up. One of the porters sells them back to the Krishnas. That's against the rules. I guess he's hungry for dough."

We were joined by a stout, middle-aged woman coming from the direction of the candy and news concession. "That's Della," McNeil said. "Ask her to tell you about her run-in with the Krishnas." I introduced myself to Della and described what we were doing.

"I hope you succeed," she said warmly. "They're awful. I had one of them arrested—Mike, the one with the glasses." She looked around. "He's not here now; he must be in Two."

"What happened?"

"I told him to get away from my store; he was interfering with trade. That's against regulations and he knows it. I have to tell them many times, but this Mike is mean. He called me a dirty name, which I won't repeat. I called the police and had him arrested. I have been in court twice, but their attorney keeps postponing. I don't know why they don't get rid of them. They must be paying off some big-shot."

"A federal judge ruled they have a right to be here," I said.

"Now, why would he do that?" McNeil asked.

"He said they have a constitutional right to practice their religion, which included passing out literature and taking donations."

142

"Religion!" Della exploded. "Call that religion? Why they are nothing but rip-offs. I should know. I've watched them for three years. Why don't these young fellows go to work like honest people? I wish that judge would come here and see for himself."

Before returning to her store, she asked for several copies of the reprint for her fellow clerks.

Immediately after Della and McNeil left, a police officer spoke to me. "This man," he said pointing to a brown-wigged devotee, "is complaining that you are distributing material without a permit. Can I see what it is you're giving away?"

The devotee, whose name-tag read "Chandra," said to the officer, "The rules are posted on that wall," pointing to the men's washroom. "You can read it for yourself. They can't distribute without a permit." The officer continued reading our reprint of the *Tribune*.

"Let me read the rules," I said, and walked over to the double sheet attached to the wall. It was headed, "Airport Regulations" and one of its paragraphs read:

> No person shall distribute literature or solicit contribu-
> tions unless he shall have registered beforehand with
> the airport manager or his authorized representative
> for each day such activities are engaged in.

Registration took place between nine and nine-thirty each morning.

I returned to the officer, promising to register the next day. "I'll tell my people to stop distributing," I added. "We'll talk to people but will not hand out anything."

"O.K.," the police officer said, "that'll be fine." He began to walk away, when Chandra stopped him. "They're interfering with our right to solicit. We have a permit to be here." He pointed to the label on his sleeve. "If they are not soliciting or distributing, they have no business interfering with us."

"Just a minute," I said to Chandra. "You want to deprive me of my constitutional right of free speech? You are exercising your right to ask people for contributions. Are you saying I need a permit to exercise my right to ask them not to? Anyone in the airport has the right to talk to whomever he pleases."

"You have no right to interfere with our solicitation. That's what you're doing."

"The rules say he can't distribute without a permit," the officer said. "O.K., he's promised not to. That's good enough for me." He

143

walked away. Chandra joined two of the devotees who had been standing nearby listening. I went to each of our friends, told them what happened and instructed them to withhold the reprint, but continue to talk to would-be contributors.

"Can we still show the reprint?" Rose asked.

"Yes, as long as you don't distribute."

We had been at the airport for an hour. Now and again I would stop to chat with our friends. They were still under tension but gradually getting used to it. Each encounter with a devotee was a little ordeal. It's not easy to inject oneself into what you know will become a tense situation. We received many rebuffs—donations were made in spite of our appeal. Each time that happened to me, I felt I had been rejected. I knew it was wrong to feel that way, yet, I felt our cause was just and that others ought to see it too.

The devotees preferred to stay close together within the forty-by fifty-foot area between the washrooms. They were like a team, spurring one another on; a success encouraged the others. But by confining themselves to this small area they gave us an advantage. Few as we were, we were able to intervene in a good percentage of their solicitations.

During the second hour there were only four devotees; two had gone. I looked for them down each side of the block-long building but did not see them. I didn't give it further thought until Ronald came back from exploring Building Two.

"Dad," he announced, "there are seven Krishnas in the other building."

"Two of them must have gone there from here," I shrugged. "I guess we can't be everywhere."

"It's a shame to give them a free hand in the other building. They are raking in the money. You should see it."

"Look, Ron," I said peevishly, "they were raking in before we came here. We don't expect to cut their "take" by much. We are making ourselves felt; that may be enough."

"Dad," he persisted "we ought to make a good showing the first day. Why don't you split up?"

"How do you mean?"

"Two go to the other building; two stay here. That way you will let them know they are not going to shift their people to get away from us."

"This is the first day," I said dubiously. "Isn't it asking too much."

"Discuss it with our friends. Let's see what they think."

144

We called our group together and Ron told them what he had seen in Building Two. "I suppose you noticed," I said, "that two of the men are gone from here. They went to the other building to avoid us. It shows how effective we've been. Ron thinks two of us should go there and two stay here."

"Good idea," Esther said, rising to the occasion. The sisters, however, looked at each other uncertainly.

"How would it be," I suggested, "if Esther stays here with Sylvia; Ron stays too, to keep an eye on things, and Rose and I go to the other building?"

"It's okay by me," Rose said. Sylvia nodded.

Before leaving I cautioned Sylvia and Esther. "You are two against four. Don't feel you have to knock yourself out chasing them. We're not youngsters. If you need rest, sit down in the lounge. I'll be back within an hour to see how you're doing. Remember, Ron is around, just in case. We'll be only a couple of minutes away."

"Don't worry," Esther reassured me. "We'll do all right."

Rose and I headed for Building Two. En route, we passed two sailors with carnations on their jackets.

When we arrived at the washroom area of Building Two, the response from the Krishnas was different from their earlier one. They greeted us jovially as if there was some joke we weren't in on. "Hare Krishna," they called gaily as they passed us in the hunt for prospects. A devotee in a black wig said as he passed by, "So you're Joey's grandfather," and grinned.

With just two of us it was difficult to cover seven devotees. Need suggested a quicker way to stop the booksellers. As they approached a prospect with outstretched hand and a "Hi, Buddy," I sang out, "Watch it, Bud, it's a pitch." It worked with many. "Gotcha," one of them called out, waving at me with a grateful smile.

One devotee in particular caught my interest. He moved carefully, seeming to select his prospects, and there was an earnestness about him which made me wonder what he was saying that might be different from Narada's pitch. He took more time with prospects. I kept my eye on him until he made a fresh contact, a young sailor carrying his gear in a huge canvas bag. I walked over within hearing distance.

Krishna: Hi, what's your name? *(The sailor tells him.)* Mine is Nakula. Can you say it? Na-ku-la *(smiling encouragement)*.

Sailor: Na-ku-la.

Nakula: See, it was easy. Where you from?

Sailor: Bangor, Maine.

Nakula: No kidding? I'm from Belfast—on the Bay. Still got my folks there. *(They talk about the neighborhood.)* Where are you bound for?

Sailor: San Diego.

Nakula: Lucky you. Nice place, San Diego. Say, I've got a buddy in San Diego; maybe you'd like to look him up. You can never tell. You might get lonely and want to meet him. I'll give you his address *(writes on card)*. What branch of the service are you in?

Sailor: Subs.

Nakula: Subs! How about that. *(changes tone)* You have a plane to catch, right? I don't want to keep you too long. We're giving away five hundred copies of this book, free. *(He opens the Gita and shows the sailor the picture pages.)* This book is five thousand years old. Can you dig that? It's not a book which is going to make you rich. It's about God. You believe in God, don't you? *(The sailor nods.)* O.K. Here, take the book but be sure to read it now. *(The sailor thanks him and puts the book into his duffle bag.)* Can you give a donation just to cover the printing cost?

Sailor: I guess so. *(Pulls out billfold and hands over five-dollar bill.)*

Nakula: Most people give us ten. *(The sailor hesitates, looks away, but then pulls out his wallet again. He gives Nakula ten dollars and takes back the five.)* Thanks, buddy, God bless you. *(No "Hare Krishna.")*

Rose, fifteen-feet away, was in deep conversation with a woman who had stopped to inquire about the *Tribune* article. Probably a traveler, I thought, waiting for her plane or meeting an arrival. I made a mental note to suggest to Rose that when we are under-manned it would be best to cut such conversations short.

Nakula had another prospect; this time a young soldier. The Krishnas favored the lads in uniform. Were they easy touches? I walked over while Nakula was on his preliminaries. "He's going to try to sell you a book," I said to the soldier. Nakula didn't look at me but held the boy's eyes. "Don't listen to him," he said, "he's a Communist." "What?" I exclaimed in surprise. Nakula ignored me. "The Communists don't want us to distribute the words of God. You believe in God?" The soldier nodded.

146

"When he says God," I said, "he means Krishna, a Hindu god, not your God." Nakula faced me: "Whatever name he goes by it's the same God."

But I had caught the soldier's attention. "This is my grandson. He disappeared into the Hare Krishnas and we're trying to get him back. That's why we're here telling people who they are." Nakula left; I told the soldier more about Joey and our search.

"You know," he said, "we were warned about these guys at the post, but I didn't recognize him."

"They wear wigs and ordinary street clothes."

"One of my buddies got ripped-off. Twenty bucks."

"How did that happen?"

"He gave one of these guys a twenty and was told to wait while he got change. The Krishna guy never came back." He thanked me for tipping him off and wished me luck in our search.

The Krishnas soon discovered a way to cut our effectiveness. Instead of concentrating in the washroom area where just two of us could cope with them, they fanned into the walkways on either side. We had to look for them; they could get lost in the crowd. But they paid a price—they lost control of the main passageway to the loading ramps. Arrivals came off the ramps, walked through the passage, and took the down escalator to the baggage level without being stopped by the Krishnas. They lost not only opportunities; more important, they lost their unity, the feeling of working together.

Time went by. I visited Building Three and found our two friends doing well. I wondered how long we ought to continue and decided that for elderly people on their first try it would be best not to strain endurance. Esther and the sisters left the timing up to me, so I judged an early breakaway would be welcomed. At 3:30 P.M. we called it quits. After just two-and-a-half hours at the airport, I was beat—not so much from the physical exertion as from the strain of confrontation and the concern for my friends.

On the way home we were in high spirits, the feeling of a mission accomplished. Each of us had a tid-bit of experience to share. Esther had been called "a nut just out of the insane asylum," Sylvia an atheist. Rose had had a dollar thrust into her hand by a prospect. Ronald described the leader of the Krishnas making several trips to the phone booths and surmised he was calling the temple for instructions. "Every time he called, he spent twenty minutes on the phone. He must have had a lot of questions."

"How many of our encounters resulted in a refusal to contribute?" I asked the group. The estimate was "about half."

"When the Krishnas scattered," Esther commented, "it became more difficult. There weren't enough of us."

"We'll build up as more people get to know what we're doing," I said. "We've just started."

19

The "Where is Joey?" People

"LET'S NOT KID OURSELVES, DAD," RONALD SAID, after we had dropped off our friends. "We weren't that effective. Perhaps it's true that half of those we talked to refused contributions—although I think that's a high estimate—but we intervened in no more than twenty percent of the cases. Fifty percent of twenty is only ten percent." Ronald was a systems analyst at a downtown bank.

"O.K., ten percent is still pretty good for a first crack. We'll get better as we go along."

"Let's talk about that. How will we get better?"

"Through practice, how else? I improved as I went along."

"I had the benefit of listening; I think I know what's wrong."

"What do you mean 'wrong'?" I was annoyed at his demands for quick perfection.

"Don't get upset, Dad. Let's be objective. Take your opening approach. You ask them to read the reprint and then you go on to say, 'I'm this boy's grandfather; we're trying to find him.' You know they are not going to read that long article—all they catch is the headline: 'At 12, He "Disappears" into Krishna.' That puzzles them: what has it got to do with them? That's not the best kind of opener."

"O.K., you got a better one?"

"Well, think back—when do you get the best reaction?"

"When I tell them I'm the grandfather of this boy, they seem to be interested."

"Some of them, those willing to hear you out and learn what happened to Joey."

149

"When I get to that point, when I tell them he disappeared among the Krishnas and their money could be going for purposes like that, I do get a good response."

"That's it!"

"What is *it?*"

"When you tell them the Krishnas are responsible for hiding Joey, that's when you get favorable attention. You make the connection between the donor and the devotee asking for the donation."

"That's true, but how does that change my approach? I still have to start the same way and get to that point as I tell my story."

"Why not start from the end?" Ron asked.

"That's nonsense."

"Is it? Suppose you start by saying, 'These are the Hare Krishnas.' You notice they never introduce themselves as such."

"That's right. In fact, they seldom mention their connection; sometimes at the end when they get the money they may say 'Hare Krishna,' like we would say 'so long.'"

"That's right and they have a reason too."

It was beginning to dawn on me. "They don't want people to know right off."

"Right! That's why the men wear wigs and they all wear street clothes instead of their dhotis and saris."

"So we should tell people right away, 'These are the Hare Krishnas.' That's bound to get attention. Those who've read about the cult will make the connection; those who haven't will wonder who Krishnas are."

"What it will do," Ron added, "is to make them want to know more about the devotee and his religion before they give their good money."

"Terrific," I said delighted.

"Then you connect the Krishnas with hiding Joey. You are giving the prospect a reason for refusing a contribution. That reduces your appeal to two simple steps: one, the grabber 'These are the Hare Krishnas'—and the clincher—'They are hiding my grandson.'"

"Great!" Then a thought struck me. "But we can't say simply, 'they are hiding Joey.' We don't know it for a fact; if we can't prove it in a law court, we can be in trouble if they should sue us for slander. I've been warned by our attorney friends."

"Well, what can you say?"

150

"That we believe they are hiding him, or we allege, or we are suing them for conspiracy to abduct."

"That sounds weak and awfully legalistic." Ron looked troubled.

My eye caught the *Tribune* headline. "Why can't we stick to that? He did disappear into the cult; that's a fact. He was sent for a visit and was never returned. We can also refer to the passport to India. That way we deal in facts only, not conjecture."

"O.K.," Ron said. "I think we've got it."

"We'll try that approach tomorrow. I'll have to brief our people very carefully."

"One more thing. We tend to get lost in the airport crowd. We need to identify ourselves so that even when we are just standing around, as we do most of the time, people will know why we are there."

"I wanted to use picket signs like the ones we had at the temple, but the City Attorney advised against it."

"It wouldn't have worked anyway; we couldn't have moved freely; our hands would be occupied. Can't we say the same thing on a lapel card?"

"You mean, 'Krishnas, where is twelve-year old Joey?'"

"That's too much to go on a lapel sign," Ron said thoughtfully. "Suppose we shorten it to 'Krishnas, where is Joey?'"

"Fine. Let's do it in bright colors to catch the eye."

I was eager to try our innovations on Monday and called out to Toby who was half-listening to our discussion, "Who've we got for tomorrow?"

"No one yet. And no one for Tuesday. But I have four for Wednesday."

That was a letdown. "I guess we'll have to wait for Wednesday."

"Look, Dad, it's important to impress the Krishnas while Braun is negotiating. We can't allow two days to go by. They'll think we're just a flash in the pan."

"But what can we do? I can go alone, I suppose."

"No," Toby called out from the living room from which she had been phoning. "If something should go wrong, another person should be there to help. There should always be at least two."

"You know what, Toby? Esther seemed to be having a good time today. I'll bet if you ask her she just might be willing to go again tomorrow."

"I don't mind asking her." She phoned, caught Esther in, and I watched Toby's face light up as they talked.

Toby hung up. "She'll go. Pick her up at eight-forty-five. Esther said it would be a shame to let people give their good money to pile up a fortune for that 'eighty-year-old what's-his-name.' Listen to what else she said. 'Those Krishnas claimed I was just out of an insane asylum; to prove they're right, I'll drive them crazy.'"

One of the attorneys I had consulted was a former business colleague. Mark and I had much in common culturally and in our veiwpoint on social problems. Although I was fifteen years his senior, we had become good friends. When Joey disappeared, he offered his help in the form of legal advice and friendly counsel. I had turned to him when we were considering employing Scarlatt.

When we decided to begin our vigil at the airport, I thought it prudent to check the legality of our plans. Mark approved the use of the *Tribune* reprint because "it told the whole story." But he cautioned against saying the Krishnas were hiding Joey, unless we had definite proof, proof that would stand up in court.

"They can sue you for libel," he warned, "and all you have at this point is circumstantial evidence. You may say, 'We believe he is being hidden,' or even, 'We are convinced,' but a flat statement leaves you open to a successful suit. Observe that the *Tribune* article sticks to facts and lets the reader draw his own conclusions. The finger does point at the Krishnas; nevertheless, the reader makes that conclusion for himself."

"What happens if we're sued?"

"There would be attorney costs and they could be considerable. Such cases are complex and long and drawn out. If you lose, the cult may claim damages—how much would be anyone's guess."

"That sounds bad."

"I don't mean to frighten you away from O'Hare—it seems to me the idea is a good one. Just be warned to be careful what you write and say. But remember this: if you tell the truth, you'll be O.K. They can still sue you; anybody can file a suit, but if you don't give them grounds, they'll be more reluctant to do so."

At nine-thirty the next morning, Esther and I were in the main passageway of Building Two where we saw five Krishnas already doing a brisk business. They didn't notice us as we took the elevator to the mezzanine floor where we would register properly.

On the way to the airport I had briefed Esther on the approach Ronald and I had developed the night before. I warned that she could not say the Krishnas were hiding Joey, explaining we could be sued for slander.

"Stick to the facts," I urged. "We sent him to L.A. for a visit to the temple; he was not returned. A passport was taken out for him for India. But, first, identify the solicitors as Hare Krishnas."

"That's what I've been doing all along," she said.

Three men were ahead of us at the airport office where we were to sign in. They were dressed in blue pants and jackets and were attended to by a tall, husky man whom they addressed as "Woody." As each signed the register, Woody handed out a numbered permit on which the solicitor wrote his or her name and stuck it to the upper part of a sleeve. The three were members of Foundation Faith, a cult of faith healers. When they were gone, I asked Woody if I could speak to him in private.

I introduced myself, showed him a copy of the *Tribune* reprint, and explained our purpose at O'Hare. I emphasized that we wanted no trouble, that our people were instructed to avoid incidents, and that our only aim was to ask people not to contribute to the Krishnas until Joey was returned.

"O.K.," he said, "you can go ahead and register. We'll give you a permit to distribute your material. Here are the rules which you'll have to follow," and he handed me the two-page brochure I had read on the washroom wall. "Notice that the permit is not transferable; only you can use it. If you run into any trouble, let me know; we'll take care of it."

While I was talking to Woody, the receptionist had caught some of our conversation. As I was signing the register, she said, "I read your story in the papers. I think it's a shame such things can happen. I hope you'll find your grandson." Her friendliness warmed me and, while Woody said nothing more, I got the impression he shared her sympathy.

Scanning the register, I noted it had ten names with the designation "ISKCON" and the temple's address of 1014 Emerson. Some of the devotees used their real names, others, Krishna names. I signed my name and address, but where it asked for the organization, I left a blank. Esther, however, wrote in: "Where is Joey?" Thus, in the days to come, we would become known in the airport as the "Where is Joey?" people. After writing in our names, Esther and I stuck our permits to our sleeves and put on our lapel cards, which said in red letters: "Krishnas, where is Joey?"

As we came off the elevator, the Krishnas recognized us, but this time there were no greetings of "Hare Krishna." They looked glum. No doubt they had assumed our appearance on the day before had been merely a one-time effort, like our picketline.

Esther and I stayed together, and for the next half-hour there was a flurry of intense activity. The devotees attempted to hold their "high ground," to stay in their preferred area, the passage between the washrooms. We were determined to stop as many donations as the two of us could. The booksellers swung their carts from one part of the area to another so swiftly that to keep up with them I resorted to the technique I had hit on the day before: to call out, "Watch it Bud, it's a pitch to sell you a book.'' It worked two ways, warning the prospective contributor, and taking the wind out of the bookseller's sails. I gave away the game with one sentence; that's death on selling. Esther picked up my cue in her own way: "Look out! It's a rip-off," she said loud and clear.

I had an encounter with baby-faced Narada which left me shaking. He had accosted an elderly man when I came up to ask him, "Do you know who these people are?" The man shook his head. "They are Hare Krishnas. He wants to sell you that book." The man looked at the book he held in his hand. "I am the grandfather of this boy," and I pointed to the *Tribune* reprint. I watched his eyes scan the headline and directed his attention to the footnote about the passport.

"Do you think he is in India now?" the man asked.

"We don't know for sure. We haven't heard from him in a year."

It was then that Narada said casually, "He's dead." I swung on him, startled. "What did you say?" He made no answer but continued talking to the man who, however, handed back the book and walked away. Narada went off rapidly in the other direction. I followed crying, "What did you say about Joey?" He disappeared into a crowd of arrivals.

I was frozen; his words, "He's dead," reverberating. I tried to dismiss them as a crude attempt to demoralize me but couldn't because they echoed my fears for Joey. When I reported the incident to Esther, she reassured me, "They're hitting back at you where they think you are most vulnerable. Forget it; it's a cruel ploy." I resumed my vigil, but every now and again I would hear those awful words.

Partly in retaliation and partly in hopes of drawing him out, I kept an eye out for Narada and caught up with him showing the *Gita* to an executive type. I had hardly begun when he interrupted me to say, "Don't listen to him. He just got out of an insane asylum." Narada's expression was bland; there was no conviction behind the words; he was merely mouthing them. I continued telling the man why we were at the airport. He walked off without taking the book; Narada's slur may have boomeranged.

Several minutes later I was to have still another confrontation with Narada. This time he had accosted a poorly dressed black man. When I came over asking, "Do you know who they are?" Narada said, "Don't listen to him, he's a racist." The words were outrageous, the tone, neutral. I continued talking, but the man, impressed by Narada, took the *Gita* and handed him two dollars. Narada said, "We usually get five; it costs that much to print it." The man said that was all he could pay. Narada pulled out a paperback from his cart, "I'll give you this one instead, O.K?" and, without waiting for an answer, made the substitution. The paperback was *Sri Isopanisad*, which the man took without protest.

I checked back with Esther. "I've been called a communist," she reported. "You know what I said to the pretty little flower girl? You live in a commune, contribute all your collections to it, eat out of a common pot, and sleep in a dorm. I live in an apartment by myself on what I earned over a lifetime of teaching in Chicago's public schools. But you call *me* a communist." I laughed. "You know what?" she added. "I think they were rehearsed to say these things about us. They don't know what-the-hell they're saying."

Though we were two against their five, within the confined area between the washrooms, about two thousand square feet, the Krishnas were vulnerable. Gradually, they abandoned the space and took to the walkways on either side. Keeping one eye on the washroom area in case they should return, I pursued them along the walkways, now and again catching up.

The opening lines I had worked out with Ronald proved their worth. "Lady (Sir), do you know who they are?" I commanded attention, sounded a bit mysterious, even ominous. A traveler asked, "Who are Krishnas?" "A Hindu cult," I replied and just these words were enough to send her away. She may have read about Hindu cults, or heard stories, or she may have been prejudiced. Then, again, she may have thought at first she was being approached by an established charitable organization, while donating to a Hindu religion had no appeal to her. At any rate, the words often had the desired effect, and I modified my opening words to, "These are the Hare Krishnas, a Hindu cult."

The next time I used the phrase was during an encounter with the apparent leader of the Krishna contingent, Maharaj. Dressed very neatly and wearing a black wig, he impressed me with the calm, thoughtful way he looked out on the scene. The scholarly type, I thought to myself. I had a weakness toward it.

When I uttered my opening words, Maharaj said to the traveler, "We're not a Hindu cult."

"If you're not," I countered, "why do you take Hindu names?"

"That doesn't make us Hindus. There are many Christians in India with Hindu names." He had a point there.

"But," I protested, "the book this gentleman is holding, the *Bhagavad Gita*, is part of the Hindu scriptures."

"That may be," Maharaj said coolly, "but the fact is our religion is universal." Interesting, I thought, that they seek to disavow their Hindu roots—something to be looked into.

The traveler, impatient with our discussion, thrust the book into Maharaj's hands and left. I wanted to continue the discussion, not alone for its scholarly aspects, but to get to know the young devotee. However, he broke off and left.

I rejoined Esther in the washroom area. "Morris," she said, "business is very slow here." We looked around and could spot only one other devotee besides Maharaj. "My guess is," she continued, "they have gone to Building Three, leaving these two to keep us occupied."

"That's what it looks like," I agreed.

"It takes only one of us to cover these two. Why don't you go to the other building; I'll stay here."

The friendly reception we had received in the airport office, the permits we carried on our sleeves authorizing us to do what we were doing, plus our growing familiarity with the place, gave me a feeling of security. I sensed too that airport employees were on our side and would be protective.

"Let's give it a try," I said to Esther. "I'll check back with you after a while."

The washroom area in Three was thick with devotees when I arrived. For the next fifteen minutes I was running from one encounter to another, succeeding to the extent that they were compelled to retire to the walkways and to the end of the building at the point where it led to the Rotunda; the Rotunda itself was forbidden to solicitors. For awhile I was content to guard the washroom area in case a devotee returned.

A middle-aged porter with a limp came up to me. "You're Joey's grandfather. I read that article." I nodded. "I'm glad to see what you're doing. These nuts have been ripping-off the public for three years without anyone stopping them. Why the hell don't the police chase them?" I explained First Amendment rights as interpreted by the federal courts. He shook his head in disbelief. "But they don't give away the books; they sell them. Just try to take one without a donation. They'll follow you all over the airport till they get your money or the book. That judge ought to come down and see for himself."

"How often do the Krishnas come down here?"

"Every day," he replied. "Seven days a week including holidays. And they work at it; they really hustle."

"How late do they stay?"

"I'm not sure; I quit at four. But I hear they stay to seven. I hope you get your grandson back," he said as he went into the men's washroom.

Just then, I noticed a young, good-looking Krishna in black wig and eyeglasses showing the *Gita* to a man in a clerical collar. I went over to see how a minister would respond to their pitch.

The Krishna—his permit carried the name of "Gopal dasa"—made the customary opening and handed the minister the "free" book. Then he asked for a donation.

Minister: What organization do you represent?

Gopal: We are a religious organization.

Minister: Are you Christians?

Gopal: I'm a Lutheran.

Minister: This book is neither Lutheran nor Christian.

Gopal: It's about God.

Minister: But what organization is printing these books?

Gopal: ISKCON.

Minister: ISKCON?

Gopal: Yes.

Minister: What is ISKCON?

157

Gopal: International Society for Krishna Consciousness.
Minister: Oh, you are the Hare Krishnas.
Gopal: Krishna is the same as Christ.
Minister: My spiritual master is Jesus. Who is yours?
Gopal: God is the same whatever you call him.
Minister: Is this book a gift?
Gopal: Yes, but we ask for a contribution to pay for the cost of printing.
Minister: If I don't give a contribution, do you want the book returned?
Gopal: Can't you give something? *(The minister hands back the book and leaves.)*

From my post at the corner of the men's washroom I saw little Deva dasi approach a woman, flower in hand. Deva was a petite, reddish-blond who never lost her temper. She was one of their hardest workers and their most effective flower-girl. Her smile could charm a contribution out of a Scrooge. She had just pinned the woman, who was reaching into her purse when I stopped her with my usual question. As I came to the part about Joey, Deva interrupted, "Joey is with his mother."

"How do you know that?" I asked her. "Do you know where they are? Tell me!" Deva would not, or could not, tell.

I followed Deva, hoping to speak to her, but she avoided me. What did her outburst mean? Had she given away information without intending to? Or was the remark simply to give the impression the boy was with his mother and nothing was wrong? Narada had said he was dead. Did the devotees say whatever popped into their heads, whatever seemed to them to serve the particular moment?

I started out for Building Two to see how Esther was doing and ran into three devotees working the area at the end of Building Three near the entrance to the Rotunda. This was the second most trafficked area, used by patrons of the two restaurants located there and by travelers going from one building to the other. I arrived as Maharaj was pointing to the inside of the dust jacket on the *Gita* and saying to a man, "This book is used in the University of Chicago. All the colleges use it."

When I began to speak about Joey, Maharaj interrupted. "How do you know he's in one of our temples?"

"He had a passport for India. On the application, it said 'Purpose of trip—school.'"

"Do you know for fact," he insisted, "that he's in India?"

"Are you telling me he is not in India?"

"It is you who are telling people he is. Do you know it as a fact?"

Cautioned by Mark's advice, I said, "I don't know it for fact, but we have evidence he is in Krishna somewhere. We offered to show it to Prabhupada but he wouldn't see us." As on other occasions, the prospect, involved in an argument, bowed out. Maharaj followed two devotees as they took off for the main passageway of Building Three. With me away, they would be back in their favorite spot.

Esther was sticking close to the washroom area in Two and keeping it clear of devotees. She expressed concern that we were not doing enough to cut down their "take." There was an undertone of boredom at "standing guard." I explained what the loss of this space meant to the Krishnas: they could not catch arrivals before they went down to baggage. Besides, I said, dispersing the devotees over the airport cut their effectiveness as a close-knit unit.

"So you see," I assured her, "if you do nothing else but keep this space clear, you are doing well. Naturally, we could do better; we could follow them wherever they went if we had more people. That will come in time."

Before I left her, we agreed to quit at one; that would make three and a half hours. I bought a chocolate bar at the candy stand and returned to Building Three. When Esther came at the appointed time, I regretted leaving the Krishnas a clear field. They'll probably stay late tonight, I thought, to make up for what they lost this morning.

In the late afternoon I received a phone call from Braun to inform me that Pandu, the GBC representative, was back from Australia. Peter Braun expected to meet with him and Drupada that night or the next. That was all he had to say; nothing about O'Hare. This was the first time Braun had called on his own initiative and, considering what he had to tell, it was rather unusual. I guessed that Drupada, informed by Mukunda of events at the airport, was worried. Not that we had hurt their collections that much—a total of six hours opposition from us meant little—but the threat that we would improve our capability, and that our tactic could be used at other airports, would concern the GBC. It could well be that Drupada had called Braun

159

to suggest the meeting, and Braun's call to me was intended to influence us to suspend our vigil until we heard the results of his meeting. One thing seemed clear—the Krishnas were beginning to move. Toby and I determined to put up a good show the next few days.

20

The Krishnas Fight Back

ON WEDNESDAY WE ARRIVED AT O'HARE WITH A
team of four: Sylvia and Rose agreed to come again, and Toby had
recruited Victor Schmidt and his wife, Birgit. A retired teacher
who had taught at the high school our boys attended, Victor was
tall, energetic, and appeared much younger than his seventy
years. He was to become one of our best campaigners. Birgit, a
former office worker, was quiet and somewhat shy in manner.

Just as we concluded registering, the Krishnas came in too,
greeting everyone with "Hare Krishna." As they waited their
turns to sign, some, with bead pouches hanging from their necks,
rapidly whispered the mahamantra. I surmised they were
making up the daily requirement of 1,728 rounds. There were
eight men and four women; three of the men I had not seen before.

To give the Schmidts a break-in period, all five of us stayed in
Building Two. Very soon we found all but three Krishnas had
vanished. Victor was confident that he and Birgit could handle
the three and urged us on to the other building where the other
devotees had most likely gone to avoid us.

Sure enough, we found nine devotees in their chosen place in
Building Three. Two planes from New York had just unloaded
and a stream of passengers poured through the main passsage-
way. The three of us went to work, the sisters giving their
attention to the slower booksellers and I giving mine to the
nimble flower-girls. For the next thirty minutes things were
hectic. As in the past, the Krishnas made a stand for their favorite
spot and were doing quite well. While I was confronting one of the
girls, the other three worked without interruption. Similarly

with the five booksellers, only two of whom could be followed by
the sisters. Underneath their surface smoothness, however, the
devotees were reacting to our presence. We made them nervous,
especially the booksellers who needed to concentrate on their
sales pitch, create an atmosphere favorable to a sale. With but a
few words we upset their approach: "He wants to sell you that
book." Their talk was canned to prepare the prospect for the
clincher; we tipped off the prospect before the Krishna's cordial-
ity and "Please have a free book" lowered the guard.

With the flower-girls our job was a bit tougher. Smiling at the
prospective donor, they pinned a carnation with a deft movement
of both hands (they didn't ask permission), requested a donation
in a single sentence, such as "Please help cure dope addicts," and
the money was passed. From start to finish this might take
forty-five seconds, at most a minute. Yet, even then, a sentence at
the right moment—"She wants your money for the Krishnas, a
Hindu cult"—could turn away a contribution. In spite of their
winning formula—pretty girl, smile, flower—they too were
upset. They too felt the loss of elan, needing constantly to watch
for us over their shoulders. So, as on previous occasions, the
devotees, one by one, surrendered the area and escaped to other
parts of the building.

After the surge of disembarking passengers, there was a lull. I
stood in the center of the washroom area and surveyed the scene.
Sylvia and Rose were on either side, some paces away. The
flower-girls had retreated into the women's washroom. Gopal
and Chandra, the two men who remained, were idle for the
moment. Suddenly the two sprang forward and began circling
me, chanting loudly in Sanskrit. Not knowing what to make of it,
I simply stood looking at them. Actually, there was nothing
threatening in their attitude; I saw from their faces they were
having fun with me. Amused, myself, by their antics, I just let
them dance round and round me in time to their chant. Travelers
stared and I heard comments like "nuts" and "crazy Krishnas."
Finally, after about ten minutes, they got tired and returned to
their book-peddling.

A middle-aged woman clerk from the news and candy concession came over to tell me that the bespectacled Gopal was under
bond for assault and for calling her and her fellow clerks
prostitutes.

"Looking at him you'd think a lump of sugar wouldn't melt in his mouth," she told me. "But you should have heard the way he talked to us."

"When does the trial come up?"

"They keep postponing. It's a month from now."

"Can I ask a favor?"

"If I can do it, I'll be glad to," she replied.

"I may have to leave to go to other parts of the building. You work nearby. Would you keep an eye on my two friends just in case the Krishnas should give them trouble?"

"I'll call the police the minute they try something funny."

"Thanks. They are elderly and I wouldn't want harm to come to them."

"You're lucky to have such friends."

"How well we know it. We need more like them," I added, hoping that perhaps she might have suggestions.

Maharaj appeared, wearing the absorbed look of the studious. He had not registered that morning and I wondered what he was doing here now. Instead of an armful of books, he carried a small notebook. Walking up to Rose, he peered at her permit and pencilled into the book; he did the same with Sylvia.

"What's it for, Maharaj?" I asked.

"You'll find out," he replied and went to join Gopal.

Rose and Sylvia came over to tell me that he had taken down their names. "Why is he doing that?" Sylvia asked.

"I can only guess," I said. "They may be gathering information for a suit against us."

"What could they possibly sue you for?"

"For one thing, interference with their First Amendment rights. That would provide an interesting case—their First Amendment rights against ours. It's also possible they may sue for slander."

"Slander?" Rose echoed.

"That we are telling lies about them. Anyone can file a suit. They may do it to intimidate us. But I would hate to see you involved."

"Don't worry about us," Sylvia said, "we don't scare easily."

But I did worry. I didn't want to see our friends taken to court. We would cover the legal expenses, but the prospect of involving our friends in legal difficulties was troubling.

Noticing one of the booksellers talking to a young man, I went over to stop a sale. "These people are Hare Krishnas, a Hindu cult," I said to the prospect.

The Krishna, whose permit read "Ananda," turned calmly to me, "He knows who we are." The man nodded agreement. "We're not a Hindu cult," Ananda continued.

I registered surprise. "All my readings tell me differently, that you are a branch of Hinduism."

"Our religion pre-dated Hinduism; it's five-thousand-years old." He had a gentle, engaging smile and excellent diction.

I began to explain what I had read, when Ananda took advantage of a pause to say, "I'd like to discuss it with you, but I'm talking to this other gentleman. May I invite you to our temple for Sunday dinner. We can continue our discussion then."

The offer was made so agreeably, it was hard to refuse. "I've been to your temple," I said.

"Well, come again, whenever you wish."

"Perhaps I may," I said. "Thank you." Though I had no intention of doing so in the midst of our confrontations, Ananda's good will prompted my response.

I never saw him again either at the airport or anywhere else. I had been impressed by his gentle self-assurance. It was the Anandas who offered a pleasing and attractive veneer to the cult. I would have loved to spend an hour or two in conversation with him to understand what the Krishna religion meant to his life.

When the time came to see how the Schmidts were faring, I made my way to Building Two. There a cluster of people, including two police officers, were milling around Victor, Birgit, and Chandra. I ran up to Victor to ask what had happened.

He was shaking with anger. "I have to go to the police station to prefer charges against this fellow," Victor said, pointing at Chandra. "He tripped Birgit and she almost fell." And with that, Victor handed me his pile of *Tribune* reprints, Chandra turned his book pouch over to Maharaj, and they all walked off with the two policemen. I watched them go, worried that Chandra's attempt was the beginning of a campaign of harassment of our friends.

A voice interrupted my reverie. "I saw the whole thing," said a man wearing work clothes and an airport employee badge. "I'm Joe, the window washer here. Aren't you the boy's grandfather?"

I nodded and asked what had happened.

164

"This lady was walking over to stop one of them Krishna guys from ripping off a sailor when this other Krishna..."

"You mean Chandra, the one who left with the police?"

"Yeah, him. He stuck out his foot as she passed him. She lost her balance and almost fell on her face. She would have got hurt real bad if she had taken the fall. Her husband called the police. I'm going to be a witness."

The devotees had resumed their solicitations, and I went back to Building Three to tell the sisters what happened. They offered to cover Three while I returned to Two.

Although the O'Hare police station was but a minute's ride away, the Schmidts were gone forty-five minutes. When they returned, Victor was still boiling. "The gall of that kid," he said. "He filed a cross-complaint against Birgit for harassment."

Birgit gave me an account of the incident. "If I hadn't kept my balance, I would have had a bad fall. Still, I didn't want to call the police. Victor insisted. You won't believe this, Morris, but I've never been in court." She was fearful. I promised to accompany her, but she remained troubled.

In spite of the affair, Victor was more eager than ever to face the Krishnas, but I had promised Sylvia she would be home by one.

On the way from the airport, Birgit reported that a devotee had taken down her and Victor's names in a notebook and she wondered what that meant. I spoke of the possibility of a suit; I could see she was worried over other court appearances. Victor, however, viewed the prospect calmly, perhaps with a touch of adventure. "I'd love the chance to tell a judge the tricks they are pulling at O'Hare. Maybe that would blow it wide open."

Just before I dropped off the Schmidts, Victor mentioned that some travelers had mistaken him for a Krishna: "Our lapel card has 'Krishnas' on it and maybe that's as far as they read." We all laughed, but I decided to change the card to read simply, "Where is Joey?"

When I recounted the day's events to Toby, she shared my concern at involving our friends in legal battles. "Maybe we ought to tell them in advance there is the possibility we might be sued."

"Oh boy," I exclaimed, "how many people would accept then? As it is, it's tough enough to get volunteers."

Talking it over again later with Larry and Ronald, we finally

165

came up with a solution. From now on, our vigilers should not register for permits or reveal their names to devotees. Those who had once registered, whose names were already known, could continue to sign in if they wished. That meant that those without permits could not distribute our material, but they could still show the *Tribune* reprint and talk to people as before. Should a traveler want a reprint, it could be obtained from one of us with a permit. I also decided to keep a daily log of the names of our friends and devotees and a description of events. If there was going to be a court case, we would need the aid of memoranda.

That evening I re-read scholarly material on Hinduism, with Ananda's words in mind. Contrary to his disclaimer, the Hare Krishna movement is a sect of Hinduism. Hindu sects, over the centuries, elevated to supreme position one or another of their many deities. Prabhupada, founder of ISKCON, was a member of the Gaudiya Vaishnavas. Gaudiya is a town in Bengal, a province in the east of India. A Vaishnava is one devoted to Vishnu, another name for Krishna, one of three supreme deities of Hinduism, the others being Brahma and Shiva.

Maharaj had also denied Hindu origins. I conjectured that either the cult was straining to make its movement unique by claiming to pre-date Hinduism, or—more likely—it was an effort to make their cult more palatable to Americans.

As luck would have it, we could not muster anyone for Thursday, but Victor would join me on Friday. That morning ten Krishnas signed in: three women and seven men. Victor agreed to cover Building Two by himself while I went over to Three. Six Krishnas were already there. Perhaps they preferred Building Three because of heavier traffic (American Airlines was there), or they were shying away from direct surveillance by the airport security office located on the mezzanine of Building Two.

As I came up, rosy-faced Narada was showing the *Gita* to a man: "This is a five-thousand-year-old history." I said nothing, waiting for him to continue. Instead Narada told his prospect, "He's a goon; don't listen to him." I couldn't hold back a laugh, suddenly remembering the goons of my union days, gangsters recruited by a certain type of employer to break up our picket lines and beat us up. The qualifications for the typical goon of that period were large size, big muscle, and viciousness. The contrast with my five-foot-six, 135-pound frame provoked my amusement.

166

"Sir," I said to the man, "I'm the grandfather of this twelve-year-old boy who disappeared into the Hare Krishnas. This young man is a Krishna, although you can't tell because he's wearing a wig."

The man looked at Narada suspiciously, then handed the book to him. Narada wouldn't take it: "You can have it, it's a gift." The man continued to hold the book out to him. I said to him, "Drop it on the floor." Evidently, the man couldn't bring himself to that; he continued offering the book to Narada. When I reached out for the volume, Narada grabbed it. Then he leaned toward me, enraged face close to mine, and shouted at top of his voice, "N'shingaday!" I jumped back, frightened. "N'shingaday!" People turned to stare at the raging Krishna, but, oblivious, Narada walked away.

What did the shout mean? Was it a Sanskrit cuss word?

From then on, it seemed to be the day for shenanigans. I had hardly resumed my vigil in the washroom area when blond Deva dasi and ring-nosed Sasi circled me, chanting. Sasi had called me "a demon who should be smashed." Was she now summoning up the "powers"? What amazed me most was that they were immune to the stares of passers-by. When I merely smiled at their antics, they soon returned again to pinning carnations.

Dozens of encounters were taking place between the devotees and me. I estimated that in two of three instances I was successful in stopping contributions. It was not long before they avoided the washroom space and took to roaming the block-long building. Alone, I had to be content to guard the immediate area and about twenty feet in either direction. If I became engaged further off, the devotees were soon back at their favorite perch, cashing in on my absence. I had to make up my mind to either knock myself out chasing them up and down the huge building or settle for saving my energy and allow them to take more money. While I was used to being on my feet—luckily I had just acquired comfortable Space Shoes—three hours of it was exhausting.

When I checked back with Victor, I found him waiting impatiently to tell me that Chandra, who had not registered that morning, was nonetheless carrying a permit on his sleeve. Victor had been unable to decipher the name on it but had gotten the number, which could be checked against the register.

"What are you going to do about it?" Victor demanded. Transferring a permit was in violation of the rules, and the guilty party was subject to arrest. I went up to the mezzanine office to report to Woody.

Woody had noticed Chandra soliciting, did not recall that he had signed in that morning, and wondered about it. A register check showed the number assigned to Kapila. Assured by Woody that Chandra would be picked up by airport plainclothesmen, I returned to Victor. Chandra had disappeared. "He smelled something," Victor said, "when he saw me speaking to you."

Victor's success in Two was much like mine in Three, with the difference that he, older than I but more vigorous, periodically made sweeps of the entire building. He said that a favorite hangout for the Krishnas was the area at the west end of Two in front of the entrance to the International Building.

He was particularly indignant at the "rip-off of young servicemen." "I came up to one uniformed man," he said, "too late to stop him from handing over a ten-dollar-bill for that junk. I tried to get him to return the book and get his money back, but he was too embarrassed. They just take advantage of these naive kids, putting on the friendship act and taking them for all they can get. It just isn't right. They shouldn't get away with it."

When I returned again to Three, I found the Krishnas making hay in their preferred space between the washrooms. As before, we skirmished until they cleared out.

Gopal, owlish in heavy spectacles, dressed in a plaid flannel shirt open at the neck to show a three-strand bead choker, followed me around, chanting. I paid no attention except to note from his demeanor that he was having great fun at what he thought my expense. On the contrary, I was amused by his boyish display.

"Where is Joey?" he read aloud from my lapel card. "Do you really want to know?"

I perked up. "Yes, I certainly do."

"Then join ISKCON and look for him."

"Where should I look?"

"Go from temple to temple until you find him."

"There are a hundred temples all over the world. Are you serious?" I thought he might be putting me on, but he wasn't; he looked earnest. "How can I join when I don't believe in your religion?"

"You want Joey, don't you? If you really and truly want to be with him, that's what you should do." I shook my head in disbelief.

"You don't want to be with him, that's it." He was just a simple kid, I concluded, suddenly remembering something Della had told me.

"Gopal," I said, "you're from Minnesota, aren't you?" He looked intently at me and I was encouraged to go on. "I wonder if your parents know where you are." A faint smile appeared on his face and he began to chant softly, then walked away.

As I slowly paced my post, one of the airline ticket clerks introduced himself: Herbert Delafield, trim, mustached, in his middle thirties. "I'm glad somebody is finally stopping them," he said. "It makes me mad how people fall for their line. We keep warning them with announcements, but it doesn't do any good."

"Announcements? What announcements?" I asked in surprise.

"See what I mean; people don't listen. Over the PA system. We tell them that those who are selling flowers and books are not authorized by any of the airlines. Since you people have been coming here, we have been making them more often."

"I'm glad to hear it; it may do some good. I guess I've been too busy to pay attention."

"Listen," Delafield said, "I think I could get Channel 7 to do a piece on you. I know Dave Cohen up there. Would you like to speak to him?"

"Yes, I would, but I'll have to talk to my son first." I was thinking of Scarlatt and his injunction against publicity.

"Let me get him on the phone and introduce you," Delafield suggested, "and you can take it from there." With that he walked promptly to his desk, called Cohen, and then handed the phone to me. Cohen was definitely interested and suggested that a Channel 7 crew come out to the airport. I told him I would have to check first with Larry.

I was excited by the prospect of telling thousands of viewers why we were at the airport. It would add pressure on the cult, and even more important, might bring more volunteers for our vigil. Our own friends would be encouraged to come out. But I would have to convince Larry first. If Scarlatt protested, perhaps Larry could shift the blame to me—can a son stop a headstrong father?

It was almost one in the afternoon when I went to ask Victor if we should quit for the day. I found him involved in an argument with Gadapati, a devotee I had never seen angry nor even so much

169

as annoyed. When I stopped his sales, he showed no sign of emotion, simply wheeling away his cart of books in search of another prospect.

"We're distributing the word of God," he was saying to Victor.

"If you want to get the word around, why don't you give it away?" Victor asked angrily. "I saw one of your boys take a kid for ten dollars for one of those," pointing to the *Gita* under Gadapati's arm.

"We can't distribute unless we get reprints and that takes money."

"Ten dollars for a piece of junk?"

"Some give us more, some less; it averages out," Gadapati said.

"Why do you offer it as a gift if you want money?"

"It is a gift. We ask for a donation to cover printing costs."

"But no one gets to keep it unless he makes a donation."

"That's not true. If a person wanted to read it and didn't have the money, we would give it to him without a donation."

"I've been here two days and haven't seen one instance of that yet. Let's face it; this is a money operation for the Krishnas. The books are only an excuse to extract money."

"That's your opinion," Gadapati said stiffly and moved away.

"It's nothing but a rip-off," Victor called after him.

The altercation disturbed me. "Take it easy," I said to Victor. "Don't let it get under your skin."

"They're frauds using religion to cover a rip-off of the public. No one should stand for that." He was still arguing with the departed devotee.

"Do you think Gadapati a fraud?"

"How should I know," he said impatiently. "If he isn't, then he's a dupe for those who are raking it in."

"Do you think you can convince him he's doing wrong?"

"I suppose not," he admitted. "But still it rubs me the wrong way."

"Listen, Victor. We've thought this thing through carefully. You have to understand what we are trying to do. We are not here to prove they are frauds, or that a devotee is a dupe for the frauds, or that their literature is junk." He was looking at me as if to say, "Don't try to lecture me buddy." I wanted to be tactful. "The first day we came here, before we started, I went over to one of their people and said to him, 'We're not against you personally and we're not against your organization. We just want to return Joey

170

to his father who has legal custody of the boy. Until he is returned we will come here to ask people not to contribute.'"

"I can see your point," Victor said thoughtfully. "You don't want to take on more than one fight."

"Exactly. We have a single, simple purpose. Not that the other isn't a worthwhile fight, and important. These devotees, in my opinion, are being exploited, and they are taking money under false pretenses. But that's not our fight; not now, anyway."

"Okay, I got you. But jeez it still burns me up to see a poor kid ripped off."

"The fact is, Victor, we are stopping a good many rip-offs by being here. Why do you think the airport personnel are supporting us?"

"Say," he said, brightening, "guess what happened? The police did pick up Chandra and another guy caught peddling books to people on the ticket line. How about that? Their cases come up at the same time as Birgit's, on October 5, same court."

"They'll have their hands full with court cases. I think, too, the fact we are here will push the security officers to enforce the regulations. It's all to the good." I looked at my watch. "It's been a long morning, Victor. When do you think we should clear out?"

"Let's stay a while longer," he urged.

21

Running Battle

LARRY AND RON HAD LINED UP SEVERAL FRIENDS
for Saturday at O'Hare. I was to remain home for shopping and
house chores, but a new development brought a change of plans.

Friday evening I received a phone call from Peter Braun. He
had met with Pandu and Drupada the day before, a meeting, he
said, which was nearly cancelled because of "our escalation at
O'Hare." I reminded him that he had always known of our plans.

"Yes, but I thought that once I got into the picture you would
leave everything to me."

I didn't argue that point, being more eager to hear what came
of his meeting with the representatives of the Governing Board
Commission. The meeting, he said, had continued far into the
evening, with the following outcome: first, neither Pandu nor
Drupada had any information of Joey's whereabouts; second,
Miriam might be in contact through someone in Krishna somewhere; and third, the GBC was willing to send out a letter
directive to all temples that Miriam should be contacted and told
that she and Joey should get in touch with us by phone. If we
wished, we could mail the letter ourselves. The focus of all this, he
continued, was that if Miriam were anywhere in touch with a
temple, not only would she learn of the directive, but pressure
would be placed on her to phone. Larry could then make his
arrangements with her and Joey; ISKCON saw it as a question
between husband, wife, and child, but it would bring every
pressure to bear to open communications between them.

My first reaction was one of triumph—our O'Hare vigil was
bringing results. But doubts followed quickly. Was this another
Prabhupada circular letter?

"Do you think they're sincere?" I asked Braun.

"I think they are," he replied. "But you'll have to call off the airport action."

"Why?" I asked, though I was not surprised at the request.

"Otherwise they will not go through with the steps I have just outlined. If they are willing to extend themselves on your behalf, they want you to call off your interference with their solicitations. By the way, they have been considering a suit against you for that." Was that why Maharaj had noted down our names a few days before?

"How long will the GBC need to complete the process of letter-writing and replies from the temples?"

"It will take a couple of days to draft the letter; it will go out by mid-week. The results should be in shortly after. You understand they can't guarantee the results." A lawyer's "caveat," I thought.

"I should tell you," I said, "that on Monday we are being interviewed on Channel 7 at O'Hare."

"If you go ahead with that," he said emphatically, "you can forget it."

"I'm not going to give you an answer now. I'll have to talk to Larry and the family. You still haven't told me the time the GBC will require."

"Well, considering the world-wide mailing and allowing for time to respond, the process should be completed in two weeks." He gave me his home number asking that I call him that evening after I had conferred with the family.

I phoned Larry, gave him a full report, and left our decision for later that evening when we would be together for our Friday dinner.

We all had serious misgivings of Krishna intentions; we had been deceived so many times.

"I think they are just buying time," Ron said. "They know where Joey is. Why all this business about sending out a letter?"

"True, they may know where Joey is," Larry responded, "but they need to give the impression that Miriam is the one who is hiding him, that they have to find her and I have to negotiate with her."

"Precisely," I said. "They have to maintain the fiction of noncomplicity."

"Okay, then, why should we help them?" Ron asked. "If they are now responding because we forced them to, let's continue until they return Joey."

"What you're saying is what I would have said in the old organizing days. When the company is cracking was no time to call off the strike. That was the time to increase the pressure. I'm not sure, however, we have the same elements here as in a strike situation."

"What have we got to lose," Larry asked, "if we give them the two weeks? What will they gain by the delay? Shouldn't we go along with their fiction to get them off the hook. We're not out to hang them; it's Joey we want."

"The situation is not the same as a strike," Toby said. "When you send strikers back before you have a contract, just on the boss's promise, it's almost impossible to pull them out again. In our case, we can always go back to the airport. As a matter of fact I can make good use of the two weeks to recruit our friends."

"What we lose," Ron insisted, "is credibility. Every time they make conciliatory noises, we soften and take a low profile. That's what happened with Prabhupada's letter, then with Drupada's, and now this. They play us for suckers."

"There is something new in the situation," I replied. "For one, there is the intermediary. If in his judgment they are now acting sincerely, we have to give that some weight. Second, they are making these conciliatory noises, as you call them, because of our vigil. That's a new element in the picture. Maybe this time they have had enough and want out. Yet, they want 'out' in their way. Shouldn't we let them off the hook?"

We decided to give them the two-week stay, but to impress on Braun our reluctance. Larry and I phoned him granting a moratorium until Sunday, October 10; if we did not hear from Miriam and Joey by then, we would be back at O'Hare. We told him of our difficulty in making this decision, of the deceit previously practiced on us, and that our willingness was in large part based on his judgment of their present sincerity and our confidence in him. He thought the two weeks sufficient, but if not, he would be in touch before it expired.

It was an anxious time. Was our long struggle coming to an end? But when a week went by without a word and without a copy of the promised letter to the temples, I began to have doubts. When I phoned Braun on Friday, he was apologetic. The letter had only just gone out; it was delayed because he had not gotten around to approving it. If the letter worked, there should be a feedback next week. He suggested I call him in the middle of next week.

174

Calmly and deliberately I said, "I hope we won't have to go back to O'Hare."

Four days before the moratorium expired, Braun phoned that the letter had been delayed and they would need more time. He contradicted what he had said in our last conversation, that the letter had then gone out.

"I helped draft the letter," he said. "It will go out all over the world and that will take a little time. It requests that both Joey and Miriam should call you. You will receive a copy."

I was barely listening to him. I had the feeling we were once again being put through the ringer. At the same time I was reluctant to give up the shred of hope; I wanted to believe.

"Listen, Peter, tell me honestly, can we trust them?"

"I can't see why they would use subterfuge to buy a couple of days grace."

"I should tell you, in all frankness, Peter, we think the letter is only a way to continue the fiction that they are conducting a search, when in fact all they have to do is pick up the phone and call the people who know where Joey is."

He did not attempt to argue my point but repeated his recommendation that we grant the postponement. I would only promise we would not resume our vigil until we had touched base with him; in the meantime, I would discuss his request with Larry.

We had a difficult time coming to a conclusion. The Krishnas were dangling before us the possibility of a call from Joey. The thought of hearing his voice again was enough to make me tremble in anticipation. Yet we had been disappointed so many times. Was it a calculated method for breaking our spirits?

In the end, we decided that with the deadline four days away, Larry would call Braun to tell him that we were convinced the Krishnas would respond only to pressure and were inclined to go back to the airport, Sunday, as originally agreed. We would wait, however, until Friday to let him know our decision. After the call, Larry reported that Braun said, "It well might be you will hear from Miriam or Joey by Friday, depending on whom the letter reaches first." Did this indicate that Joey was not with Miriam? Was it an admission that they were in ISKCON?

Friday came without our having heard anything; in spite of skepticism, we agreed to extend the moratorium to Wednesday, October 13. We felt that we ought not alienate our intermediary. On the thirteenth, Larry and I called Braun and, in his absence, left a message that we were going back to O'Hare the following morning. That evening Braun called. "Perhaps," he said, "the letter even now is reaching them and you will hear a response."

This whole fiasco left me with a deep sense of defeat. It had seemed for awhile that the cult had had enough. It was only much later that I began to understand why they had dangled hope before us at this particular moment in time. Our suspicions should have been aroused by the fact that the GBC had confined itself to their letter and world-wide search. They had not dealt with the terms of a settlement, the subjects of my earlier conversations with Braun: that we refrain from publicity after Joey's return, drop our damage suit, provide for Joey's continuing contact with the cult. Their omission should have warned me they were not serious and only stalling for time. But the question remained, why did they want the eighteen days? What would it do for them? That continued to puzzle me until I ran across a forgotten clipping from the *Chicago Tribune* of October 1, 1976, reporting that:

> Federal Judge George N. Leighton told City attorneys Thursday that Chicago ordinances on soliciting at O'Hare will have to be rewritten because it is unconstitutionally vague....Leighton said he will supply a written memo within the next two weeks commenting on specific requirements of the law.

These two weeks coincided with the moratorium. Had the cult been afraid that our presence at the airport, reported on TV and in the news, would hurt its chances for a favorable ruling from the Judge? If so, was Braun implicated?

The Society did not send us a copy of its letter to the temples, despite the promise to do so. In the Robin George case, too, such a letter had gone out, all the while Robin was being transported from temple to temple to hide her from her parents. Now we had the dubious distinction of meriting two search letters, one from the Swami himself.

But we had learned something—the cult feared our vigil. I speculated that if Braun had dealt with others than Drupada and Pandu, both of whom had been in Los Angeles when Joey "disappeared" and possibly implicated, our search might have ended.

176

At any rate, it was back to O'Hare for us, and this time, we surmised, it would be a long siege.

22

"He's A Jew"

ESTHER, VICTOR, AND I RETURNED TO O'HARE ON Thursday, October 14. After a lapse of almost three weeks, Woody, the security officer, and Sonya, the receptionist, were surprised to see us. I told them what had happened, of the moratorium, and our dashed hopes. Their sympathy, I felt, justified my confidences. Sonya told us that Mary, who worked at the USO lounge, had asked after us, wondering whether we would return. "Mary has been fighting the Krishnas ever since they came to the airport. She was even written up in the *Trib*." I was sorry I had not heard of her before.

Registered, our permit tags on our sleeves, we went down to the restroom area of Building Two. The Krishnas looked surprised; evidently they had not been informed of developments.

Seeing Maharaj, I asked him if Mukunda had told him of the failure of negotiations. He replied amicably enough that he had heard that efforts were being made to settle the conflict but knew no details. As I filled him in, Maharaj listened intently, but made no comment. "We had hoped we would not have to come back, that Joey's return would have been arranged," I said finally. "We don't know what sense it makes to hold on to him in the face of all that's happening." I didn't know how much Mukunda was told by the GBC, but I still hoped Maharaj would relay the information I had given him. In spite of disappointments, we counted on Mukunda to push for a settlement.

After twenty minutes of skirmishing, the devotees scattered from the restroom area, distributing themselves over the two

178

buildings. Victor agreed to go to Building Three, Esther stayed in Two, and I decided to get to know Mary of the USO Lounge, which was located at the west end of Two.

I found her working at her desk in the lounge, surrounded by a few tables and chairs, a coffee bar, and a TV. From the hearty welcome she gave, I felt immediately that I could trust Mary.

"I hate to say it," she told me, "but I'm glad you're back. Now, don't get me wrong—I hope you find Joey. Still, you're the only ones who've been able to stop them." Mary was familiar with Joey's story since she clipped every newspaper article concerning the Krishnas and kept them in a file. Her interest had come out of complaints from servicemen who dumped the cult's literature in the lounge and told her how they had been stuck. To warn them, she had put a sign on top of a stack of the sect's books reading: "Religious Freedom or Big Business?"

"The trouble is they grab the uniformed men as they come off the buses. These kids don't have a chance. They come crying they've been ripped off. We've gotten money back when one is willing to make a case and can recognize the Krishna who took him. Most, however, are ashamed to admit it and dump the book in a washroom or in the garbage. The porters fish them out and sell them back to the Krishnas for a few cents each. The devotees even came to me to buy them back. Did I tell them where to get off!"

"Why don't the base commanders warn the kids before they get on the bus?" I wanted to know.

"I was told they do. But I don't think it registers. Anyhow, when the Krishnas pull their con game—you know, 'Hi buddy, where you from?'—they've got 'em hooked. These kids are lonely and suckers for that shtick."

"Sonya, in the airport office, said you had been written up in the *Tribune*."

"That was a long time ago." Mary went to her files and pulled out a clipping dated November 4, 1973; it had Anne Keegan's by-line. The heading read, "GIs ripped off by sect, USO charges: Pay $10 'for the word.'" The article quoted Mary:

> There have been massive complaints about this Hare Krishna organization. They seem to prey excessively on our servicemen, whom they find soft-hearted and sort of naive, I guess.

179

> They are taking them for up to $10 for these books and
> all they are is gibberish. You can't even understand it.
> The boys leave them here in disgust. I've got a table-
> load of them and that's only one-fourth of what we've
> collected.

I complimented her on her courage in single-handedly trying to stop the practice. Before I left, she invited me and my friends to drop in to the lounge for coffee and rest. During the weeks which followed, we took advantage of her offer, grateful for the chance to rest at her "hearth."

Back on the floor, I found Esther keeping the central area around the washrooms clear of devotees, but able to do little else. So, for the next hour I made the circuit of Building Two several times, clearing devotees out of both ends where they liked to gather when the restroom space was closed off. Our confrontations assumed a set pattern. If I came up as a devotee was in the process of selling a book, I would seek to dissuade his prospect; usually I was successful, whereupon the devotee took off for another part of the airport, looking over his shoulder to see if I followed. If I appeared as a Krishna was scouting for a prospect, he would leave quickly, sometimes using the stairs where I would not follow. Again, I would circle the building to find them. Since there were ten of them that morning, and three of us, they made a large number of sales, but the most profitable areas of the airport were covered by us, and the time spent in running was lost to them. Their morale suffered; we could see it in their faces.

At 11:00 A.M., I went through the Rotunda into Building Three to visit with Victor. He wasn't in the restroom area, but it was clear of devotees. Seeing Herb Delafield at his ticket counter, I went over to talk. He was glad to see me and wanted to know what had been happening in the past three weeks. When I told him we were now back for the duration, he called Channel 7 and left word for Pete Bardwell to call me at home. Then, filling me in in turn, Herb told me the Krishnas worked long hours during our absence from the airport, often staying until nine at night.

Just then Victor arrived, out of breath but with a happily flushed face. He told us triumphantly that he had just convinced a contributor to return a book and get his money back.

"Victor," I said, "how would you like a cup of coffee and a chance to rest your old bones?" I told him about Mary at the USO, urging that he take a break while I took charge of Three.

180

While Victor went to rest up, I found Deva and Madhusa at work in the prime center area. When the two women saw me, they ducked quickly into the ladies washroom. Just outside the door was a large canvas bag filled with copies of *Back to Godhead;* on top were the girls' coats. They really feel at home here, I thought, waiting for the girls to reappear.

"Are you Morris Yanoff?" The tall young woman's question startled me. "I've been looking for you for the last week. Where have you been?" When Gera-Lind Kolarik then introduced herself as airport reporter for the City News Bureau, I agreed to meet her later in the USO lounge. She wanted to do a story on our vigil and explained that the City News Bureau reported Chicago events which otherwise might not reach the news media. Her story might be picked up just as written or it might prompt an editor to dispatch a feature writer to do a fuller write-up. It sounded like a possible news breakthrough for us, and it was.

Though I didn't actually see Kolarik's final story, it created interest. The following morning Bob Faw of Channel 2, CBS, came out with his TV crew. An excited crowd quickly gathered around us in the main passageway between the restrooms. The Krishnas had registered fourteen that morning, more than usual, and many of them were in the area, contesting it against Victor and me. I briefly told Faw what we were doing and pointed out the devotees. Directed by a Krishna to Gadapati, Faw interviewed first him and then me.

An incident, fortuitous and even amusing in a way, exposed a side of the cult's collection methods that I would not even have imagined. As the crowd was milling around the TV men, I noticed a devotee approach a short man with a bony face to offer him a *Gita.* I asked the little man, "Do you know who they are?" "I know," he said impatiently. He had listened to the bookseller but a minute when he pulled a ten dollar bill from his wallet and ostentatiously handed it to the devotee. Tucking the book under his arm, he began walking away when Herb Delafield called to Faw, "I know him; he's a Krishna. He's shilling for them." Faw hurried over to the little man, the TV crew following, and asked him, "Are you a member of the Hare Krishnas?" He replied, "What business is it of yours?" "I'm a reporter," Faw said, while the camera pointed at him and the man. "Are you, or are you not, a Krishna?" The man's eyes took in the people around him and returned to Faw. We heard him say "yes" in a low voice and then

181

hurry out the door before Faw could ask other questions. I wondered if the incident would be included in the broadcast.

Not long after the TV crew left, a newspaper photographer arrived. His editor at the *Chicago Sun Times* had sent him to take pictures of our encounters with the Krishnas; Kingsley Wood, one of their reporters would call me to get the story. He snapped me talking to the flower-girls after I had stopped a contribution. The photographer asked for each of our names, and when Deva dasi, who looked very young, gave hers, he asked if her parents knew where she was. She answered that her father had just visited her and approved of her being in Krishna. When he asked for her father's address, she refused it.

It had been an eventful morning, but it wasn't over. Victor had a devotee arrested for threatening to kill him. As Victor was urging a traveler to refuse a contribution to one of the flower-girls, Yajnava ran up to him shouting, "I'll kill you, I'll kill you!" Was it an explosion of exasperation or a serious threat? Was a pattern of menacing behavior developing? Chandra had tripped Birgit; Saci had shouted, "You're going to be smashed."

As an elementary precaution, I again warned our people not to follow devotees into stairwells or to isolated places in the airport. On the other hand I could not imagine a Maharaj or a Gadapati resorting to violence.

Just as we were about to leave, a good-looking young man introduced himself to me as Tom Most.

"I'd like to help you," he said.

This was the first offer to come from a stranger; naturally, I was pleased. He was a seminarian, he said, and worked part-time. He had been accosted by one of the booksellers.

"I told this Krishna I believed in Jesus. He said, 'That's fine, we are for him, too,' and insisted on a donation for the book. I looked at the book and saw it was Hindu. It made me mad that he would lie to get money."

"I know what you mean," I said. "I have heard them make that pitch to others who have said they were Christian."

"I want to prevent them from fooling others. I can't help you now, but when I have free time, I'll be down here."

That evening Toby and I waited impatiently for the CBS news. At five o'clock the anchorman announced that the six o'clock news would show "One man's war against the Hare Krishnas." At six-fifteen Bob Faw introduced the segment by reporting that a twelve-year-old North Side boy, Joseph Yanoff, had disappeared in November 1975 and a search was in progress to find him. The camera picked up the scene at O'Hare. There followed in sequence: me talking to a woman traveler who had just been pinned with a carnation; Victor speaking indignantly to a man about brainwashing; Gadapati telling Faw the sect was a victim of an argument between husband and wife over their child; and, finally, me replying to a question by Faw, "They say you are harassing them," to which I said, "We're simply telling people who they are. They have their right to talk; we have a right to talk; we have a right to tell people of our search for my grandson who we are convinced is being hidden by them. They have a hundred temples throughout the world; where are we to look? We came here in the hope that public pressure will eventually force them to give him up." Faw made no reference to the shill. He concluded with a quotation from a Krishna who said that my problem was that I was too much attached to my grandson.

When the newscast ended, the phone rang; it was Rose. I called to Toby to get on the other phone.

"Wasn't it exciting?" Rose asked. "When I heard the announcement at five that it would be on at six, I called Sylvia and some of my friends to be sure to listen."

"What did you think of the newscast itself?" I asked.

"It was good for our side. Even though they denied hiding Joey, Morris had the chance to tell our side of it. Most important, it keeps the issue before the public. The Krishnas won't like that."

"Do you think the publicity will help us get volunteers?" Toby asked.

"I'm sure it will. I plan to call one or two of my friends. I spoke to Sylvia. She and I will come two mornings a week."

"Wonderful," Toby said delightedly.

When Rose hung up, I called Victor. "What did you think of the newscast, Victor?"

"O.K., good publicity for us. But Faw left out the part about the shill. They should've left it in."

"How did you like seeing yourself on TV?"

"It was funny looking at myself on TV; I couldn't believe it was me."

We did not go to the airport Saturday—I needed the day for shopping and household chores. On Sunday, however, we were there in force: Simon, a printer-friend, and Pat, his social worker wife, Ronald, and two of his young friends. The time for registration, 9:30 P.M. having passed, I could not get a permit. For the first time we outnumbered the Krishnas who had only four: Saci and three booksellers, including Chandra. Our six had all the important points in the two buildings covered: the two main restroom areas, the entrances to the Rotunda, and the entrance to Building One, the international airlines terminal. The Krishnas were compelled to work along the walkways and seating areas; they did so individually and in pairs, no longer as a group.

Chandra proved true to form that day. I was in Building Three when Ronald came to inform me that the police had received a complaint from a devotee that we were harassing the Krishnas, interrupting them and interfering with their freedom of speech. We went to Two where the police were awaiting me; one of the officers repeated Chandra's charges.

"Officer," I said, "we are not interfering with their right of free speech; we are merely exercising ours. They ask people for donations for their books and flowers. We tell who they are, since they don't, and inform prospective donors of my missing grandson. Whether they get a donation or not is up to the individual."

Chandra interjected, "You interrupt us while we're speaking."

"You get your chance to make a pitch," I replied, "but we are not going to wait until you get their money. We want the contributor to have a chance to hear our story before he makes up his mind."

Chandra and I argued until the officer said to him, "I don't see what we can do about it. So long as these people are orderly, they have as much right to speak as you do."

"What about the fact they have no permit to be here?" Chandra said shifting his ground.

"Officer," I said, "we settled that with the airport office. We need a permit only if we solicit, or distribute literature. We are doing neither; just talking to people."

"What about the leaflet he is holding in his hand?" Chandra asked.

"I'm not distributing it. I hold it up so people can read it, but I don't hand it out."

"O.K.," the officer said, "just so you don't distribute." He began to walk away with the second officer when Chandra called after them, "You pick on us for doing nothing, but you won't lay a finger on them."

184

Chandra, however, wasn't through. Fifteen minutes later he came down from the mezzanine accompanied by a man with a badge pinned to his chest. He identified himself as Lorenzo, in charge of security on Sundays, Woody's day off. "The rules require you have a permit before you can do what you are doing," he said to me.

Ronald spoke up, "The rules say we need a permit only if we solicit, or distribute literature."

"We had this out with Woody," I added.

"Look," Lorenzo said, "I don't want any trouble. Let's go up to the office and I'll try to reach Woody."

Ron, Chandra, Lorenzo, and I took the elevator to the airport office. Lorenzo, unable to reach Woody by phone, insisted that we stop our activity. "If Woody gives me instructions that you can be here without a permit, that's all right with me, but I have to enforce the rules as I see them." Ron argued with him but couldn't move him, and rather than antagonize an airport official, we gave up for the day. We had worked hard to get a good turnout, but to no avail.

On Monday morning I was in the airport office early to talk to Woody before the Krishnas arrived. It was vital to establish our right to be at the airport without registering; we did not wish our friends to reveal their names for fear the Society would include them in a suit against me. Although I was not unduly alarmed as to the outcome of a suit, I did not want our friends inconvenienced and put in jeopardy. So I was tense as I described to Woody yesterday's incident. I was soon relieved; Woody blamed himself for not having informed Lorenzo of our activities. We were the only ones who came to the airport to dissuade people from giving, he said, and Lorenzo assumed that anyone who accosted travelers, for whatever purpose, needed a permit. He would issue the necessary instructions.

I registered, got my permit, and immediately after, thirteen devotees filed in. As luck would have it, I would be alone until 10:30 A.M., when I expected a friend. I also had a promise from Tom Most, the seminarian. After stopping to say hello to Mary at the USO, I headed for the central area of Two. The devotees, seeing I was alone, did not disperse.

However, that day I carried a new weapon. Until now, our attention catcher had been the *Tribune* reprint with its headline, "At 12, he 'disappears' into Krishna." On October 14, the *Tribune* carried a front page story of two Krishna leaders indicted by a

New York grand jury on charges of "unlawful imprisonment" of a Queens woman, Merilee Kreshower, 23, and a Boston man, Edward Shapiro, 22. The indictment included an attempt to "extort $20,000 from Shapiro's father, a prominent Boston physician," in return for his son. I mounted the three-column article and pictures of the two accused. Topped by the headline, "2 Krishna Leaders Indicted," it made a dramatic exhibit for prospective contributors.

My first encounter that morning was with Chandra, who had handed a volume of the *Srimad Bhagavatam* to a middle-aged man. When I caught the man's eye, I said, "These are Hare Krishnas, a Hindu cult. They have just been indicted in New York for attempting to extort $20,000 from a doctor who wanted to get his son out of the cult." I held up the *Tribune* article for the man to read. He took one look, another at Chandra, abruptly handed back the book, and left. Chandra went over to Maharaj; there was a consultation joined in by three others. When they resumed soliciting, I was soon engaged with a Maharaj prospect. I repeated my statement about the indictment but was interrupted by Maharaj: "That doesn't mean they're guilty. It's a frameup." I addressed myself to his prospect, "True, it's only an indictment, but you'll notice it was made by a grand jury after it heard the evidence." The man asked to read the story and as I handed it to him, Maharaj walked off.

I returned to the main passageway where six devotees were busy. Again I latched on to Chandra. Before I could say anything, he said to his prospect, "Don't listen to him; he's a Jew." He drawled the last word contemptuously—"djeuw." I was shocked and angry, but forced myself to continue. Chandra did not wait for the outcome. Minutes later, he came up to me with a mocking smile. "Yanny, why did Hitler kill the Jews?" My anger flared. "Why didn't he kill the rest of us, hey, Chandra, you son-of-a-bitch?" He grinned and went away; he had drawn blood. He joined another Krishna, the smile still on his handsome face; the two talked and laughed as I glared. That Chandra, I thought, if there is a filthy trick in the barrel, he'll be sure to dredge it up.

There was also Govinda—tall, thin, tireless. When I showed the news of the indictment to a woman traveler he had stopped, he smiled knowingly at her, "Shapiro and Kreshower, a couple of Jews who don't want their kids in Krishna."

At ten-thirty, Nathan showed up as he promised. Now seventy-two, a retired community center worker, he still served as consultant to Jewish organizations. I briefed him, gave him the new material, and suggested he watch until he felt sure of himself. He soon began to work on his own, and when I proposed to leave him in Two while I went to Three, he readily agreed. Aware of his heart condition, I urged him to take frequent rests and showed him where he could sit and still keep the main area under observation. After an hour I returned to find him very upset.

"You know," he said, "all my life I have battled anti-Semitism, but I've never met it on this personal level. I'm burned up; I want to do something drastic."

"Take it easy, Nathan," I cautioned. "These kids are using it as a ploy; they aren't Nazis."

"That's how the Nazis got started, using kids like these who didn't know it would lead to crematoriums." He was visibly agitated. "I can't continue. My heart is pounding; I took a pill. I'm afraid I'll have to quit," he apologized. "I'll try to make it back another time."

Nevertheless, on one occasion the devotees' slurs boomeranged. Resenting an appeal to anti-Semitism, a stout, elderly woman who said she was Catholic came to my aid. She had been waiting the arrival of her son's plane; for the next twenty minutes she went from prospect to prospect saying, "When they speak of the Lord, they are not thinking of Jesus, but someone with the name of Krishna." Before leaving she said, "I'll pray for the safe return of your grandson."

She gave me an idea. The devotees often used expressions like "We're doing the Lord's work," or "You believe in God, don't you?" I pasted on paperboard a picture of Krishna from the front cover of *Back to Godhead* in which he was pictured in a jewelled red turban, yellow pantaloons, rings on fingers and toes, pearl strands on one ankle, the flesh softly rounded at neck, arms and shoulders, and lips bright red. When a devotee's pitch included a reference to God, I would show the picture. "When he says 'God,' this is whom he means—Krishna." The reaction from the prospect was surprise and puzzlement; from the devotee, silence.

There were unforseen consequences. Madhusa, squat, dark-haired, the most outspoken of the flower-women, came up one

187

morning in a great rage. "That man," she said pointing to Saul, one of our people, "insulted our God."

"What did he say," I asked.

"I won't say; he knows what he said. You tell him to cut it out." I beckoned Saul over and asked what happened. "Nothing. All I asked her was if this (holding out the picture of Krishna) was a man or a woman."

"It's the way he said it," Madhusa boiled. "You tell him, Mr. Yanoff, to stop that." When she calmed down, she informed us that "Krishna is the supreme male." She was, in fact, quoting doctrine: in relation to Krishna, all are female; he alone is male in the universe.

Tom Most phoned me that night. He had been in Building Three when I was in Two with Nathan. He reported, "When I saw a Krishna approach a traveler, I prayed that God harden his heart. When someone was about to give, I went over to tell who they were and what they stood for."

That evening Toby and I discussed the anti-Semitism at O'Hare. "I was surprised," I said, "that Nathan was so upset. I, too, was shocked when I first heard the remarks, but I've become used to almost anything the Krishnas throw at us."

"It may be," she said, "that he has had some bad experiences, and a remark like that brings up all the horrors. If it didn't happen to him, perhaps it was to his family."

Toby, during the civil war which followed the Russian Revolution, had faced that age-old horror. The Jews of the little towns in that part of western Russia were often victimized by marauding bands. When our children were old enough, Toby told them of a time of terror.

"One day—about two years before we came to America when I was about seven years old—Jews fleeing from the town next to ours warned us the White Guards were coming. The people of our village ran to the forest to hide, but my mother, who had seen her friends come back from there with frozen hands and feet, took my sister and me to a neighbor whose house had a cellar. There we hid with a couple; the man was so very old he didn't even realize what was happening. He kept moaning and his wife tried to shush him. We were afraid the White Guards would hear him and we would all be killed. When night came there was loud banging

188

on the door. We shivered in fear. But then we heard Jewish voices through the door and knew we were safe."

"There is nothing in Krishna doctrine that smacks of anti-Semitism," I said, "—at least not that I've come across. According to a survey by Judah, that prof who wrote the book about them, fourteen percent of their number are Jewish. You remember Lerner? His son is high up in their hierarchy."

"It doesn't prove they are free of anti-Semitism," she said. "I understand that Collin, the leader of the Nazis in Chicago, is half-Jewish. Some Jews may despise their origins and join the anti-Semites to purge themselves."

"In one respect, though, the Krishnas are like the Nazis. ISKCON is run on the führer principle. The Swami's word is law."

"Morris, do you remember what Sandra Kallin told us? She thought that if they were ordered to kill, they would. Something like the Manson family."

"Toby, please. Let's stop scaring ourselves."

23

We Make Headlines

THE FOLLOWING MORNING, JAMES BOWMAN, RE-
ligious editor of the *Chicago Daily News*, came to Building Three
with a photographer. Recognizing me by my "Where is Joey?"
lapel card, he introduced himself. I suggested that he listen to an
argument between Nakula and a young Canadian with a back-
pack, Jay Cestnik of Ontario. Cestnik complained that Nakula
wanted a donation for a book he had offered "free." The photographer began to take pictures, and Bowman, pencil and pad in
hand, listened.

"You said you wanted me to read it, didn't you?" Cestnik asked.

"We do want you to read it," Nakula replied, "but we would like
a contribution to cover the cost of printing." I had met Nakula the
first day we came to the airport and observed the earnestness
with which he spoke to prospective givers.

"You didn't say anything about a contribution when you gave
me the book," Cestnik protested. "You said, 'We're handing out
free books today.'"

"It is free," Nakula insisted, "but if we don't get contributions,
we won't be able to print more."

"Do you want the book back?" Cestnik held it out and Nakula
took it. "You are a religious society; you want to spread your faith,
don't you? You should be glad to give your literature to people
who want to read it. You shouldn't make a donation a condition."

It wasn't clear to me what Cestnik's motives were for continuing
the dispute. Did he want the book, or was he miffed that he had
fallen for the "free book" ploy? Bowman kept taking notes and the

190

photographer, pictures. Nakula was aware of the reporter, but conditioned to go through his routine, he seemed unable to shift gears.

"It's like I said. We distribute our books for people to read. If you can't afford a donation, why don't you say so."

"Whether I can or not isn't the point," Cestnik insisted. "You gave me the book and told me it was a gift and I took it as a gift. When I started to walk away with it, you hit me for a donation."

Bowman turned to Nakula: "Is the book free, or isn't it?" Before he could reply, Gopal, who had been watching quietly, interrupted: "It's free." He took the book from Nakula and gave it to Cestnik.

"May I ask who you are?" Bowman asked. Gopal gave his name. "Are you saying this man can walk away with the book without making a donation?"

"Yes," Gopal replied. "Like Nakula said, we'd like a donation but it's not mandatory."

I believe Gopal realized it would be awkward for the Society if the *News* published a story that its literature was being sold. Selling is a violation of City ordinances; only the concessionaires had the right—they paid rent. The Krishnas had to maintain, at all costs, that they were giving the books away as a religious function and that donations were voluntary.

Bowman took me aside for a brief interview: he was already familiar with the events which brought us to O'Hare. Afterward, he went over to Gopal, who stood with book pouch slung over his shoulder. I followed. In answer to Bowman's questions, Gopal said he was twenty-four, from North Dakota, and a permanent resident at 1014 Emerson, the temple's address. He received from three to ten dollars for a book, he said, and expected to take in about a hundred dollars in eight hours. I knew this to be a considerable understatement, following the cult's policy of belittling its collections. From my observations, a bookseller sold about eight books an hour for an average, modestly, of five dollars per book—giving him $320 in eight hours. Govinda had boasted to one of our helpers that on a day when we had been absent, he had taken in five hundred dollars.

Bowman asked Gopal why he wore a wig and got the standard reply: "People freak out when they see us in temple dress. We want to make them feel comfortable talking to us."

"Why don't you tell them who you are?" Bowman asked.

"We tell them if they ask. Even if we told them we're Hare Krishnas, they wouldn't know the difference anyhow."

There was a pause and I took the opportunity to ask Gopal, "Why did you tell a prospect this morning not to listen to me because I was a Jew?"

At first he denied it, but Bowman kept pressing until he said, "Well, he is a Jew, isn't he?"

"Suppose he were a Christian, would you mention that?"

"He's prejudiced in favor of the Jews and against the Krishnas," Gopal replied. "People should know that."

Maharaj came up to Gopal, took him aside, and I heard him whisper, "Don't talk to the press." I repeated it to Bowman, who asked Maharaj his name.

"Did you tell Gopal not to talk to me?" Bowman asked Maharaj.

"If you want information about the Society and its philosophy, you should talk to the president of our temple," he replied.

"My questions," Bowman said, "have been only about what is going on here at O'Hare. Can he answer those?"

"Mukunda is the only person with authority to give information to the press." He spelled Mukunda's name for Bowman and gave him the temple's phone number. "What Yanoff is doing here is illegal," he asserted. "He won't get away with it."

"What do you intend to do?" Bowman asked.

"That's something you will have to talk to Mukunda about. He's interfering with our First Amendment rights under the Constitution."

"What rights does Yanoff have?" Bowman asked.

"He has the right to talk but not to interfere with us. He has his rights up to a point."

"What point is that?" Bowman pressed him.

"He can talk to a person before we do, or after, but not interrupt while we are talking."

Bowman spent another fifteen minutes speaking to travelers who had been approached by devotees, asking why they gave, or refused.

The Saturday edition of the *Daily News* carried the announcement: "A 69-year-old man has been battling the followers of Hare Krishna on one of their busiest turfs—O'Hare Airport. Find out why in Monday's *Daily News*."

The Monday edition, for which we waited impatiently, carried Bowman's long article as well as a picture of Gopal jabbing an

192

accusative finger at me. Especially interesting to me was Bowman's report of what travelers said to him:

> Andrew Bella, of South Bend, emptied his pocket of 60 cents after a young Krishna woman pinned a flower to his lapel. "She wanted $5 to help somebody," said Bella.
>
> Bob Antisdel, of Edwardsburg, Mich., gave the same woman 50 cents—"and she got mad," he said.
>
> Hal Batten, 45, from Des Moines, said he had been approached "50 or 100 times" by Krishna followers in his air travels. He said they "confront and almost physically hold you" when making their pitch.

Kingsley Wood's articles, written from the interview I gave over the phone, appeared the following day in the *Chicago Sun Times*. It had the picture of Joey with his trumpet and a photo of me arguing with three of the flower-women. Melodramatically headlined, "Stalks O'Hare for His Missing Grandson," it began:

> He is a 69-year-old grandfather. Day after day, he stands in the United or Eastern concourse at O'Hare Airport holding a newspaper clipping about his 12-year-old grandson's mysterious disappearance in 1975.

Wood, who took my suggestion to contact Mukunda, reported him saying:

> He doesn't bother us too much," Makunda said of the grandfather. "It's like when you go camping and there are mosquitoes. He even told me he has no grudge against the members of our bona fide religious movement who work in Chicago.
>
> He said that if he steps on our toes here, we'll react and put pressure on the Krishnas in Los Angeles to get the boy back. But the honest truth is that we're trying to help the grandfather and father find the boy. We don't know where the boy or his mother are.

Travelers at O'Hare gave me clippings of Wood's story from the *Detroit Free Press* and the *Baltimore Sun*, both cities with temples. I wondered how many other papers carried his syndicated articles.

We had hoped that our airport tactic would be picked up by other victim families and anti-cult organizations. We tried to stimulate them by sending a letter describing our procedure and enclosing clips of both the *Daily News* and *Sun Times* articles. It was only many months later that some others followed our example.

The next day twelve Krishnas registered. Our vigil was composed of Victor, Moira, a petite woman of forty-five who also became one of our stalwarts, and me. Moira was the daughter of the Glatmans, a retired dentist and his wife who, too, had been helping us.

That morning when I noticed a devotee whose face was not familiar, I introduced myself and learned his name was Brispati. Of a good height, lean and athletic, he might have looked at home at West Point. Brispati told me he had been raised in New York and, since that's my home town, we reminisced about well-known spots in the old city. Later when I intervened with one of his prospects, he said to the woman, "He's a communist. We're trying to stop communism." I laughed and told the woman who I was. She, no fool, saw that the charge was solely to divert attention from the issue at hand—whether or not to donate. She didn't, and Brispati became angry. To ease the situation, I asked in the tone of the inquiring reporter, "What makes you think I'm a communist?" He stalked off, still angry.

That day I ran the whole gamut of Krishna verbal attacks. Nakula, for example, said to a potential giver, "He's an atheist."

It was, however, an incident with Gururama which disturbed me. Unlike the "clean-cut" type usually sent to the airport by the Krishnas, he was a stubby little fellow with a solemn, homely face. On one occasion I had introduced myself to him, but he wouldn't tell me his name in return. When I persisted, he dropped a Jewish phrase. Today, seeing him trying to sell a book, I intervened in the sale. "He's a Jew and a communist. That's why he doesn't want you to read these books," Gururama told his prospect. As usually happened, people shied away from controversy and he lost out.

Afterward, I confronted him: "How come you, a Jew, go in for anti-Semitism?"

He faced me with a savage look, "You're a bloody, sectarian Jew! If your grandson had been sent away to some bearded rabbi,

194

you would have been happy." The tone, the facial expression were venomous; it jolted me. Where other devotees had called me a Jew with the blandness of salesmen selling toothbrushes, he exploded. Why, I wondered? Was he struggling against his own feelings as a Jew? Was I the butt of his festering conflicts? It would take a Dostoyevsky to understand him.

At times the counterattack was merely silly, as when the tall, stately Gadapati said to a prospect, "He wants you to give the money to him; he's jealous."

There were moments of sanity as when Gopal, with whom I got into a brief discussion, agreed that to enlist Joey into the Society at age twelve was incorrect. "You can't make a decision like that at twelve," he admitted. "The age of religious consent in Illinois," I said, "is eighteen." "That's more like it," Gopal agreed.

Gadapati, who supervised the devotees when Maharaj was absent, took Gopal aside and I overheard him say, "Follow instructions; just say 'Hare Krishna' to him." And yet, somewhat later, Gopal made a friendly comment to me. On such small events did my hopes rise for breaching the walls of hostility.

At noon I took a break for coffee. On my way to the USO lounge, I notice Chandra sitting dejectedly, legs stretched full-length, staring before him. This was the first time I had seen a devotee idle.

Entering the USO, I waved to Mary, who was seated behind her desk. Moira was sitting alone at a table and I joined her with my cup. She was bursting with indignation, "What a bunch of bastards, they are!"

"Did you have a run-in with one of them?" I asked.

"Do you know the tall fellow with the hook-nose? Here, I took his number—0509."

I checked the number against the morning's list of sign-ins. "That's Charvaka."

"Well, I went over to talk to a man he was trying to sell a book to. He asked the man, 'Do you believe in Jesus Christ?' The man said he did. Charvaka then said, 'The Jews killed Jesus. This woman is a Jew. Don't listen to her.' Imagine, in this day and age! I never dreamed I'd hear a thing like that."

I told her of my experience with Gururama. "I think Charvaka may be Jewish too," Moira said. "I heard him mention his real name to someone. I can't remember it now, but it sounded Jewish. It's incredible to me that a Jew would speak against his own people."

To cheer her, I told of Gopal's criticism of Joey's admission into the cult at twelve.

"You know, Morris," she said, "I think they respect you for what you are doing even while they are fighting you."

"You really think so?" She surprised me.

"I can see it in their attitude towards you."

"Well, if true, I hope it pays off in some way. Do me a favor, Moira. Write up that incident with Charvaka. We may be sued by the Krishnas for harassment and we will want to show the provocations we met."

A tall, thin devotee in temple dress and with shaven head and tilaka between his eyebrows came off the elevator in the main area of Three, pushing a handtruck with books. As he stood waiting, I went up to introduce myself, catching only the last part of his name, Rupa. When we got into a discussion over the philosophy of his movement, he painted a dark picture of the world: overpopulation, poverty, violence, atomic weapons. Science, he said, was being used for evil ends; industrialization had a demoralizing effect: "Prabhupada said that machinery breeds idleness. We should model our society after Vedic village life, based on land and cow culture. The cow is our best friend but we slaughter it."

"How can you go back to a primitive economy," I asked, "to a time when the earth's population was five percent of what it is today? There were less people in the whole world at the time the Vedas were written than there are in India today."

"If we can't, it's because of our emphasis on material goods. I used to have an apartment of my own, four rooms filled with furniture, TV, hi-fi, a car, and a bank account. Now I sleep on the floor of a bare room; I have one change of clothes, I own nothing, and I'm happy. What I now want out of life costs nothing. Those who value material things always want more and are jealous of those who have more. There's the cause of violence and war."

It was in my mind to say, "If so, why does your spiritual master ride in a Rolls Royce and take rooms at luxury hotels?" But I was afraid he would think I was baiting him. "There is an over-emphasis," I agreed, "on the mere acquisition of material goods. I also know people whose lives are dedicated to wealth accumulation. But that's only one side of our society. There are beautiful things in life, things like music for which one needs hi-fi; books, for which we need libraries, and so on. Industrialization has given us many good things. There is no need to throw out the baby with the bathwater."

I felt an affinity to this young man. In my younger days I was moved by the poverty around me to join movements for a more equitable distribution of the world's goods. This man, similarly motivated, voluntarily accepted poverty and looked for fulfillment in mysticism. I believed that if we could replace the extremes of wealth and poverty with sufficiency for all, there would be harmony in society and an end to war. He saw the solution in doing without and in worship of Krishna.

"Your music and books," he said, "are forms of sense gratification. They don't bring spiritual realization and the perfection of life. We too have music and books, but they are devoted to Krishna. If one is engaged in Krishna consciousness, then, automatically, sense desires subside and one is free of petty materialism."

"But what is wrong with sense desires which urge us to listen to a Beethoven or read a novel by Tolstoy?"

"They serve only the body and its desires. We are not our bodies; we are spirit souls and we have to do what serves our spirit souls. Prabhupada said in *Easy Journey*—you should read that—the only important thing for human beings is adopting the principle of spiritual realization, that's the sole obligation. If one is busy listening to what is called good music or good books, he neglects the one, single, obligatory duty—the duty of spiritual perfection. But once he has achieved that, he has gained everything; he doesn't need Beethoven or Shakespeare because what they can give is insignificant in comparison."

I understood his words—but what did they really mean? Did chanting the mahamantra two hours daily give him more than I received from the Chorale Symphony? Freddy Loewe, who had spent time in the Boston temple, had said, "It's hard for people like you to understand a completely different culture, that happiness can come through chanting the holy name of God, Krishna, from religious dancing and ritual, even from eating food offered to Krishna."

"Do you by any chance know where my grandson is?" I asked Rupa.

"You know, we would not hold anyone against his will."

"I believe you, but how can a child of twelve, especially if he is in a foreign country, leave the temple?" He made no reply. "The worst thing for us is not hearing from him in over a year."

"I sympathize with you," he said. "I don't know if he's in Krishna, but if he is, you needn't worry; no harm will come to him."

"Will he get schooling?"

"Naturally. Krishna children from the age of five attend gurukula."

"Will that prepare him to take his place in the real world, or is he being educated for Vedic village life?" I couldn't restrain my bitterness, but Rupa took no notice.

"In my opinion, he is being better prepared than if he attended a secular public school, as I did. If someone is educated with a view to his God consciousness, to the existence of his soul and its relation to Krishna, to God, that child will handle life in the material world better than other children. What we give him is a set of values by which everyting can be measured."

"Would he be trained to make a living?"

"A vocation is part of the Vedic system of education. Not everyone has the aptitude to become a Brahmin, a priest. He will be given training according to his abilities and inclinations."

"Suppose his aptitudes were toward medicine or engineering? Would the gurukula have the facilities to prepare him?"

"Ways will be found. We have many devotees who hold positions in such occupations." Yes, I thought, those who joined after receiving their schooling elsewhere. "But his character training will never be lost, no matter what work he follows. You may be sure he will not work for the sake of accumulating wealth or for his self-gratification."

I was exasperated by Rupa's bland assurances. "How can he be prepared for a world from which he has been withdrawn?" I persisted. "He sees no newspapers, no TV; he doesn't mix with other children, or adults other than devotees."

Rupa remained undisturbed: "If he doesn't view TV or movies, it's because there is little or no spiritual benefit in them. Children need protection from the cold world until they are prepared to cope with it. Krishna consciousness prepares them."

Just then, Deva and Madhusa peered around a corner and, seeing me, ran off. Excusing myself, I left Rupa. It had been a rare occasion. Seldom did the devotees engage in a sustained discussion on a give-and-take basis. The Society, I supposed, attracted all kinds—the foul-mouthed Chandras and the gentle Rupas. In moments of despair I feared the Chandras of the movement would prevail.

That evening I followed Rupa's suggestion and dipped into Prabhupada's *Easy Journey to Other Planets*, a copy of which I purchased at the Krishna parade. Rupa was expounding doctrine, all right:

> Bhakti-yoga is therefore the great panacea for all...singing dancing, and chanting the names of God...all the misgivings in the heart will disappear, the fire of material tribulation will be extinguished, and transcendental bliss will be ushered in.

Written in 1970, before there were moon landings, the Swami affirmed that man cannot go to the moon in his material body, but can go to it and any of an infinite number of planets in his spiritual form. This is accomplished by blocking the "vital force" from leaving through the body openings and centering it between the eyebrows:

> At this position, the yogi can think of the planet he wants to enter after leaving the body. He can then decide whether he wants to go to the abode of Krsna... from which he will not be required to descend into the material world, or to travel to the higher planets in the material universe. For the perfect yogi...transfer from one planet to another is as easy as an ordinary man walking to the grocery store.

And so on for a hundred pages about how to escape material existence, travel at will over interstellar space—a bonanza for those who practice bhakti yoga (the yoga of devotion)—bliss in this world and blissful travel after death.

Try as I might, I couldn't imagine Joey receiving such revelations.

24

Devotees and Demons

TOBY, NOW BETTER ORGANIZED, WAS SCHEDULING our friends over two-week spans. She offered a choice of dates and, if someone had to cancel, she asked for a new commitment. Encouraged by the vigilers' positive reaction to their experience, she became a bit bolder, phoning people with whom we had been out of touch for a long while. She told about Joey (although most had read or heard about him), and won more than sympathy— their agreement to help. Her list grew with names furnished by those who had already done a stint at the airport. These had told their friends of encounters with the Krishnas and aroused a desire to help recover Joey, and, also, to counter a public deception.

Nonetheless, it was still no easy task for Toby to find people willing to walk up to strangers and ask that they refuse a donation to the Krishnas. This smacked of conflict, and many had no stomach for it. To the timid, Toby suggested they go as observers and take part only if they felt comfortable. Those who overcame their fears were exhilarated. "Can you imagine," said little Libby, aged sixty-eight, "this big, six-foot Krishna takes one look at me, and runs."

Mukunda came to the airport for the first time on October 21. I was glad to see him because it proved our effectiveness—and too, I hoped to talk to him. Dressed in neat business suit and wearing a black wig, handsome Mukunda might have been taken for a corporation executive on a field trip. I walked over to offer my hand and he took it.

200

Formal preliminaries over, he complained that one of our women vigilers had said, "They're a fraud," to a potential giver. He pointed to May Ronch who, with her husband, a retired metal dealer, had come to the airport for the first time.

"I will speak to her," I promised. "My instructions to our people are to stick to facts and avoid offensive remarks."

"Some of your people say we are brainwashed," he continued.

"I don't use that expression," I replied. "I'm not sure what it means." Although I felt that the expression ought not be used, I made no promise to correct it. I did not like to police our friends any more than was absolutely necessary. Driving to the airport, I always briefed them about our simple routine: "Identify the devotees as Krishnas, tell of Joey's disappearance into the cult, ask they don't contribute until he is returned." I was convinced this factual, direct way of making our appeal was best and least likely to give the sect ammunition for legal action. Yet I knew that people liked to put their individual stamp on whatever they did, and, inevitably, would react in kind to insults.

We were not conducting a vendetta which would continue after Joey came back, and I wanted Mukunda to realize that we were reasonable. I held to the belief that eventually he would bring his temple's situation to the Swami's attention and secure Joey's release.

"It's a shame we have to be here at all," I told him. "I assume you know why we are back after the moratorium?"

"We received a letter from the GBC instructing us to have Miriam or Joey communicate with you should they be present in any temple."

"Well, nothing came of it," I said. "We had hoped that this time the GBC would put us in touch with Joey. You may know we had an intermediary." He nodded. "Well, he held out hope we would succeed this time. That's why we went along with a moratorium." I gave him an outline of our negotiations with Braun, without naming him, describing our pledges of non-retaliation and readiness to accommodate to Joey's spiritual needs.

"I don't know where Joey is," Mukunda asserted. "He may be in some group on the periphery, and they may even use one of our temples on occasion. We have no control in that kind of situation."

"It's easier for ISKCON to find him, than for us. After all, you were responsible for his disappearance; you inducted him without his father's consent; you forcibly took him away from his father on the temple lawn in L.A."

He became indignant. "The Evanston temple had nothing to do with it. Why pick on us for what took place in L.A.? Go to them."

"We believe ISKCON is a monolithic organization and that the parent body is concerned with what happens to any of its branches. Besides, we live here, not in L.A., and our friends are here to help us."

"We're not monolithic; Evanston is autonomous," he protested.

"Don't you send money to India?"

"We haven't sent any in a long time. The only money we send out of Evanston is for printing of the literature we distribute; that money goes to L.A."

Very interesting, I thought. Every time Saci signed in to register, she wrote "World Relief" on her permit.

At this moment a husky airport worker got into a shouting match with the Krishnas, accusing them of "rip offs and peddling junk." He tried to grab books out of devotees' hands but was restrained by a friend who eventually led him away.

"You know, Mukunda," I said, "there is a wall of hostility against you here."

"That's because the police and the airport encourage it."

"Don't you think our case contributes to it?"

"We haven't been hurt much by your being here," said Gadapati, joining us. Both Maharaj and he came and went during our conversation although Mukunda did most of the talking.

I appealed to Mukunda. "You're a father. Can you understand how my son feels, and how we feel, not having had a word from Joey in a year, not even a postcard to say he is well. It could have been posted from anywhere."

A devotee passsing by heard part of my remark: "Maybe Joey likes it in Krishna and doesn't want to come back."

Mukunda said to him, "Mr. Yanoff just told me they haven't heard from the boy, so they wouldn't know what he thinks." I was pleased by these words hoping they indicated sympathy.

"What about the suit in L.A. for money damages?" Mukunda asked.

"If we get Joey back, we would consider vacating it."

"Braun said you wanted money."

Braun, evidently, wasn't keeping his intervention a secret. "Yes, we told him that Larry would like to be reimbursed for his costs."

"You said you would not seek publicity after Joey is back. Does your son feel that way too?"

"I can assure you he does." Mukunda was asking the questions I hoped he would.

"Does he share your opinion about Joey's spiritual state—that he would be permitted to continue in Krishna consciousness?"

"We are not seeking a traumatic experience for Joey. If he decides after his return to continue and to visit the temple, we would not stand in the way."

"Maybe you would bring him and after a while get to like it yourself."

I smiled wryly. "So many strange things have happened to me in the last year—who knows?" I was being as gracious as I could.

Gadapati and Maharaj, who had been listening, left to resume bookselling. Mukunda brought up the eviction the temple faced, blaming us for their predicament.

"We're not responsible," I replied. "The fact is that for two years you failed to comply with the City's standards of health, safety, and off-street parking. Perhaps our case did affect the climate of opinion in Evanston, but the 'special use' permit was denied on legal grounds—your failure to make corrections."

"We were on the point of complying," he said, "when they made their decision against us. True, we should have done it sooner; my predecessor did not get around to it. But we were getting it done when the City pulled the rug. It was your case which brought out their prejudice."

"It's hard to judge these things, to know what goes on in people's minds when they make decisions like these. But, if what you say is true, then news of Joey's return could have a reverse effect and help your efforts to stay in Evanston."

Mukunda pointed to the *Tribune* reprint of the New York indictment I held in my hand. "That won't hurt us," he said. "The trial will give us the opportunity to expound our views and make new converts. You've been saying to people that we sent Joey to India," he went on. "You know, the travel ticket was never picked up or paid for." How did he know that, I wondered? Scarlatt could not determine if Joey actually left on the Pan-American flight, or on any other flight. How much more did Mukunda know?

"We don't know if he got to India. We've charged only that a passport was taken out for him and that his destination was given as India. We have stated frankly that we *don't* know where he is but are convinced from all the evidence in our possession that he is in Krishna somewhere." I made a final appeal before leaving. "If you can do something, do it now."

He looked thoughtful: "It's up to Krishna."

"Help him a little," I said, and left to join my friends in Building Three. Out of delicacy I had avoided encounters with the devotees in Two while Mukunda was present.

The conversation raised my hopes. I had given Mukunda fresh arguments to broach whomever in the hierarchy was his contact. Mukunda's most persuasive problem was loss of income; we would have to make it more convincing in days to come.

At noon I took a coffee break. As I was chatting with Mary at the USO, Ellen joined us. I had known her husband thirty years ago when he was an organizer for the Fur and Leather Workers Union. Now a widow in her sixties, Ellen was bursting with life. A running stream of words bubbled from her—stories of her relatives, comments on the news, the immediate scene—everything was a subject of lively interest.

She was laughing. "Y'know what? I'm gonna die. There's news for you. One of the Krishna boys said to me, 'Lady, you know you're gonna die.'"

"Who said that?" I asked.

"That young fellow with the glasses. Gopi, I call him."

"Gopal," I said.

"Gopal, Gopi, what's the difference? I said to him, 'We're born to die. It's what happens in between that counts.'"

"Was he threatening you?" Mary asked.

"It didn't sound like he was. He just repeated, 'Lady, you're gonna die.' I said, 'Nobody knows when they'll go. You're a young man but you may suddenly drop dead. I may outlive you.' 'I've got Krishna,' he said. 'You know what you can do with him,' I said. He was offended and walked away. How do you like that?"

"What do you think he meant by it?" Mary asked.

"I guess he was trying to make me feel bad because I'm old."

"Could be," I said. "But it may be part of their religious beliefs."

"To poke fun at old people?" Mary asked.

"No, to show his superiority to you, to us, who are not in Krishna. They believe the body is nothing; like a suit of clothes. It dies, but the spirit soul, a tiny particle, continues and transmigrates to another body."

"Like reincarnation," Ellen said.

"Depending on your karma, your fate, the way you conducted yourself during your lifetime, your soul may go into one of

8,400,000 forms. You can become a pig, or a cockroach, or whatever, in your next life."

"You're kidding!" Ellen exclaimed. "Do they really believe that? But isn't Gopi going to die, too?"

"His body, yes. But his spirit soul will be freed forever from the cycle of birth and death because he's in Krishna consciousness. He'll stop migrating and live for eternity with Krishna."

"Where?" Mary asked.

"On Goloka," I said.

"Goloka?" Ellen echoed. "Sounds like a new parlor game."

"It's Sanskrit for 'the place of the cows.' That's where Krishna lives—with the sacred cows and the cow maidens—gopis."

Ellen roared. "Gopis! That's what I called him, Gopi, a cow-girl."

I wrote Faye Levine, author of *The Strange World of the Hare Krishnas*, in hope she might have suggestions for our search. With the consent of the temple president, she had spent a month living as a devotee in the Brooklyn temple. Her book, published in 1974, was my introduction to the daily life of a devotee. In reply to my inquiry, she proposed that since there were only four temples in India, we look there. She also wrote:

> My final feeling about the Hare Krishnas was that they were somewhat interesting, but very creepy....There is no question but that a month with them will have an insidious effect on the thinking of an adult, which could sloppily be called 'brainwashing.'

We saw that "creepy" quality at the airport. The devotees showed complete absorption in themselves and blindness to impressions they made on others. For example, when the Krishnas circled me at times and began chanting in full voice, travelers gaped but the devotees remained blissfully unconcerned. Taught that our world is illusionary (maya), they were living in their own. Everyone but themselves was contemptuously called a "karmie" (materialist) or a demon.

Levine recounts a conversation with Bali Marden, Brooklyn temple president. He had described Prabhupada as a "world-genius greater than Jesus" engaged in "an international ideological battle."

"Who are the parties to this battle?" she asked.

"The demons and the devotees."

"Who are the demons?" Levine probed.

"Everyone who is not a devotee."

It was no doubt this war against "demons" like me that allowed Narada to overstep the most ordinary decency and calmly to lie, "Joey is dead"; or, similarly, the three flower-women chanted at me, "You'll never see Joey again." When I traced Narada's shout of 'N'zhingaday," I found it was, properly, "Nrsimhadev," the destroyer form of Krishna. Half-lion, half-man, he disembowelled his enemies with his talons and garlanded himself with the bloody intestines. In shouting the word at me, did Narada wish me a similar fate?

One morning, a woman devotee with a little boy and girl came through on the way to a plane. She stopped to greet the Krishna solicitors, and I, attracted to the shaven-headed boy, kneeled to talk to him. Madhusa screamed, "Don't let him touch you. He's a demon!"

Such callous disregard of another's feeling could not be put down to antagonism alone.

There were also efforts to reach me or make me "understand"— always through their doctrine. One day Madhusa approached me and held out a copy of *Back to Godhead* opened to a page headed, "The Prince Passed on Too Soon."

"Here's a story you should read," she said, as if giving me a message from Krishna himself.

When I promised to do so, her swarthy face lit up. Madhusa (whose real name was of Polish origin) was the oldest of the flower-women, about thirty, and the least successful; she did not have the good looks of the others.

That night I read the colorfully illustrated story. An Indian king had everything but a son—none of his many queens could give him one. A great sage who was visiting the palace asked the king what he needed most to make him happy. He granted his wish for a son, cautioning he would bring both happiness and sorrow. From jealousy, the child was poisoned by other queens. As the king grieved, the sage returned:

> "O King," the sage said, "what kinship does that dead body have with you? Or you with it?....Just as the waves of the ocean push together and pull apart grains of sand, so the waves of time cause people to meet and

separate....The distinctions we make between people on the basis of family or country are imaginary.

"...I could have given you the supreme transcendental knowledge...but when I saw that your mind was absorbed in material things, I gave you a son."

Madhusa was sending a message: "What is Joey to you, and you to Joey? Forget him as you would a grain of sand that fell into your shoe. His atom of spirit soul is destined to be attached to one or another body through infinite time." I knew Madhusa had a child of her own. I wondered what happened to him.

Gururama, in one of our rare conversations, said, "Joey made a spiritual decision. Instead of materialism, he chose spiritual life. His mother helped him make that decision. Why should he be in the material world when he can have the spiritual? It's the best thing for him." Gururama seemed to take for granted that Joey was in the sect.

"How can a child of twelve make his life's choice to become a celibate devotee?" I protested.

"If he had chosen a rabbinical school, you would have been happy, wouldn't you?" he shouted, face contorted with contempt and anger. "You are prejudiced against our religion."

"What kind of a religion is it which hides a child from his father, which sees us in agony over a lost loved-one, and hasn't the compassion to send assurance of his well-being?"

"Your grandson has Krishna," he declared. "He doesn't need you or his father or any of your family."

His words reminded me of a pronouncement by Prabhupada in *Back to Godhead:*

> If we want to please Krsna, we have to be prepared even to kill our so-called bodily relations. All Vedic civilization is arranged in such a way that we may become detached from so-called family attachment.

25

Religion or Rip-Off?

IN BUILDING TWO ONE MORNING I OBSERVED GOVINDA hastily walk away from a young sailor. Sensing something odd, I walked over to the boy, who stood holding two books and looking through his wallet.

"Anything wrong, sailor?"

"I don't know," he said, shaking his head. "I'm trying to figure this thing out." He counted some bills in his hand and looked through his wallet. "God damn, that son-of-a-gun took me for fifteen bucks."

"How did it happen?"

"He sold me this book," pointing to the yellow-jacketed *Gita*, "and I was going to give him a five, but all I had was a twenty. He said he'd give me change. Next thing he gave me this other book and put these bills in my hand." He held up the five singles. "Where'd he go? If I find that s.o.b., I'll shove these books down his throat."

"Do you want to return the books and get your money?"

"Sure do."

"I know who he is. Let's go through the airport to find him."

As we went looking for Govinda, I told the sailor who I was and what we were doing. He was Carl Mathewson of Appleton, Wisconsin, on his way to submarine training at New London.

"He didn't say he was a Krishna," Mathewson said. "He said this book was all about God. He said nothing about it being Hindu."

"Didn't you look at the book before you bought it?"

208

"Just the pictures. He kept turning the pages and saying it was all about the Lord and how to serve him."

We had gone through both terminals and were back in Two when we saw Chandra. "That guy is another Krishna," I said to the sailor. "Let's try to give him the books and get your money."

Mathewson told the story to Chandra, but he refused to take the books. "Look Bud," he said, "you didn't get these books from me," and went off.

Mathewson looked anxiously at his watch. "I'm close to plane time." I suggested we go up to the security office. He agreed provided it would not take more than fifteen minutes. Woody asked him to fill out a complaint form.

"Look," Mathewson said to me. "I don't want these books. You take them and if you get my money, send it to my address. O.K.?" I agreed and he ran for his plane.

"What are you going to do about his complaint?" I asked Woody.

"File it. We have hundreds. We can't do anything unless the complainant is willing to testify. Look here." He pointed to a question at the bottom of the form. "Are you willing to testify regarding this matter?"

Mathewson had left it unanswered. "Naturally," Woody said, "he isn't going to come in from New London, Connecticut, to testify. Even Chicago residents won't appear in court."

"Then why fill out the complaint?"

"Most don't. I'd guess only one out of twenty takes the trouble. This guy thinks that somehow we'll do something without his help."

I saw Madhusa accept a twenty-dollar bill for a carnation, crumple and put it in a corner of her bag. The giver was leaving when I asked, surprised, "Aren't you going to wait for your change?" He looked at me, puzzled. Madhusa appealed to him, "You gave me a dollar, didn't you?" Now aware, the man rummaged through his wallet. "It was a twenty," he said angrily. "I meant to give you a dollar."

"You gave me a dollar," she shouted. "This man"—pointing at me—"is trying to make trouble." The traveler now loudly demanded his money, and I urged Madhusa to look into the corner of her bag. She did—and pulled out a dollar bill, and another. "You see," she said, holding them up for all to see. A crowd had gathered; soon a security man joined it. I explained the situation to him but before he could act, Madhusa pulled out the twenty. "It was crumpled up," she said, "and I couldn't see it." The traveler snatched the bill, thanked me, and left.

Alone, Madhusa raged at me, "You're a demon. You'll be sorry."

On another occasion, money was refunded from an unexpected source. One morning I saw Randy, a tall, thin boy of about sixteen, holding two books and peering about as if looking for someone. When I asked if he needed help, he explained he had come from Kenosha with his parents—they were sitting nearby—to see off some friends. He had been approached "by this man with the books" and was offered one, free. When tapped for a donation, Randy asked, "How about two dollars?" When Randy gave him a ten dollar bill, the devotee thrust another book into his hands and hurried off.

There were only two booksellers that day, Maharaj and the indefatigable Govinda. From Randy's description, it was the latter. We left Randy's folks waiting in Two and cruised the two buildings looking for Govinda. Randy explained that he worked spare time on a golf course and could not afford to lose the money. We questioned the flower-women in Three, but they said they had not seen Govinda. When we returned to Two, we found Maharaj and, on my suggestion, Randy told his story to him. The parents came up to add their appeal. Maharaj asked the boy, "How much did you want to give?" He replied, "Two dollars for this book." "O.K.," Maharaj said, "here's eight dollars, give me back the other book." I said to him, "That was a decent thing to do." He made no acknowledgment and left me wondering if he acted out of propriety or pressure.

Krishna methods of collecting money created an undercurrent of violence, especially when young people were involved. Near the entrance to the Rotunda, I came upon a confrontation between a soldier, who, having looked through the *Gita*, demanded that Maharaj return his money.

"The book is yours now," Maharaj said. "I didn't force you to make the donation."

"He has a right to ask for a refund," I interjected.

The usually well-poised Maharaj snapped back, "Why don't you mind your own business?"

Before I could reply, a big man wearing a Texas-style hat, towering above Maharaj, said to him, "You give that soldier-boy his money or I'll shake it out of you." To several onlookers, he said, "I know these bastards. We have them at the Dallas airport. They're rip-off artists."

A fight between four sailors and some devotees was barely avoided by a last moment capitulation. I met one of the sailors, McCarty, holding a copy of *Shrimad Bhagavatam* under his arm while looking at some bills in his hands. I arrived just as Nakula was leaving.

"You know," I said, "you can get these books in the USO lounge for free if you want them. They were left by other servicemen."

"Hell!" the sailor exclaimed. "That guy short-changed me. I told him I'd give him a buck for the book. I gave him a ten and thought he gave me a five and four singles but the son-of-a-bitch gave me six ones."

"Do you want your money back?" I asked.

"Hell, yes!"

One of his buddies spoke up, "I want my money back too. I'm mad they ripped off McCarty."

"Did you buy the book from the same guy?"

"No, from a little guy." He described Gururama. The remaining two also bought books from him and now wanted their money returned. The five of us went in the direction taken by Nakula and caught up with him at the center of Three. McCarty angrily demanded his money.

Nakula attacked me. "He's a godless character. He doesn't want you to read God's word."

Gururama, in the vicinity, came over to see what the commotion was about, and the other three sailors pounced on him. "You made your contributions willingly," Gururama said. "I didn't force you, did I?"

"We got a right to change our minds," one of the three said. "Here are your books; we want our money."

The devotees resisted; the sailors became belligerent. When it seemed they would come to blows, the devotees gave in.

Dramatic as were these offenses, I felt the Krishnas were wrong on an even larger score: thousands of travelers thought they were giving to a worthy cause, led to believe so by the devotees withholding their organization's name and couching their appeal in words acceptable to the donor. Each of the flower-women used whatever appeal she thought would get results. With Saci, it was "World Relief," although I never heard where or

211

to whom relief went. Others did better with "Help our mission-
aries"—no details given.

I came up to Deva as she pinned a woman, sweetly saying,
"Please help the needy."

"Just a moment, lady," I said, "these are the Hare Krishnas, a
Hindu cult."

"We are authorized by the airport," Deva said, pointing to the
permit pasted to her book pouch. The PA system warned many
times during the day that solicitors are not authorized by airlines
or airport; the permit was merely a means of identification. The
public wrongly assumed that solicitors are screened by the
authorities and represent established charitable and religious
organizations, a reasonable assumption considering the airport
is not the street where any panhandler can make a pitch; it's an
enclosed, policed area. When I spoke to the woman, I shook her
assumption, but Deva, pointing to her official tag, reassured her.

Madhusa pinned a carnation on a poorly dressed black man
and asked for a donation "to cure drug addicts." The man,
embarrassed, tried to move away but she persisted "for whatever
you can afford." He dug into his pocket and came up with some
small coins. "That's all I have," he said. She scooped them out of
his palm and gave him a copy of their magazine which he waved
away.

I said to her, "You saw how poor the man was. Why did you
insist on a donation?"

She replied earnestly, "The money in his pocket is material;
with us it becomes spiritual. It's Krishna's now. Anyhow, he
would have spent it on liquor or something like that."

Maharaj surprised me one day by asking, "How do you know
the moon is 235,000 miles from the earth? Have you measured it?
Science has been wrong many times." We had been discussing a
Los Angeles Times interview with the Swami, in which he said
that, according to "Vedic literature," the moon was 1.6 million
miles beyond the sun. Maharaj was a graduate of Columbia
University of New York, a scholars' school.

Gopal thought the TV showing of the moon landings were
faked. Madhusa, her sallow face knitted in thought at my
prodding, recalled from her school days that during its dark
phase the moon is between the sun and the earth. When I quoted

212

the Swami's contradictory decree, she said, "If he says the moon is further than the sun, he knows. Our brains are not able to see things like his can." I recalled Faye Levine quoting Prabhupada: "If you begin a sentence with 'I think', you better end it in the closet."

On November 13, among the fifteen devotees who registered, the name of Sally Suskind appeared. The name was familiar to me from Mukunda's news conference of nearly a year ago. Sally was a young Krishna who had been deprogrammed. In answer to a reporter's question about her, Mukunda declared triumphantly, "She is back with us." Now she was at O'Hare and I hoped to talk to her.

She had joined the cult at age seventeen, while still in high school. After two years her frantic parents engaged Ted Patrick to bring her out. Patrick seemed to have succeeded. At a press interview with the *Jewish Post* in April 1975, Sally issued a signed statement addressed to the FBI and its Canadian equivalent (the Suskinds lived in Toronto):

> It speaks of horrors in the Hare Krishna movement, of being psychologically kidnapped by the group, of being willing to kill her parents if she had been told to, of mind control, of earning as much as $200 a day by selling and begging, of living in fear.

> It concludes: "I once again feel like a useful member of society. If, in any event, the Hare Krishna movement...psychologically or physically kidnaps me back, I am requesting immediate action by the authorities to come and physically remove me from this, because in such case, regardless of what I may say or do at the time, I will not be acting under my free will."

> For two years, she said, she was deprived of sleep, fed poorly and overworked. She sold the Krishna books eight hours a day, carrying heavy loads on a back that is so weak it needed a brace for two years.

> ...She loves the devotees at the temple, she says, and wants to help them get out. "They're innocent," she says. "We're all innocent."

213

A strange cry: "We're all innocent." She was not accused of any crime. Of what did she feel guilty? Of bringing grief to her family? Of having been sucked into the cult through her innocence?

The reporter sensed a note of disquiet in the parents. Sally at times absentmindedly resumed chanting, they said.

Today I met up with her in Building Two where she was pinning carnations. She looked about twenty-two, petite, and with long black hair. "You're new here, aren't you?" I said, walking over. "I am Joey's grandfather." She threw me a fearful look and quickly walked away. I did not see her again. Soon after, she was booked for soliciting in the International Building, a prohibited area.

Meeting her depressed me. It brought to the fore the very issue we were still trying to avoid: what problems might we and Joey face when he returned?

I felt I should contact Sally's parents; perhaps they were trying to find her or wanted word of her. The Toronto directory had three addresses for Philip Suskind, her father. I wrote but received no reply. I then wrote the *Toronto Star*, which had also carried her story. There too I drew a blank.

26

The Krishnas Get Rough

NOW IN THE SIXTH WEEK OF OUR VIGIL, THE PUB-
licity and reports of those who had been at the airport contributed
to a more favorable response. Best of all, we had several
"regulars" who committed themselves to come once or twice each
week.

The sisters came two mornings a week. As always, Rose stood
at the exact center of the Krishnas' chosen ground and held high
the mounted reprint of the *Tribune* article about Joey. Those who
caught the headline sometimes asked what it was all about. One
of our vigilers suggested that a poster, the size of the sheet Rose
held, with the slogan "Please don't give to the Hare Krishnas"
would be more effective than a news clipping few could read from
a distance. Moira's husband, an advertising man, agreed to make
it. At my suggestion, he included a rough replica, in color, of the
Gita's yellow cover and a carnation, to aid viewers make the
connection. The poster became popular with our helpers and we
had several more made. Those who had formerly felt useless
waiting around for devotees to appear, now spread the message to
thousands of passers-by. Many stopped to offer encouraging
words, some with stories of their own about the cults. There were
even tenders of money.

Ben Glatman, a retired dentist, and his diminutive wife,
Frances, helped change the vigil pattern. Until then we had
confined ourselves to mornings. Although I was prepared to stay
longer, I had to take the others home. The Glatmans proposed
coming two afternoons a week in their own car, offering to bring
other volunteers who preferred those hours. That opened for

Toby new possibilities of recruitment among those who found it difficult to be ready in the early morning. It was a breakthrough.

Moira told me her parents, the Glatmans, were shocked by the anti-Jewish jibes. "They were deeply involved in the anti-Nazi movement," she explained, "and when they are hit by something like this, they see the concentration camps opening again." Unlike Nathan, whose heart could not endure the stress, the peppery Glatmans found another reason to come: to oppose anti-Semitism.

Charvaka, who on an earlier occasion had outraged Moira with the words, "The Jews killed Jesus," had Ben arrested for "assaulting" him. Ben was seventy-two years old. An officer, summoned by Charvaka, asked Ben for his version of what had happened.

"A traveler tried to return a book to this Krishna, but he wouldn't take it back. I said to the traveler, 'I'll take it off your hands.' When the traveler handed me the book, Charvaka said he would beat me up if I took it."

The officer asked Charvaka, "Is this true?" Surprisingly, the devotee said yes. Realizing how matters now stood, he decided to change his charge from "assault" to "harassment." The officer insisted they both come to the police station.

At the station, Ben overheard an officer saying to Charvaka: "We know you have an arsenal in the Evanston temple," and Charvaka's reply, "We have been attacked with guns in some cities; our weapons are for self-protection."

"On the way to the station," Ben reported, "Charvaka chanted 'Hare Krishna' all the way; he was scared. The officer requested we both drop our charges—I had charged him with threatening me—and I agreed, on the condition that he talk to me man to man. He consented, and you know, he's really not a bad kid; just screwed up."

With the Glatmans coming twice a week, Jim Malin volunteered for other afternoons. He had read news of the vigil and, having known Larry at college, phoned to offer help. He was a tower of strength. About thirty, tall, soft-spoken, he was a trained social worker interested in the plight of underprivileged youngsters. Unemployed at the time, he was working as a volunteer in a neighborhood youth center on Chicago's West Side. When he came to O'Hare, he often brought one or two of the center's teenagers.

216

Jim was interested in the psychological makeup of the devotees; he gave particular attention to Govinda, who at that time began to develop a peculiar trick. When prevented from making a book sale, he would snap the open book like a pistol shot, an inch from our faces, laugh crazily, and run down the length of the airport. After a week, he was caught by a tough plainclothesman who said to him, "If I catch you doing that once more, I'll kick your ass from here to that door." Jim, after observing him over a three week period and talking to him in short snatches of conversations, thought he was a lonely boy trying to get attention with his antics.

"He's not as crazy as he seems," Jim said. "He talks sense when you show him sympathy. I wanted to know more about him, but he shut up when I tried to probe into his family life."

Govinda was the cult's work-horse. He roamed tirelessly over both terminals and appeared in the most unlikely places, always selling books.

"He's proving himself," Jim said. "You may have noticed that while the devotees generally work in pairs or groups, he works alone. I suspect that if he weren't a Krishna, he would be in trouble. He's found a channel for his frenetic energy, and the temple's structured life may be his salvation."

Jim was good at stopping donations. His dignified appearance, his polite, earnest appeal, inspired belief in the listener. Devotees avoided him. The Glatmans, Moira, the Schmidts, the sisters, and Jim formed the backbone of our vigil.

However, we were not without a skeptic in our ranks. Indirectly, we heard that one of our friends "would not waste his time anymore." He was of the opinion that our efforts were useless; although the vigil "might be good therapy for the Yanoffs, it will not deliver Joey." We were only helping the airport authorities, he asserted, who wanted to be rid of the Krishnas. It was not clear how he came to these conclusions; perhaps he was merely rationalizing his reluctance to help out.

Such talk, however, might spread defeatism and we had to counteract it. On the way to the airport, I carefully explained to our friends the thinking behind the enterprise. I illustrated, with figures, what the normal income for the cult should be and the loss incurred by our presence. "While you have seen weird practices by the devotees," I said, "and heard them say strange things, the Society is a business. Otherwise, it would quickly go under. There are sound business minds in the governing body. Somebody up there is weighing the costs of our vigil in lost revenue and reputation. Our effect is cumulative; at some point the scales will tip in our favor. We are asking for nothing more than the return of our child. We are not threatening their existence or their right to believe as they choose."

Fortunately, there were no other defections; we now had thirty of our friends participating. By then, too, they had new motives for opposing the Krishnas: insults they had suffered, rip-offs they had witnessed, and a conviction they were countering a threat which could strike at any family. The last was voiced by Moira, who had a seventeen-year-old son.

I was driving her home after a morning at the airport. With us was a neighbor, a woman who resided in my co-op apartment complex.

"I think my son doesn't know where he's at," Moira said. "He's dropped out of school and is experimenting with drugs, mostly hash. I sometimes wonder, suppose the Krishnas reached him at this point in his life, when he is vulnerable?"

"It's a worry," I said. "I've just read a book by a Berkeley prof, J. Stillson Judah. His book is called *Hare Krishna and the Counterculture.* He estimates that ninety percent of the devotees have been on drugs in one form or another, and, of those, forty-six percent could be classed as 'heads,' regular users."

"What happened to them when they joined the cult?" Moira asked.

"Judah explains that the drug users in many cases were looking for a religious experience through drugs, something to take them out of this world, which they saw as ugly and evil. When they found they could accomplish that purpose by chanting and ritual, they gave up drugs."

"So, in a way, experimenting with drugs prepares them for the cult?"

"Or, you might say," I replied, "that young people who seek to escape from their problems will use drugs or other means, such as cults."

"I don't know whether I'd rather have my kid on drugs or on Krishna. When I talk to these young devotees, I could cry. I've tried to get through to them, but as soon as I get down to anything personal, they walk away. All they want to talk about is Krishna. I guess they feel safe doing that. At least with my kid I can talk to him and feel I'm getting through to another human being, not to a zombie who repeats what he has been told and who has no ideas of his own."

"If he were in Krishna, you probably wouldn't get to talk to him at all."

"Why not?" she asked.

"They have this dogma of non-attachment to the material world as a pre-condition for Krishna consciousness. The only proper attachment is to Krishna. Any other is off-limits—especially when it comes to family. Family members are classified among the demons who try to take the devotee back to the ugly, material world, the world of maya, illusion. The family being the strongest of all ties, this is the one the Krishnas have to sever to hold on to the kid. There you have the most frightening aspect of the cult, alienation of the child from the family."

"Do you think that is why they refuse to talk about their personal lives, why they talk only Kirshna?"

"It may also mean they feel guilty about it and may find it too painful a subject."

We were nearing her home, and I asked when she could come again. "Count on me for Tuesdays and Fridays," Moira said. "You know, when I started it was to help you. Now I feel I'm doing something for all young people."

One Sunday morning a Krishna photographer, head shaven but dressed in street clothes, came to Building Two, and whenever we confronted a devotee with a prospect, he ran up to snap a picture. Slung over his shoulder was a black box, which I assumed was for recording conversation.

It was a day when the devotees got rough. Athletic Brispati grabbed my Tribune reprint card and flung it across the restroom space, looking at me as if to say, "What are you going to do about that?" I said nothing, but went up to the security office. I had to act promptly or matters would quickly get out of hand. (Later, Ronald told me that Gururama had done the same to him.) Security sent Officer Byrne and his partner to help me find Brispati. He was neither in the spot where I had left him, nor was he to be found in the other building. As we retraced our steps, I finally caught sight of him in the Rotunda. I shouted to the officers, "There he is!" Brispati took to his heels and didn't show up again for several days. Gururama, tipped off, also disappeared.

I guessed that the Krishna photographer was gathering evidence for legal action against us, and my guess was confirmed by the cult's Chicago attorney, Al Cohen, whom I had first met in Federal court in the suit to change the airport's regulations. This time we met him at the police court where three devotees were to be tried: Chandra, for tripping Birgit; Yajnava and Maharaj for soliciting in restricted areas. Cohen asked for a postponement; a new date was set for three weeks later.

"This is par for the course," the arresting officer said as we huddled together. "When they have gotten all the postponements they can, next thing they'll ask for a jury trial—that's another postponement."

"Why do they do that?" Birgit asked.

"To make you sick of coming back again and again, so you'll quit."

"We won't quit," Victor said. "We'll see it through." Joe, the window washer, our main witness, nodded agreement.

"We get criticized," the officer said bitterly, "because we don't stop the rip-offs. What can we do when the judges go along with them? In your case, you live in the city and Joe gets paid by the airport, so he don't lose pay. But see what we're up against with an out-of-towner. Chances are he won't even make a complaint. The Krishnas know it and play the game for all it's worth."

As we left the courthouse, I saw Cohen alone on the way to his car. I followed hoping to get him to intercede with the Krishnas and to find out if he knew anything of their intentions regarding us.

"All I know about your case," he said, "is what I read in the papers." I looked my disbelief. "It's a fact."

"Why do you think they are holding on to my grandson? Is there something we've missed? If you have any suggestions we would appreciate hearing them." He offered none and gave the feeling he wanted to end our conversation. "Sometimes I have ugly thoughts that Joey may have been done away with to hide evidence of their complicity." My anguish must have reached him.

"They're not that kind," he reassured me.

"One of the devotees told me he was dead. Another time, three of the flower-women said I'd never see Joey again."

"You are hounding them," he said coldly.

"But why do they say such things?"

"I don't know."

"We are simply urging people not to give until he is returned."

"You are interrupting them, interfering with their right of free speech. They have sound films to prove it. You may be the subject of a suit."

"We have a right to tell people our story," I insisted. "They employ insults, anti-Semitism, even violence."

"They are not fascists, you know."

"Perhaps not," I said, "but I'd like you to see what they are teaching kids like Joey," and I pulled from my portfolio a page of quotations from Prabhupada. He accepted it.

Before leaving, he said, "You'd better get yourself an attorney."

I assumed that a suit would be filed shortly; a week went by and another, but no papers were served on me. The threat gave me a great deal of concern. A suit would be a drain on our financial resources, and time spent with lawyers and in court would take us away from the airport, slow down our vigil. Without me, the morning shift might not materialize. My worst fears, however, were that my friends would be dragged to court.

On the other hand, I reasoned, there could be a positive side to such a development. Virtue could be made of necessity. The suit would bring more publicity: "Krishnas sue to limit free speech to Joey Yanoff's family." The cult, which had gone to court frequently to defend its First Amendment rights, would now be on the opposite side, trying to restrict ours. We would have the chance before and during the trial to tell the public of the practices we had been witness to; we would recite instance after instance of deception, of money taken under false pretenses, of unwanted books pushed on unwilling victims. Perhaps the exposure would impel the Attorney General of Illinois to conduct an investigation and lead to revocation of the Krishna's license to solicit.

I had noticed that the sect grossly underestimated its income in its public statements. The Evanston temple president told a reporter that for a two-year period beginning November, 1973, the temple collected $250,000 from the sale of books and magazines. Seventy percent of that went for printing, he said; the net for the two years was $75,000. I made my own calculations. I took an average of eleven devotees—eight booksellers and three flower-women—working every day, nine hours. Undisturbed by us, the booksellers could sell eight books each hour at an average price of five dollars. The women could pin twenty flowers at an average donation of one dollar. The total for the day came to $3,420. The books, produced in large runs, I estimated to cost $1.50, the magazines fifteen cents, and the flowers, a nickel; total materials cost, $930. This would give the sect a net daily income of $2,490. Three hundred and fifty days in the year (allowed for the closing of the airport to solicitors for the Thanksgiving and

221

Christmas holidays) yield a net income of $871,500. That was from the airport alone. The temple had forty-two residents— men, women, and a few children—so that the per capita income from this one source was $20,750 annually. Considering the austerity in which they lived, a legitimate question to pose to the public and the court would be: "Where does the money go?" Another question: "What kind of religious group employs one-third of its able-bodied members every day in money-raising?" Still another: "Why did devotees apply for state welfare?"

I realized, of course, that in the event of a court battle, our efforts would have to be increased beyond what was now required. We would need additional help and funds. We had sounded out our business friends, however, and been assured of assistance in the formation of a city-wide support committee. Our struggle would take on new proportions.

During the third week after our courtroom meeting, Cohen visited the airport to see for himself the scene of conflict. I was talking to Bob, a young airport employee, in the main passage-way of Three and did not notice Cohen immediately. Bob was describing a "rip-off" he had witnessed and how he had com-pelled the devotee to "cough up what he took from the sailor."

"Where the hell do you get off with that kind of stuff?" an angry voice interrupted. It was Cohen, bearded, in casual clothes, shirt open at the neck.

"Who the hell are you?" Bob asked.

"Never mind who I am. I heard what you said. That rough stuff don't go. You're infringing on their rights to be here."

"The hell I am. Any time they rip-off a serviceman, I'm going to make it hot and I'd like to see you do anything about it."

"Give me your name," Cohen demanded. "I'll soon show you."

Bob resorted to obscenities; Cohen replied in kind. They shouted, faces close up. "Come on outside," Bob challenged. Cohen appeared willing. I was amazed that he, an attorney, twenty years older than Bob, would engage in a brawl. I was afraid he would be hurt and I tried to cool things. Cohen wouldn't respond; Bob was more compliant to my pleas. A raging Cohen left with a parting shot at me, "You're going to be crushed." I called after him to wait. I wished to explain that Bob was not one of our group, that I had just met him for the first time. He rushed off boiling, without a backward look.

222

27

Letter from Spain

THE WEEK OF NOVEMBER FIRST STARTED WELL
for us. Only five men devotees signed in; our vigil had six. With
that number we were able to man all the key points of both
buildings and compel the Krishnas to cruise where the traffic
was thin. From our positions, we kept them under observation,
intervening when necessary to stop a donation.

It was a bad day for the Krishnas. They were on the run all
morning, most of the time trying to avoid us and without much
success. Airport employees watched delightedly as the young
devotees ran from our "little old ladies."

The other religious cults had gradually taken over Krishna
turf. Foundation Faith, blue-clad faith-healers with names
beginning with "brother" and "sister," dominated the center
areas; the Jesus people, terribly earnest and long-winded, worked
the lounges; and a lone Moonie girl (who wouldn't admit her
affiliation) wandered everywhere wearing a frozen smile and
peddling a long-stemmed plastic flower. But, unlike the Krishnas,
these cults had few solicitors.

Evidence accumulated that the Krishnas were being hurt. No
longer did they register with morning greetings of "Hare
Krishna." They lined up soberly, as for a hard day's work. More
often now, we found them lounging, sometimes dozing, with legs
outstretched. For the first time, too, the women took breaks at the
lunch counters and carried carbonated drinks to their seats. At
such times, I would place myself two rows away content to watch
and rest.

The change showed itself in conversations with devotees. I asked Chandra, as Gopal listened, "Why doesn't ISKCON return my grandson? We don't enjoy coming here any more than you welcome us."

"If I knew where he was," Chandra said, "I would get him and return him to you. But do you know for a fact he is in Krishna?"

I described at some length the circumstances of his disappearance and the pieces of evidence which convinced us he was in Krishna. For the first time, they really listened. Instructed not to say anything to us but "Hare Krishna," the steady deterioration of their position forced them to ask themselves the forbidden question: "How did we get into this mess?" No matter how devoted, they did not like to spin their wheels. Running from our elderly friends, laughed at, ever on the defensive, they must have dreaded the daily confrontations. Nor could they any longer secure respite when we left after our morning shift; the Glatmans and their crew, or Jim Malin and his, took over in the afternoons.

One Sunday night, after an uneventful day when only two devotees appeared at O'Hare, our home phone rang at about 10:30 P.M. When I answered, a man's voice, deliberate, menacing, said, "Don't go near the airport."

"Who is this?" I asked.

"If you value your health and safety, don't go near the airport anymore." He hung up.

I had been warned of such a possibility, but nonetheless I was upset. Late as it was, I phoned Paul Bullock, our attorney, who advised that I notify the police the next morning.

"What about informing the press," I asked. "If we publicize this threat, the Krishnas will be put on the spot and won't dare."

"No," he advised. "You will become the butt of pranksters and kooks. The FBI manual warns against any publicity in such circumstances."

I then called Peter Braun. He was not at home; his wife was shocked at my news. Braun phoned a half-hour later. "They have their crazies," he said. "I'll call the Society tonight to warn them against violence. Such a development will harm everyone concerned." He went on to give me welcome news. "Your vigil is succeeding and there should be a break in the direction you are looking for." He warned, however, I would probably be sued for harassment.

What was one to make of it? On the one hand, we were succeeding; on the other, we were to be sued. Could the phone threat and the suit be last-ditch efforts to scare us off? Next morning I phoned the downtown police headquarters. Asked who I suspected, I told of our vigil and the circumstances which led to it. The officer suggested that, should I receive another call, I was to arrange with a neighbor to phone 911 and ask that the call be traced. "Chances are we won't succeed. These guys are too smart to hang on the line, though it might be worth trying." He urged I watch out for suspicious people and to check my car before entering it.

After the call I left to pick up Rose. I looked carefully to right and left, and, feeling a little foolish, raised the hood of my car to inspect it for "devices." I didn't know what to look for—I guess for anything which looked out of place. When I dropped Rose at the airport entrance, I glanced in my rear-view mirror to see whether I was being followed on the way to the parking lot.

That morning Charvaka also spoke to me menacingly. When he got turned down by a traveler after I intervened in the sales pitch, he smiled slyly at me: "Your goose is cooked."

"What do you mean by that?"

"Chant Hare Krishna," he said and went off.

Strangely, this gave me some comfort. They're talking too much, I realized. They're trying to intimidate me. If they really intended to do something to me, they would shut up.

I watched a TV movie that evening, *Death Wish*. In it Charles Bronson meets violence in the streets of New York with his own brand of counter-violence, a one-man vigilante committee. He knots four rolls of quarters into a stocking to use as a flail. Its effect when smashed into the face of a mugger was made too plain on color film. The next day I went to my bank for four rolls of *nickels* (an adjustment made for my size), placed them into the foot of one of Toby's winter stockings, and did a test swing. I was thrown off balance by the weight. I reduced it to two rolls, knotted the stocking to give me a grip, and kept the contraption in the right-hand pocket of my coat. From then on, whenever I left my house, or my car, my hand reached for the knot-end.

A few days after the threatening phone call, Mukunda came to the airport. Standing in the entrance to the Rotunda conferring with the devotees, he looked every inch the executive in business suit and impeccable black wig. I was twenty feet away observing the Krishnas deferentially greeting him, listening attentively to what he said. He made no acknowledgment of my presence, not even a nod. I played it "cool" too, although I was disappointed. I had hoped he would follow up our discussion of three weeks ago, which then seemed so promising. Looking at him—poised, pleasant-faced, very middle-class, I wondered if he could have ordered the phone threat.

On November 16 only the three flower-women checked in: little Deva, Madhusa, and Saci. When we followed them to Building Three, they left their bags of magazines and flowers outside the women's restroom door and went to a phone booth in the lounge area. The three crowded into one booth, as Madhusa talked into the phone. We wondered what was up. After fifteen minutes they returned, gathered up their belongings and left. I followed for some distance to make certain it was no ruse. This was the first occurrence of it kind, the first time they had left without even attempting to solicit. Before departing ourselves, we arranged with Mary to call me if they returned.

The next morning the same three were back with Maharaj; we had six. The four repeated yesterday's pattern: they phoned the temple and left the airport, not to return.

On the way to the USO lounge, I was stopped by the police officer who had been in court with us. "Yanoff, you'll be interested in this. Five of the men devotees shipped out yesterday."

"Shipped out?"

"Yep. Took a plane for another city. One of them was that little guy, Guru something. I guess they're not much use here."

I could not hide my joy. "How about that! Maybe we have them licked."

At the USO Mary gave me a message to call Toby. Toby was excited. *Tribune* reporter Anne Keegan had called that morning to say that Miriam had called the paper the night before from Barcelona, Spain. Joey was with her, she said, and they wanted to be interviewed in Barcelona. The night reporter had jotted down something of what she said: that she did not appear at the custody suit in Chicago because she did not expect a fair hearing; that she had not been served in Los Angeles with the writ of habeas corpus. She would give the full story, she promised, to the

Tribune's reporter in Spain. The night man, aware that Keegan had done a story on the case, referred the information to her. The *Tribune*, she told Toby, had no reporter in Spain, only a stringer—part-time correspondent—in Madrid, and they were not about to run up expenses for a minor story in Barcelona. If Miriam changed her mind, Keegan said, and submitted to a phone interview, Larry would be contacted for his response.

"What do you make of it, Morris?" Toby asked.

"We've finally smoked her out. The Krishnas must have ordered her to get us off their backs."

"With an interview to the *Tribune?*"

"That's what's crazy about it. We'll have to puzzle it out."

"I'll phone the boys and ask them to be over tonight."

"Do that. We'll have to think it through."

I picked up a *Back to Godhead* and turned to the page listing their temples—there was none in Barcelona.

A month earlier we had received a tip from an American journalist with contacts inside ISKCON that Miriam, Joey, and Lainie were at the Paris temple. When we got over the shock of surprise, we had asked ourselves, "What can we do about it?" We couldn't just fly over to Paris to check it. If Larry walked into the Paris temple to ask for Joey, we knew from experience what would happen. Should he hang around the streets hoping for sight of him? And if he saw Joey, how would he get him home? We had a tip, but what was its practical value? Now, Miriam's call from Barcelona provided a missing part of the puzzle.

That night when our family put our heads together, we concluded Miriam had been sent from Paris to Barcelona because that city had no temple. That way the cult dissociated from her; she probably would deny being in Krishna. She could give the reporter some kind of story of how she got to Barcelona and how she had lived during the last sixteen months. No doubt she would have Joey say he is well and wants to stay with his mother, perhaps send a message to his father to drop the search. The Krishnas, we conjectured, wanted to prove Joey was alive, well, and happy where he was, believing perhaps that this would be enough to make us end our vigil. The face-to-face interview was essential to the scheme because the reporter could meet Joey, take pictures, and hear his wishes from his lips.

If that indeed was the plan, it was naive. We were convinced that Joey would say whatever he was told, just as Miriam would. The effect on us of this maneuver was the opposite of what the cult intended. It confirmed the correctness of our strategy. Miriam came out of hiding because the Society wanted to be rid of us. Well then, it would have to learn that only one thing would do that—Joey's return.

Arriving at the airport the next day, we waited for the other shoe to drop. Two men and four women Krishnas showed up, among them Mukunda's lovely blond wife. Spurred by yesterday's events, Toby had mustered five of our friends for the morning, and the Glatmans and Birgit for afternoon. Overwhelmed, the devotees left early, only Govinda remaining as lookout in case we should depart. If we did, I assumed he would phone the temple and the others would return. That tactic pinned our people to the airport, although they had nothing to do but watch Govinda scampering into the most unlikely places, peeking at us from the mezzanine and making faces when we noticed him.

Woody informed me that the airport would be closed to solicitors for the Thanksgiving traffic, from November 23 through the 29. It was welcome news; we badly needed a rest. The Krishnas, he said, had protested and secured an injunction, but Judge Leighton had ruled in favor of the airport's decision.

The next day, November 19, five devotees signed in. We started out the day with two vigilers and increased to five when several of Larry's friends arrived later in the morning.

"He's a Jew," Maharaj said of me to a black man, "that's why he doesn't want you to read this book." I hadn't heard that for some time.

"But, Maharaj, you're Jewish, too."

"I'm non-denominational; God is the same whatever you call Him."

The other shoe was finally dropped by Miriam on November 24, during our Thanksgiving break from the airport. That day Larry called from school to say he had received a four-page registered letter, postmarked "Barcelona." "It's a long letter; I haven't time to read it to you and it's too complicated to explain. I'll be over right after school."

"Does Miriam say anything about Joey?" Toby wanted to know.

"She writes he's O.K., but I can't tell if he's with her or not. She says nothing about returning him. Most of the letter is an attack against me and a defense of her actions. She says she sent copies to the newspapers, so you may get a call from the *Tribune*."

Three hours later Larry put the letter in our hands. It opened with the following:

I have recently come to learn of your ambitious campaign to defame me and the members of the Krishna Consciousness movement. Having visited some Krishna temples, I have been requested to contact you and give you some news of Joey.

"I had no chance to get an unprejudiced hearing from the court," she wrote in explanation for not appearing at the custody trial in Chicago. Besides, she had been recuperating from surgery. She had watched the attack on Larry on the temple lawn, she said, but justified it because "no one actually knew your identity." She accused him of "racism" against "another minority group for their religious beliefs." At some length she charged Larry with neglect of Joey except for such occasions when he wanted "to show him off."

The kernel of the letter lay in these words: "Joey is now a happy child and doesn't want to return to you," and "Joey has a right to choose his religion, to believe in God." The letter concluded, "I consider myself a devotee of Krishna, of God, and follow all the practices of Krishna Consciousness."

The hard line was disappointing, especially the omission of any proposal for the boy's return, but the fact remained—the cult had instructed her to write. She had offered no explanation for keeping silent for over a year; even now, there was nothing from Joey himself.

Why was the letter written? "I think," Larry offered, "its purpose is to induce us to give up our efforts. They had hoped to do it with a *Tribune* interview; they are trying again with this letter. Much of what she writes has no relation to the truth; it's intended for *Tribune* publicity."

"The Krishnas are saying," Toby added, "that yes, they've got Joey, but he doesn't want to come home, so forget it."

"The Krishnas want us to believe this is Miriam's doing," I said. "They are trying to make a separation between themselves and her."

"But how can they?" Toby asked. "The fact that she is in Barcelona at their expense implicates them. How could she have gotten to Europe without their help?"

"There is a return address on the envelope," Larry pointed out. "Why? The letter asks for no reply." Thinking aloud, he con-

229

tinued, "They're hoping the letter turned us off. And if it doesn't, they want to know why."

"It's the way we figured," I said. "One way or another, they want us out of the airport."

"We still don't know if Joey is with her," Toby said, "or where he is. It's him we want to hear from."

"The thing to do is talk to Joey," Larry said. "It may be difficult for her to refuse to let him talk to me. Why don't I write asking that Joey phone me?"

"That's it," I agreed. "Maybe we'll learn something from him that she is concealing."

"What about the lies in the letter?" Toby asked.

"There's no purpose in answering them," Larry said. "I know Miriam; trying to reply will only raise the heat level. The point is to establish contact with Joey."

"What will you tell him if he calls?" Toby wanted to know.

"That he has to come home, that the court has given me custody."

"It could be a rough phone call, Larry," I warned.

"I know, Dad. They can get him to say anything. I'll tell him, 'Come home and we'll talk,' and I'll tell Miriam that until he's back we will continue at the airport."

The letter went off the next day, Larry suggesting that Miriam and Joey phone Sunday between eight and nine in the morning (midnight Barcelona time), or, if the letter arrived too late, the following Sunday. He added that if there were no call, he would assume her letter was nothing but a ruse to get us out of the airport.

28

Mukunda Comes Through

TUESDAY, NOVEMBER 30, 1976. WE WERE BACK AT THE airport after the Thanksgiving vacation. Six devotees registered: the three flower-women, Maharaj, and, after a long absence, Chandra and Gadapati.

Maharaj was surprised to see me. "Why are you here? Didn't you get the letter?"

I wondered if he had seen a copy. "Yes, we received a letter from Miriam but it doesn't offer to return Joey. That's what this is all about." I quoted from memory sections of the letter to show that both were in ISKCON; from his questions, it appeared he had not read the letter. He left hurriedly for a phone.

Coming out of the Rotunda and entering Building Three, I ran into Deva and then Madhusa. Both asked the same question as Maharaj. Just as we had thought, the cult was counting on the letter as a means of getting rid of us. Both women denied Miriam was in Krishna; they referred to sections of the letter describing Larry's neglect of Joey, but knew nothing of other parts. It appeared that they had been told only what the Society wanted them to know. When Maharaj returned, I informed the three devotees that Larry was writing to the address on the envelope to ask that Joey phone.

"We have a mutual interest," I said. "You want us out of the airport, we want to leave—we are not here for our pleasure. The sooner we get Joey, the sooner we will be gone."

Maharaj asked, "If Joey is returned, will you sue us?"

How they gyrated, I thought. One moment, he wasn't in Krishna, the next, they were worried what would happen if they released him. "We have made our position clear," I said. "You were present, Maharaj, when I told Mukunda that we are not looking for lawsuits but for a child." He listened attentively; a change of attitude had taken place. I said I considered him a leader among the devotees and hoped that through him and Mukunda our position would be made known to those who could effect a solution.

Our conversation over, the devotees conferred among themselves, had a long conversation over the phone, presumably with the temple, and left the airport. When our second shift—Jim Malin and two of his friends—came on at 1:30 P.M., the devotees had not returned. Jim later reported that at 3:15 P.M. the men came back without the women, and, after several encounters, left at 5:30 P.M.; the only one who gave trouble was Chandra.

On the morning of December 1, I was sitting between Jim and Birgit in the courtroom waiting for the case against Chandra to be called. As the airport police had predicted, the sect had asked for a jury trial, which was to take place that day. All the cases against the devotees were up for trial. Thus, quite a few of them, including Mukunda, were in the congested corridor outside the courtroom. Having come from the airport, they were in street clothes. Al Cohen, beard and head of hair looking more unruly than ever, had taken his place. Seated in front of us were two airport police and Joe, the window washer.

While a jury was being sworn in for a case which preceded ours, I tried to occupy my mind by following the proceedings, but it was pulled back to the events of the previous days. Though I had been wrong before—wishful thinking often distorted my judgment—I felt that our long struggle had taken a decisive turn. I had an awful yearning for Joey, to hear once again his special burst of laughter, listen to his stream of questions. Now that I felt the end of our search approaching, my impatience was difficult to bear. The lawyers droned on; the judge spoke barely above a whisper. Birgit fidgeted nervously; Jim looked on placidly. I heard someone calling my name and, looking up, saw Cohen in the aisle motioning to me. I squeezed past Jim and followed Cohen to the rear of the room.

"Mukunda would like to talk to you about getting Joey back," he said as he walked into the corridor. I had a sudden heady rush as I gladly followed to where Mukunda was standing apart from the devotees out in the hall.

232

Mukunda: *(looking serious)* I've been in touch with India until two in the morning trying to get this settled. Prabhupada has intervened, and I think we can bring it to a conclusion. Joey is coming back. But we must have assurances.

Cohen: They are putting themselves in a vulnerable position— you know, that Queens case *(referring to the indictment of the two Krishnas for "unlawful imprisonment" of Merilee Kreshower).*

I: *(trying to remain calm)* I understand. What assurances can we give other than our word?

Cohen: I'm not sure that any document would hold up. *(Any agreement made under duress, while they were holding Joey, could be repudiated by us.)* However, let's get together in my office. I'm free any time of the day or night to work it out.

Mukunda: I would like to get this settled as quickly as possible.

I: What time frame are you thinking of?

Mukunda: This week; maybe the next couple of days, if possible If we're going to do it, let's get it over with.

I: *(restraining my excitement)* We're for that, too.

Mukunda: We still have to work it out with Miriam. We don't want her to think we are acting arbitrarily. But she will do what Prabhupada thinks best. She will come to Evanston with Joey.

I: You know, she said in her letter she is completely devoted to Krishna. Did you read her letter?

Mukunda: I didn't get a copy, but I heard some of it.

Cohen: Will Miriam be able to see Joey?

I: *(cautiously)* We will have to work it out in relation to the custody order. We are concerned for Joey's transition, that it should not be a traumatic experience. We expect to have medical advice.

Mukunda: I could help with that. I know how to speak to devotees; they come to me with all kinds of problems. I have a knowledge of psychology.

I: Your help could be important.

Cohen: You're not going to sue us, are you?

I: You know we have a suit going in Los Angeles. Under certain conditions, we are prepared to vacate, as we told you and the intermediary.

Mukunda and Cohen: Peter?

I: We told him that in return for dropping the suit, Larry wants to recover the monies he paid out for legal and other expenses. We will furnish an itemized list.

Mukunda: You know this has cost us a lot of money.

I: We didn't ask for it; you brought it on yourself. I hope your organization learned something out of all this.

Mukunda: What happened in L.A. was due to individual devotees taking things into their own hands. You can't blame the movement.

I: Bhima was not any individual; he was the president of the temple. He knew Joey's legal status when he swore Joey disappeared.

Mukunda: There are all kinds of people around a temple, especially in L.A. It's loosely arranged, people coming and going; it's hard to keep track.

I: Joey lived in the men's dorm; Miriam in the women's. However, let's get away from all this. It's not our present concern.

Mukunda: I'll call you later in the day to let you know definitely what the arrangements are for Joey's return. I would like you to call off your people from the airport.

I: *(thinking fast, wanting to encourage him, show appreciation for his efforts, yet afraid to let up the pressure)* We'll call off our people for today as a gesture of good faith, but tomorrow's schedule stays until we hear from you.

Cohen: We would like to get your cooperation in securing a continuance of today's trial to early in January. Could you help us on that?

I: I will have to speak to Birgit Schmidt, but I can't do anything about the City's cases against the others.

Cohen: What about Victor Schmidt's case against Yajnava? *(He had threatened to kill Victor.)*

I: He's not here. He must have forgotten, or didn't know he had to appear.

Cohen: He probably didn't understand that when he filed the complaint he's supposed to appear.

I: Wait for me, I'll be back. I'll talk to Birgit.

When I got Birgit and Jim into the hall, I described the conversation I had just had. They beamed with delight. Birgit gave her consent to the postponement; while they waited, I returned to Mukunda and Cohen. I asked Mukunda, "Exactly what will you let me know this afternoon?"

"The time of Joey's arrival and the plane information."

"O.K. With that understanding, I'm going to call the airport now and ask our people to leave. As soon as I get the flight information, I will consult with my family. If things are as you say, that Joey will be back in the next few days, I'm pretty sure we will go along and stay away from the airport."

"I hope to get him here in the next couple of days," Mukunda said.

"Where is Joey now?" I asked.

"I think he is with Miriam in Barcelona."

When Larry came in, he wore a wide smile. It did my heart good to see him like this; he deserved better than what fate had been dealing him. He asked to hear exactly what Mukunda had said and so I described in detail how I had been called out of the courtroom by Cohen and Mukunda's fateful words, "Prabhupada has intervened. Joey is coming back." When I told of Mukunda's desire for "assurances," Larry burst out, "The bastard! He wants assurances? Did he apologize for the lies they told us? Did he explain Prabhupada's letter? Did he show any sign of being sorry for what they did to us?" His eyes glared with hurt and indignation.

"You know," I said softly, "Mukunda is not the main culprit."

"I suppose not," Larry agreed resignedly.

I continued my report of the corridor meeting. When I repeated Mukunda's complaint, "This has cost us a lot of money," Toby exclaimed, "Did he say that?"

"Do you remember," Ron said, "when Mukunda told the *Sun-Times* we were like mosquitoes on a camping trip—we didn't bother him?"

"What about Joey?" Larry asked. "Did he say anything about him?"

"Only that he was with Miriam in Barcelona."

"Nothing else about him?"

"I think that's all he knows."

When I had finished, Larry asked, "What happens now?"

"We wait for Mukunda to phone the flight information. If it's what he said it will be, that Joey will be here in the next few days, I think we ought to suspend our vigil."

"I guess we've got to work with Mukunda. Let me know just as soon as you get the flight information."

Toby and I waited at home for the call which would end our long quest. For once our reasoning had proved correct. To extricate itself from the charge that it was involved with Miriam in a conspiracy to abduct and conceal Joey, the sect had sent her to

Barcelona, had her engage an attorney, and, when the *Tribune* idea failed, write to Larry. Whoever devised the cult's plan for dissociating itself had failed to take account of the catastrophic decline in the revenues of the Evanston temple and the demoralization of its solicitors brought on by our O'Hare vigil. Mukunda, seeing us back at the airport, lost patience with letter writing between Miriam and Larry. Taking the bull by the horns, he went directly to the Swami in India. He must have convinced Prabhupada that our assurances could be relied on. Things were falling into place at last.

No call, however, came from Mukunda; instead, Cohen phoned. Things were moving slower than expected, he said. Calls had been put in to Miriam's Barcelona attorney, but because of the time difference they were unable to reach him; messages had been left for him to call back. Cohen proposed that we meet tomorrow in his office with our attorney and call Barcelona then. Miriam's attorney was concerned about contempt proceedings against her for violating the writ of habeas corpus, and wanted guarantees of immunity from prosecution. My heart sank—something had happened since our courthouse talk.

"What is this business about Miriam's attorney?" I asked indignantly. "There was nothing in our conversation this morning about her attorney."

"Don't worry," he reassured me, "everything Mukunda told you is in force; it's a problem of coordination. There are things to be discussed: should she come straight to Chicago? Who will meet her? How shall her rights be protected?" My anger mounted; they had reneged again. "Whether you believe it or not," he continued, "Mukunda stuck his neck out by going over the heads of the movement in the U.S. Prabhupada has been brought into the picture. Mukunda's risk is my risk. I will see to it that everything is done in the most expeditious, kindest, most reasonable manner. If I get any feeling that I am being used as a front, I won't stand for it."

I could sense what he was angling for and I came down heavily against it: "Since no flight information has been given us, we will be out at O'Hare tomorrow morning."

He flared up: "If you come out Thursday and Friday, Mukunda will be undermined in his position; his word will be worthless."

"I'm sorry about that. We had a clear understanding in the courthouse that if we received the flight data on Joey's arrival, we

236

would consider withdrawing our vigil. We have no such information."

He threatened he was ready to draft legal proceedings against
me for harassment.

"You escalate," I said, "we'll escalate. Don't roil the water." I
was struck with an idea. "Let's have a moratorium on both sides,
then. Neither of us will go to O'Hare."

"We've just had a moratorium for Thanksgiving week," he
protested, and complained of loss of income to the temple, of
police badgering, and the Evanston eviction suit. I suggested he
speak to Mukunda about a moratorium and call me back.

He called three hours later—Mukunda wouldn't buy the moratorium. And so I told Cohen we would be back at O'Hare the next
day. "Two months ago we gave the Society almost three weeks on
the promise they would locate Miriam and Joey; nothing came of
it. Your promises are meaningless, and we will not be sucked into
negotiations over Joey's custody. ISKCON and Miriam are in
violation of the custody order; they are holding Joey illegally.
They have to return him. We are willing to talk to her attorney to
assure him we intend no reprisals. But we will not call off the
vigil."

Cohen granted there had been no talk of Miriam's attorney that
morning, but insisted the movement did not wish to be dragged
into a family dispute. There would be no negotiations over
custody, he promised. Mukunda didn't question our good faith,
but it took time to work things out.

"This morning," I reminded him, "Mukunda was in a great
hurry. He wanted the matter cleared up in a couple of days. What
happened to change that?" I was shouting at Cohen.

There was no answer to that question, nor could there be, from
Cohen. He was not about to tell me that some higher-up had
overridden Mukunda, and was insisting on a more adequate
cover-up of the cult's complicity; that Miriam and her attorney
had to be placed in the up-front role in the process by which Joey
was to be returned.

"Listen, Al. I'll be leaving the house eight-thirty in the morning
for O'Hare. If you or Mukunda call to give me Joey's arrival time,
we'll call it off. If you should have the information later, call my
wife, she'll know how to reach me at the airport."

Cohen did call at eight the next morning, but it was not with the
news I had hoped for. We were to call the Barcelona attorney,
Louis Castillo. "He doesn't speak English, so have a translator

237

present," Cohen advised. "Call him at 10:30 A.M. our time, that's when Miriam will be in the office with him. They want assurances against reprisals." He made no mention of the airport; neither did I.

That morning, the Krishnas registered three men and the veteran flower-women: Madhusa, Saci, and Deva. We had only four, but the devotees looked dejected when they saw us. Though they stayed, they made little effort to peddle their wares. They lounged in the seats and the women visited the soda fountain for pop.

They were friendlier than they ever had been. Perhaps they sensed our confrontations were coming to an end and thus had no stomach to continue the run-and-chase game of the last two months. No doubt they had been given pep talks of how Yanoff would be slapped with a suit and cleaned out of the airport, but when nothing came of it, it must have added to their demoralization.

I can guess why such a suit was never filed. The sect's attorneys may have recognized that the Krishnas' complaint of harassment had little merit. The devotees argued that we interrupted their pitch, which may have been true in some cases, but travelers had not complained. Most were prepared to listen to both sides. That was all we asked for: a chance to speak before a contribution was made. I think, too, the Krishnas were afraid that a court hearing, with the press on hand, would expose their collection methods and the huge sums they gathered. That could prompt an official investigation. They must have decided to keep that can of worms closed.

Chandra, the bad boy of the Krishnas, was unusually friendly. "Did you hear from Bhagavan?"

"Bhagavan?" I had not heard his name before.

"He's the GBC man in France. He would have jurisdiction over this matter." He made no attempt to conceal ISKCON's involvement. Unknowingly, Chandra had just confirmed the rumor that Joey was in France which we had heard some five weeks before. He must have gone with Miriam from Paris to Barcelona.

Yajnava, who had threatened Victor, joined us, contributing the thought that Lainie might be in the Los Angeles gurukula, recently opened when the one in Dallas was closed. Gadapati also came over to chat. Their guard was down and now we were like friendly enemies. I could even sense a certain admiration for us. Did our love for Joey, our willingness to sacrifice for him, find an echo in buried memories of their own parents' love?

Yajnava, without muffling his voice, asked Gadapati, "Are we going back to New York?" Crack collectors, they had been sent to New York when our vigil became effective, so as not to waste their talents. In premature expectation of our leaving O'Hare, they had been returned; now they wondered if it was back to New York again.

Gadapati was especially talkative this morning. Raised in New York, college-educated, he expounded Krishna doctrine: the world was filled with misery—war, overpopulation, hunger, pollution, drugs, violence. The only worthwhile course was to find your spirit soul and unite it with Krishna. Listening, I could only continue to marvel at what a bleak view these young people had of life.

From Gadapati I also learned that Mukunda had been in touch with India on our behalf. "I heard him talk to Jagadisha," he said.

"Jagadisha? I thought he headed up your schools in the U.S.?"

"That's him. He's in India now, Prabhupada's secretary."

Larry called in the afternoon to say he had taken off the morning from classes to go to our attorney's office for the Barcelona phone call. When the call was placed, however, Miriam was not there in her lawyer's office. Attorney Castillo explained she was staying with Joey in a small town outside the city from which transportation was difficult. In this manner we received independent confirmation that Joey was indeed with Miriam. Castillo suggested Larry call the next day at 11:30 A.M. Chicago time when Miriam was certain to be present.

Cohen, however, did talk to Miriam in Castillo's office. He phoned Larry to say all she wanted was his personal assurance that there would be no legal steps against her.

The next morning, Friday, December 13, at 8:15 A.M., Cohen called just as I was about to leave to pick up our friends for the airport. "O.K., here it is," he said. "Joey and Miriam will leave on Air France, Flight 015, departing Paris 10:00 A.M. Wednesday, December 18, arriving Chicago, 4:29 P.M." At last! I closed my eyes, unable to speak. "No call to Spain is necessary."

Even in the midst of my happiness at this news, there was a taste of bitterness. Yesterday, on Cohen's insistence Larry had lost a day's work, the price of a phone call to Barcelona and his

239

attorney's time, to give assurances to Miriam. Now it was taken care of by the cult's attorney; they treated people like puppets.

"Why the delay?" I asked. "Wednesday is almost a week off. Mukunda promised their arrival for this week."

"She has a few things to clear up. We don't have any control over her. What she does in Chicago is not my concern. She'll have to hire another attorney when she gets here. Now, what about the airport?"

"Hold on," I said. "This is not the time-frame Mukunda promised." I was keenly aware that we had avoided extended negotiations by transatlantic phone, only because of our presence at O'Hare.

"Look, I'm sick," Cohen exploded. "I got out of bed to give you this information. Speak to Mukunda; work it out with him." He hung up.

I sat thinking: what should I do? Friends were waiting at this moment to be picked up. It would have been helpful to consult Toby but after a night's insomnia she was fast asleep. The long struggle had taken its toll of her meagre physical resources. Larry, at this hour, was on his way to school. I dialed Mukunda, thinking, "I'll play it by ear."

I began by saying that the date of arrival was not according to our discussion at the courtroom. Mukunda complained he had been up three nights making the arrangements for Joey's return. His temple had been made to suffer for what others had done. A lot of dirt had been thrown at them. "She is going to give the boy back," he assured me. "She may get an attorney to protect her rights but she is giving the boy back. That's the way the arrangement was made."

"When will the boy be turned over?" I asked.

"Immediately on arrival, Wednesday. But please remember, something will have to be worked out. Joey is a devotee; he eats no meat, he wants to chant, he will want to visit the temple. Of course, it will depend on him. We want to help." He suggested meeting after their arrival in a quiet place at the airport to discuss these matters. He had given thought to the details of the transfer. He seemed sincere.

"Perhaps we can get a room at the airport hotel," I said. He thought that was a good idea.

"We have no intention of doing anything phony."

"I'm noting down what you're saying," I cautioned him.

"Go ahead," he urged. "I'm known as 'Honest Mukunda.' A meeting will be arranged as soon as Cohen feels well, probably Sunday. Joey's needs can be discussed as well as matters relating to the press, ISKCON's position in Chicago, and so on. We want to look good in Chicago."

I wound up agreeing to stay away from the airport until Wednesday. I phoned our friends with the news; they were gleeful, sharing my feeling of victory. Still, I had to sound a sober note. "They've reneged before; they may again."

"We'll be back again," Rose said, and I could have kissed her.

Still, I was in doubt about the correctness of my decision. From the pattern of negotiations so far it was clear that only when we were at the airport did the Krishnas move. When we stayed away, the sect and its attorney found obstacles and reasons for delay. In agreeing to Mukunda's appeal, I was relying on instinct, a feeling that we had to cooperate with him. We did not know the nature of the opposition he faced. Perhaps some of the Krishna leaders were prepared to hang on until we tired. They might fear Joey's return more than the effect of our vigil. Mukunda had finally reached Prabhupada and was able, as a result, to promise Joey's return "in a couple of days." I knew he was sincere; I could see it in everything he said and the way he said it. And yet, though Mukunda was our best hope, there were still others powerful enough to thwart all our well-laid plans.

29

Home at Last

SUNDAY EVENING LARRY AND I WERE TO MEET IN Larry's apartment with Paul Bullock, our attorney, and Krishna lawyer, Al Cohen. We planned to discuss Joey's return, assurances of non-reprisal against the cult, and handling of the news media. As Bullock was late, we chatted with Cohen and found we had things in common: our concern for civil rights of minorities; our views on politics.

Larry and I first met Paul Bullock more than two months before at the offices of a large, downtown law firm. A close friend suggested that we might be missing some legal angle for making it hot for the Society. If such an angle were available, Bullock's firm, with specialists in every field, would find it. Sure enough, at an exploratory session, Bullock, an expert in criminal law, proposed that we get the State's attorney to accept our case as kidnapping, naming the Society as accomplice. "A case like yours," Paul said, "will get a lot of publicity and help induce the State's attorney to accept it." We, however, decided against that route because of the cost and the chances of failure. Besides, we were depending on our airport vigil.

When Bullock arrived, Cohen began with a simple statement of great meaning for us: "Joey is coming back to you regardless of the outcome of our talks tonight. He will be back Wednesday." Larry thanked him, adding that if they kept their promises, they could be certain we would do all we had agreed to.

Cohen expressed misgivings to the transfer taking place at the airport. "It's too public; the press may latch on to it. You never know how this stuff leaks out." Throughout our negotiations that evening, he showed extreme sensitivity to information of Joey's return leaking to the media. Cohen proposed that Mukunda and he meet the plane, explain to Miriam and Joey the arrangements, and he bring Joey from the airport to Larry's apartment. Convinced of his good intentions, we accepted.

He brought up the matter of reprisals against Miriam—she had violated a court order and could be held in contempt and jailed. Larry said, "I am a teacher of emotionally disturbed children. I am dedicated to help such people. Do you think I would add to Miriam's problems? We will not prosecute her."

The last item on our agenda was concerned with the news media. Cohen wanted our silence: there could be nothing given to the press except perhaps the bare announcement that Joey was back. He indicated that our attitude on this question would affect negotiations with Los Angeles on a settlement, referring to our damage suit. He objected particularly to mention of our activity at O'Hare: "It gives people the idea they can get anything they want by doing the same; for that matter, that any group can be subject to the same treatment." He wanted no report that Joey had been in their French temple.

Larry voiced objections; we would not lie, we had a responsibility to tell the truth to the people who helped us, and to victim families with whom we had been in touch. Since we could reach no agreement on this point, we settled instead on a temporary solution: for seven days after Joey's return, we would say only that he was back and refer all other questions to our attorney. After Joey's return, we would discuss the issue again.

There was no attempt to put our agreement in writing; both attorneys said that by its nature it had no force except good faith. When Cohen took his leave, there were cordial handshakes; we had been brought close. Afterward, Bullock told us that the seven days would give us a chance to become reacquainted with Joey and give direction to subsequent negotiations, not only with treatment of the news media, but with regard to Miriam's visitation rights and Joey's spiritual needs.

"Paul," Larry said, "what do we do about Peter Scarlatt? I haven't yet told him about the new developments."

"I know Peter pretty well," Paul said. "I think it would be better to go ahead without him. There is nothing he can contribute in this situation. You're getting your boy back on your own. Scarlatt should be happy to hold on to the five thousand you gave him."

When we were alone, Larry and I relaxed in a glow of contentment. Though there was still a long way to go, for the moment we felt good. We were getting Joey back, not by snatching him or through a sheriff's order, but with the cooperation (true, under pressure) of those who had been involved in hiding him. This was the best ground on which to restore the boy to normal life.

Though it was late when I got home, Ronald and Toby were waiting. "Joey is coming home Wednesday!" I shouted.

"Whoopee!" Ronald yelled.

Toby's eyes were wet. "Our little boy is coming home," she murmured with a tenderness so long withheld from its object. "Tell us everything that happened tonight."

When I finished, Ronald said, "We've got to give him a 'welcome home' party. Larry will bring him here, won't he?"

"Of course. His plane arrives at about four-thirty. Cohen and Mukunda will be talking to them for a while, and there's the trip from the airport. They should be at Larry's by six or so. I would say seven-thirty or eight, here."

"Why don't I make a streamer to go over the table," Ron suggested. "How about, 'Welcome home, Joey. We love you.'?"

"I don't know," I said doubtfully. "We're kind of feeling our way. Maybe it should be low-key the first time, until we know him better. He will have changed. He may even be hostile."

"Still," Ron said, "we shouldn't hide our feelings for him."

"What about food," Toby interrupted. "We must get the things he is allowed to eat."

"We know what he cannot eat," I said, "everything else, he can."

"How simple you make it, Morris," she said impatiently. "Joey mentioned a cookbook. I have an idea. Morris, why don't you stop off at the temple and get one of their cookbooks?"

"Oh, come on," I said indignantly. "I can just picture myself asking someone like Saci—she's the one who said I should be smashed—'Good evening, Saci. Do you happen to have a Krishna cookbook?'"

"If you give her a donation, why not?" Ronald laughed.

"Well," Toby said, "I'll work out something, I wonder how well they fed him?"

"We'll soon see for ourselves," I said.

244

Two days later the boom fell. Larry received a call from Larry Berg, the child custody specialist in Bullock's law firm, that Joey was not coming Wednesday. Berg had been contacted by Miriam's newly retained Chicago attorney, Phil Seeman, who had ordered her not to come to Chicago until he had an opportunity to study the records of divorce and custody. Seeman said Friday rather than Wednesday was the day of her arrival. We didn't believe him; we didn't know what to believe. Our bitterness was overwhelming.

I was convinced Cohen had not deceived us on Sunday evening. He must have been overruled, just as Mukunda had been earlier. Whoever was calling the shots must feel the cult was still too exposed. At the Sunday meeting we had balked at the demand for media silence. Some powerful Krishna must have said to himself, "What happens after seven days? The Yanoffs can blast us then. With Joey back, our bargaining chip is gone. Furthermore, an agreement between the Yanoffs and ISKCON's Chicago attorney confirms our involvement. Miriam and her attorney must be brought front and center."

Cohen called to urge we not go back to the airport. He claimed to have warned us all along that he could not speak for Miriam; in fact, he had wanted to postpone our Sunday meeting so that she could have her attorney present. He insisted ISKCON wanted to keep the agreement, but felt we were blackmailing the Society over what was essentially a family matter.

"Who got Miriam her Chicago attorney?" I wanted to know. Cohen admitted that he had. I was frustrated and angry: "Who is paying him? Who gives her money to go abroad, to travel to Barcelona, to hire an attorney in Spain, to bring her here?"

"How should I know?" he replied peevishly. "I haven't done anything to betray you," he insisted. "The agreement we made Sunday is O.K. All we want is for her attorney to make his input."

"Let me speak frankly, Al. You were sincere on Sunday and intended to keep the agreement, but someone who calls the shots in ISKCON repudiated it. In view of the circumstances, we will resume our vigil."

He was indignant at "this kind of pressure," and again threatened to sue. I told him if he challenged our First Amendment rights to tell our story, we would organize a city-wide defense committee to fight the suit. "I think you will be sorry you escalated the conflict," I added. He protested he was not challenging our right to speak, only the way we were doing it.

The next morning we had six people at O'Hare; there were no Krishnas—the first time it had happened. At the sign-in table Woody shook his head in disbelief. "They had fifteen yesterday when you were away. What's going on?" I told him why we had stayed away the last four days, and why we returned. "You just can't trust them," he said.

Mukunda called that evening to urge we not go to the airport. "We at ISKCON don't control Miriam," he said. "She is not a robot; she is an independent person."

"Isn't she a devotee?" I asked.

"Yes, but we can't force her to do anything; she is coming to Chicago of her own free will. Seeman is representing her." Then he assured me, "Joey is coming back to you."

Wasn't he aware of the contradiction? Miriam had held on to Joey for sixteen months without a word to us. What prompted her to return him now, if not ISKCON's orders?

"If Seeman gave you a date for Joey's return," he continued, "would you call off your action at O'Hare?"

"No," I said angrily, "we are staying this time until we see Joey." I blamed the Society for the broken agreement, not him or Cohen. I recalled the many deceptions practiced on us. "Your GBC representatives, Drupada and Pandu, continued to the end saying they did not know where Joey was."

The following day, a Thursday, again no devotee appeared at the airport. On Friday, however, four women and two men signed in. When they saw us, the women gathered up their bundles to leave. As they were walking toward the exit, I stopped Madhusa. "Do you know why we came back?"

"No," she said.

"Don't they tell you?"

"We are devotees," she said simply, "and do as we're told."

"Would you like to know what happened?" Since she made no move to leave, I told of Sunday's arrangements for Joey's return, of the preparations made by Toby to have the kind of food Joey was allowed, and of our bitter disappointment. She listened without comment, but when she joined Saci, they were in animated conversation.

Seeman, I assume after conferring with Miriam, submitted to Berg a list of conditions for Joey's return. Berg called to discuss them with Larry: Joey was to live with Larry but spend weekends with Miriam at the Evanston temple; he could have contact with her at any time by phone or letter; he was to be permitted to keep his diet and practice his religion at home; he was to be kept from school but have a private tutor; there were to be no press attacks against Miriam or ISKCON; the vigil was to be terminated and all legal action dropped (a reference to Larry's suit in California). Lastly, Miriam could initiate litigation over legal custody. In effect, the conditions gave Larry temporary hold of his son, isolated him from his peers by keeping him from school, ensured the sect's continued domination over him while Miriam contested the order which gave Larry custody. No doubt she depended on Joey (until he could be reintegrated into normal life) to tell a judge he wanted to be with his mother in Krishna.

We had done serious thinking after the failure of the Sunday agreement with Cohen and came to the conclusion that if the cooperation of the cult was to be secured, we would have to keep press silence. This, above all, was what ISKCON wanted. With attacks against them on the East and West coasts (the Shapiro-Kreshower and Robin George cases), a fresh press assault in the Midwest on an issue for which they had no adequate defense would be more than they could handle. Analyzing the Sunday meeting, Larry and I realized we had overreached in withholding a pledge of press silence. After all, we could inform our friends and the families of victims by phone or letter. The other "musts" were an end to our vigil and immunity for Miriam. As to Joey's future, we were in the dark as to his needs. We assumed he was deep in Krishna beliefs and, if we wished his cooperation, we had to make allowance for his practice of the cult's rituals and visits to the temple. If, however, Joey were to be brought once again into the mainstream, he had to be introduced to the usual experiences and associations of a boy of his age. These became our guiding principles in negotiations for his return.

Replying to Seeman's list of conditions, Larry refused to disturb the custody order, he agreed to Joey's right to observe religious rites including temple visits, agreed to press silence, to vacate the airport, and refrain from suing Miriam. However, he would not drop the suit against ISKCON and insisted that Joey attend school.

At Berg's insistence, "because negotiations were proceeding sincerely," we stayed out of O'Hare on Saturday, December 11. In return, Seeman promised to give Berg the flight information for Miriam's arrival, which he now set for "Sunday or Monday,"

247

although an earlier commitment had been for Friday. One of our difficulties was to educate our attorneys in Krishna promises; like us, they accepted them at face value. Seeman promised to phone the exact flight information later in the day. When he did phone, he reported to Berg he had failed to reach Miriam and therefore did not have the flight time. We told Berg we were going back to the airport and this time he agreed with us; he had learned quickly.

When Cohen heard through Seeman of our decision, he phoned Larry in a blazing fury, threatening immediate initiation of a suit and that he, personally, would instruct Miriam not to come to Chicago. "Besides," he said, "the schedule calls for her to come Wednesday, not Sunday or Monday. But if you don't vacate O'Hare at once, she will not come and it will be your fault." So, while Seeman, Miriam's attorney, could not reach her, Cohen, the Krishna lawyer, did. In the cult's name, he could instruct her what to do, contrary to the statement made to me that once her attorney was appointed, he, Cohen, was through. Like a yo-yo, the sect intervened when its interests were at stake and it pulled back when its complicity in hiding Joey became too apparent. At such times it would declare Miriam independent. If asked, I'm sure Miriam would have put it as simply as Madhusa, "We are devotees and do as we're told."

Larry had kept the teachers at his school informed all along of developments. Several had participated in our vigil and shared our joy at news of Joey's imminent return. When they heard of the Krishnas' broken promise, they arranged to cover the airport in their spare time. That Sunday, the seven devotees who came to the airport were shadowed by an equal number of teachers.

On Monday, before I left for the airport, I received a call from Cohen. "Do you have pencil and paper?" Oh, my God, I thought, not again. "Here it is: Miriam and Joey are coming from New York under the name of 'Jefferson' on American Airlines, Wednesday, arriving eleven in the morning."

"What are you trying to do," I burst out, "drive us crazy?"

"Larry promised that as soon as you knew the flight information, you would quit the airport," he replied.

I asked if Joey was being turned over to us at the airport. He said that arrangements were being worked out by Seeman. I made no promise to Cohen about the airport. I consulted with Larry and called Bullock, instructing him to work out an

248

acceptable agreement along the lines laid out by us. If it was obtained, he was to call me at the airport. Soon after eleven, Berg, not Bullock, called to tell me that Seeman and Cohen (he was back in the act) wanted a court-sanctioned agreement. That, said Berg, meant delay and the probability that the court would not approve an agreement made under these circumstances. Berg explained what I already knew: the Krishnas and Miriam were holding Joey illegally and any agreement with conditions was invalid and in the nature of blackmail. Berg advised we turn it down and go ahead with our vigil.

Out of curiosity I asked Herb Delafield to check the flight information Cohen had given me that morning. He did, and reported that no "Jefferson" was listed on either of two American flights from New York to Chicago arriving at the time Cohen specified.

Larry heard from Berg that a new condition had been added by Seeman: that Joey be permitted to spend summers at the cult's farm-temple south of Paris. It was an indirect admission that he had been hidden there and not in Paris. Larry and I decided not to reply to the new proposal but to insist that all conditions be laid on the line with a definite date for Joey's return. We would then give our answer.

Larry and I discussed whether we ought to treat as binding an agreement made before Joey's return. I wondered whether we should take the attitude the law takes toward a criminal holding a hostage: make any promise you must to save the hostage but don't feel obliged to carry it out. Larry found it difficult to think in such terms; he tended to react to demands according to his ability and willingness to fulfill them.

Our attorneys suggested a criminal conspiracy suit against the cult; they were outraged that a religious society would bargain a child for immunity from public exposure. We would have liked to follow their recommendation but refrained for two reasons: the cost, which already was more than Larry could bear, and our belief that the cult would have to come to terms sooner or later.

On Thursday, December 16, 1976, notice was given that the airport would be closed to solicitors for the Christmas holidays from December 17 to January 4. To make an impression on the Krishnas which would last through the holidays, Toby scheduled three shifts for that day: our retiree friends for morning and afternoon, Larry and his friends in the evening. She also called Doris to ask her to organize a vigil at Balboa Park in San Diego, an important collection point for the cult.

When the devotees caught sight of us that morning, the women left; Maharaj and Govinda stayed. When I met Maharaj, I asked, "What's been happening?" My question was a general one, since I hadn't seen him in four days.

"Ask Phil," he replied.

"Phil?"

"Phil Seeman." Before I could question him further, he walked off. So Seeman was on first name terms with the devotees. I wondered if he had worked for the cult, or for Cohen, before he became Miram's "independent" attorney.

In the evening, I learned what Maharaj had meant. Berg relayed Seeman's complete proposal to Larry:

1. Joey will be brought to Larry's home Wednesday, December 22, at 5:00 P.M.

2. Miriam will pick him up Friday evenings and return him Sunday evening, an arrangement to last to February 15, when she will return to France.

3. Joey will spend July and August at the French farm-temple.

4. Joey will consult a psychiatrist twice a month.

5. Neither Larry nor his family will release anything to the news media about Joey's return.

6. Joey will be permitted to practice his religion at home, including chanting and following his diet.

7. Miriam will have the right to talk to Joey by phone and to correspond with him.

8. No public school for Joey until September, 1977.

9. No legal action against Miriam.

10. No action against the Krishnas at O'Hare.

It was our attorneys' judgment that the agreement was not enforceable by law; they urged its acceptance to get Joey home. Larry told them to proceed.

The days which followed were most difficult to bear. Would the new agreement be kept? What would Joey be like? Would he hate us for forcing his return? If so, what would it be like living with a hostile child? Would our long travail be a prelude to something worse?

When Wednesday evening came at last, Toby, Ronald, and I sat by the phone waiting for Larry's call. At 5:30 P.M. we were beside ourselves with anxiety and called him.

"Joey just came in a few minutes ago," Larry said happily. "Yes, yes; he's O.K., he looks fine. Miriam and Mukunda's wife brought him. No, no problems; everything went smoothly. They are explaining his diet. I'll be over with him as soon as they leave."

Half an hour later the doorbell rang. Standing there when we opened the door was Joey! He was two inches taller, hair closely cropped but not shaven and with pigtail on top. He wore street clothes, and aside from the beads around his neck, he looked much the same as when I had put him on the plane to Los Angeles so long, long ago. We hugged. Though his manner was warm, animated, I noticed his rapid eye-blinking, a sign with him of anxiety. While we watched him hungrily, he explored the house.

"This is a new picture," he remarked on seeing one of Ronald's graphics. "These are new dining room chairs."

"And we have a new table," I said, "which opens for twelve; something Bubbie wanted for years."

After his exploration, made perhaps to cover his unease, he sat with us at the table and talked.

"Did you go to India?" I asked.

"No."

"But you had a passport to go there."

"I was told I couldn't go because my father came with cameras to the Los Angeles temple. My mother and I went to New York for awhile and then to Boston."

We all had so many questions that we began chiming in one after another.

"When did you get to France?" I asked.

"In March, I think."

Larry wanted to know: "Did you see Paris? That's a beautiful city."

"Only for a couple of weeks altogether," Joey said ruefully. "We went there on visits from the farm. I went once to see a doctor."

Toby was immediately concerned. "What was wrong with you?"

"My allergy came back when I was in Barcelona. I was all right on the farm, though. The air was clean there."

"What did the doctor do for you?" Toby asked, still not satisfied.

"He told me to take four herbs all at the same time. They were from Switzerland." Joey giggled as he added, "But only three came and the three couldn't work without the fourth. He was a quack."

"Then why did you go to him?" Larry asked.

Joey laughed. "Bhagavan—he's the head of the movement in France—sent us to him. Bhagavan believes in herbs."

"Where is Lainie?"

"We left her at the farm."

"Alone?" Toby said quickly.

"The devotees will take care of her until my mother comes back."

"How did Lainie get to France?" Toby wanted to know.

"The devotees brought her. She came after we were there awhile."

When Joey had loosened up a bit more, he began describing his life at Chateau d'Oublaise, a farm about one hundred and twenty miles south of Paris. It was an old building on two hundred acres of farmland and forest. There were shopping trips to the provincial center at Chateauroux and to the nearby town of Lucay le Male; but these were few. For the most part, the Krishnas kept to themselves.

Joey estimated there were about a hundred poeple living on the farm, many of them children; forty of these, Americans. (How many, I wondered, were being hidden from parents?) Joey's best friend in Krishna was Aseshe, a boy of fourteen of Spanish-French parentage; he spoke English and was the only boy of Joey's age. Joey had gone to classes, but did not describe what was taught. He told us he helped grow flowers for the deities and complained of the cold in the poorly heated chateau as well as the icy morning showers the children had to take. Laughing, he told a funny story of a reluctant horse who couldn't be made to work, and had us laughing joyfully with him.

We listened and we looked at him lovingly. Joey seemed the same affectionate child as before. If he felt resentful at having been forced to come home, he wasn't showing it. Still, there would be changes in him that were not yet apparent to us. Only time will tell, I thought. But for now he was home again—home at last!

Epilogue

JOEY'S SAVING VIRTUE WAS A ZEST FOR LIFE; WE depended on it to bring him back into the mainstream. From an early age, his curiosity and inventiveness were boundless. As a three-year-old he used to lug heavy volumes of the World Book encyclopedia from the shelf to thumb through for pictures, asking "What does it say?" He liked to close himself into our catch-all closet and rig up Rube Goldberg contraptions from mops, tools, whatever. Given a choice of entertainment, he would most likely pick the Museum of Science and Industry—the "push-button museum," he called it, because many exhibits were set in motion that way. Whenever I took him there, Joey would lead me unerringly through the maze of halls to those exhibits he wished to visit for the umpteenth time. Could a mind like his be shackled to hours-long chanting and Prabhupada's expositions of ancient Vedic texts?

He had not gone to the cult to escape misery or boredom or, like many of the devotees, to replace drugs with a new high in Krishna consciousness. He was brought in by his mother with the help of the sect. Miriam probably thought she was saving Joey from the "wheel of birth, disease, old age, and death." Perhaps, too, she wished to show her dedication by giving the cult her only son.

To restore Joey, we counted on the very things which made him a happy child before he disappeared—school, friends, family, and the round of activities of a boy of his age. The sect, on the other hand, held him by a strict regime of chanting, cult diet, rituals before the deities (three doll-like figures on his dresser), and weekend visits to the Evanston temple where Mukunda gave him

253

special attention. Miriam, who had moved to the New York temple with Lainie, phoned him daily to check on his spiritual obligations. Occasionally, she mailed packages of temple food and fresh costumes for the deities.

It became apparent, too, that he had been prepared to resist "deprogramming." Seeing Ted Patrick's book on my desk one day, he said, "He deprogrammed twenty-four devotees, but twenty came back." Another time, he asked for the Bible, found the Ten Commandments, pointed to "Thou shalt not kill" and said, "You kill cows." "But Joey," I protested, "that commandment applies to humans, not animals. The Jews of that time sacrificed animals on their altars."

We welcomed discussion, convinced it was the best way to get him to think for himself. But now and then we came up against a side of him which was very distressing. In one instance, he and I were watching the early evening news about two months after his return, when a picture was flashed of a terrible elevated train accident in the Loop.

"I'm a little worried," I said to Joey. "Your father is visiting that part of town and would be coming home just around this time."

"There is nothing that can be done about it," he said matter-of-factly. "It's a person's karma which will decide if he will die at that moment." How far, I thought, he has strayed from our ways of thinking.

On another occasion I suggested that when Joey next visited the dentist, he should inquire into a new chemical treatment supposed to make teeth decay-resistant. Joey said flatly that he wanted no chemical and when Larry described the method, he broke in, "I don't have any cavities and I won't get any."

"How can you be so sure?" Toby asked.

"I refuse to discuss it," he said angrily and offered to finish his dinner in another room. Such arrogance was new to us—and upsetting—but I guessed what prompted Joey's reaction. The cult taught that *prasadam*, food first offered to Krishna, immunized the body against disease. It pained us that Joey accepted such crude superstitions.

We made more progress by avoiding confrontations. He would not eat at the same table with us because we served meat. Without debate, at his suggestion, we put up a bridge-table alongside ours from where he could take part in our conversation, something he would not miss. Several months later he joined us at the family table, but stuck to his diet of vegetables, fruit, nuts, and certain dairy products like yogurt. Before eating, he politely requested silence while he bowed his head before a portrait of Prabhupada torn from *Back to Godhead*, and made his "offering" to Krishna in Sanskrit. Patiently, we waited without comment for him to finish.

In keeping with temple custom, Joey slept on the floor. When he spent a night at our house, instead of the spare-room he had always used, he asked if he could place his pallet next to my bed. Taking it as a show of affection, I was pleased.

One Wednesday morning soon after his return, he phoned me. "Grandpa, could you come over and stay with me?" This was the first time he had ever made such a request. With Larry at work, he was alone, thrown on his own resources. He was in limbo—not at the temple, except for weekends, nor yet at school. He had been separated from his Krishna friends, but had no new ones. "Frivolous sports," including all games and TV, were forbidden him because his thoughts must be fixed on Krishna. Poor kid, I thought, as I sped to him on my bike, what a rough time he's going through.

Larry rejected Miriam's request that Joey be given a private tutor. Aside from its prohibitive cost, Larry wanted the boy to be among other children. Joey expressed fears that he would be made fun of, but they were allayed by placing him in a small, local private school whose teachers assured him there would be no difficulties.

Some school situations, however, could not be avoided. Once, asked to join his class for a symphony concert, Joey, trained to shun "sense gratification," refused. But how do you turn away a schoolmate who throws a basketball at you, saying, "Let's play, Joey." It wasn't long after that he invited his father to see his team play a rival school.

In spite of bars against relations with non-devotees, he resumed old friendships with a twelve-year-old girl who lived on his street, and with his best chum, Kyle. He also made friends at school and relished telling us of the puppy romances in his classroom. Though Joey was disdainful of these innocent forms of "illicit sex," we heard about them in detail.

He was reintegrating along many lines. Formerly he had enjoyed TV programs such as Sesame Street. At first, Larry saw him merely stealing glances at the forbidden screen, but gradually the viewing habit returned. "Sense gratification" not withstanding, when he saw his old bicycle in my basement, he inflated the tires and rode off. Taken to the zoo, he trotted around happily revisiting its familiar occupants. In a dozen ways, the threads of his former life slowly reknitted themselves.

On a Sunday evening, five months after his return, when Larry went to pick up Joey at the temple, he found the boy's head shaved, with only a clump of hair left on top. Larry angrily protested to Mukunda, who tried to make light of the matter.

"How do you think Joey's classmates will treat him when they see this?" Larry demanded. "What are you trying to do?"

"Joey asked for the haircut," Mukunda said.

"Even if he had, I should have been consulted."

On the way home, Larry made plain to Joey the purpose of the maneuver. "They want me to punish you and make you hate me. They want the kids in your school to make fun of you so you will want to leave it. I don't trust the Krishnas. I don't think you should go to the temple anymore. Think about it and we'll discuss it again before next Sunday."

Two days later, substituting for Larry, I picked up Joey at school. The principal told me Joey had asked permission to wear a hat in class to cover his shaved head. She assured him it wasn't necessary, that the children would understand. When I asked him what happened, he said, "Only two kids laughed at me."

Deprived for so long of movies, Joey asked Larry if they could see a science-fiction film the following Saturday. On the way home, he asked Larry whether he would be going to the temple in the morning. "How can I let you go," Larry asked, "when I don't trust the Krishnas? I heard that they talk against our family, against me, that I teach you sex." Joey appeared undisturbed and did not pursue the discussion. The two spent Sunday at the Adler Planetarium, another favorite of Joey's.

When a second Sunday went by without his attendance at the temple, Miriam called him. Joey was upset afterwards, but even got over that rather quickly. Two days later, Berg, Larry's attorney, called to say that Phil Seeman, Miriam's lawyer, was charging violation of the agreement and threatened to sue. Berg asked Larry to come to his office. The next afternoon I met with Larry in his high school lunchroom. He looked worried.

"Dad, I now owe our attorneys several thousand dollars. I don't know how long it will take me to pay them off. They charge $70 an hour for each attorney's time. If I have a meeting, the bill can run up to $500."

I was shocked. "That's a lot of money."

"Every time Seeman calls Berg, it's added to my bill. If it should come to a court case, can you imagine the cost? Yet, we can't send the kid back to the temple."

"Does Joey know what's up?"

"I told him. He hates to see trouble on his account. As far as I can see, he wants to leave things alone. From what he told me about his temple visits, he spends much of the time in the kitchen. He skips their classes; they bore him. Some Sundays he's been late because he chooses to watch TV before he goes."

"I've been doing some thinking," I said. "Mukunda doesn't want us back at the airport. I believe he'll tell Seeman to drop the idea of a suit."

"Do you think our friends will want to go to the airport again?"

"We'll cross that bridge when we come to it."

I had several phone conversations with Mukunda. We would defend ourselves in court if we had to, I told him, but we would be at the airport the day Seeman filed suit.

"You're trying to blackmail us," he exclaimed. "Phil Seeman is not our lawyer; he's Miriam's."

"Who's paying him?"

"He's doing it for free." I let that pass without comment. "You control the situation, Mukunda. You're temple president. This time you can't say it happened in Los Angeles."

"I don't control Miriam. She's the one who wants the boy back in the temple."

"You can tell her you don't want trouble in your temple."

"I promise you," he said, "and you can tell your son, there will be no more incidents like the hair-cutting. Mahapad did it whimsically without my permission." He had forgotten he had told Larry that Joey asked for it. He extolled the sect's virtues at length and said, "One day your son will realize Joey's devotion to Krishna and let him go."

Angered by his words, I said, "Mukunda, your Society, without the consent of his father, initiated a twelve-year-old child with vows to become a celibate monk for life. Why don't you let him grow up and make his decision when he is mature enough."

257

"In the meantime, though, he should come to the temple on Sundays."

"My son doesn't trust you guys." We went round and round repeating ourselves, Mukunda persisting in his position.

A week passed, and another, but on July 2, Berg phoned that Seeman had delivered to him a copy of the petition he would be filing in court on Thursday, July 7. On Tuesday, I drove to the airport to look around. I found Deva and Madhusa in Building Three pinning carnations; they were surprised to see me. "We're coming back to the airport," I announced and told them why. I went on to Building Two, but seeing no Krishnas, went to the USO lounge to visit Mary. We embraced warmly. She told me of the current pattern of Krishna activity. "There's no one to stop them now," she mourned. "Still I hope things work out for you and you don't have to return." I retraced my steps and ran into Gopal with three others who, he said, were from the Minneapolis temple. I told him the reason for my visit: "We'll be back here Thursday when Seeman files."

On Thursday, Larry called—jubilant. "Berg just phoned that Seeman is delaying filing for a few weeks because Miriam is worried about the effect of a court case on Joey."

"They've backed down!" I cried.

When at the end of the first year of Joey's return, my seventieth birthday rolled around, my sons organized a celebration at Larry's new home, the first he had owned. They planned a sing-along, the songs relating to epochs of my life, for example, "Union Maid" for my marriage to Toby.

To prepare for the occasion, the men of the family gathered around my desk one evening to write a script to go with the songs, each to be introduced by a vignette from my life. When Joey was critical of our efforts, Ronald said in exasperation, "Maybe *you'd* like to be emcee?" "Why not?" Joey replied. And so it was.

The following Friday, Ronald brought a draft of the invitation. For the place of the celebration, he had written, "Larry's house." When Joey suggested, "Make it Larry's and Joey's house," we all were delighted.

The evening of the affair, guests overflowed from the large, octogonal living room into the foyer and dining room. Ronald on banjo and Larry on guitar led the singing. Joey, script in hand, stood on a low platform prefacing each segment with the phrase,

"And now our hero..." He was poised; ad-libbed when necessary. Toby and I faced the room filled with our friends, many of whom had taken part in the airport vigil. I thought I saw tears in the eyes of some; they had caught the drama of the moment—the lost one had really come home. At the end, they sang a rousing tune to Ronald's words:

> As sure as his own name is Morris,
> Let everyone join in this chorus.
> Raise your voices on high
> For one hell-of-a-guy,
> The champion crusader, Morris.

A year later, Larry remarried. When the list of those who wished to toast the bride and groom was prepared, to our surprise, Joey asked to be included. As he raised his glass of ginger ale, we held our breaths, wondering what he would say. "When my father first told me he was going to get married, I wasn't exactly excited by the idea. But when I got to know Roberta, I liked her, and I know it will make my father happy." He turned to Roberta and his father, "So welcome to the family, Roberta. L'chaim."

More than three years have passed since Joey's return from France. Now sixteen, he is taller than I. His face has lost its softness; around cheeks, mouth, and jaw, the skin is taut. It seems that suddenly he's a young man.

Now a high school senior, he takes part in school plays and is a school aide. He works evenings and weekends at a drug store, banking his earnings toward studying film-making in college. He has friends at school and in the neighborhood. They play softball and pinball machines, go to the movies, listen to rock.

Visiting my son's home one Sunday after tennis, I found Larry and Joey cleaning roof gutters and drains. I was amused that Joey insisted on going up the ladder to save his Dad from the risky part of the job. Joey loves his home and plans to attend college from there. Perhaps he's had his fill of wandering.

We can now talk of his Krishna experience with greater objectivity. Recently, during a discussion comparing Eastern with Western religion, I asked him, "What was the most important thing you gained from your time with the Krishnas?"

"How to work with my hands," he replied. "You know, I never knew that tomato plants have to be held up with sticks." I waited as he seemed to reflect a few moments more. "And I learned how to do without," Joey said, "how to get along with little."

"That's good," I said with a new respect for my grandson. "That's very good."